Transformed Lives

Taking Women's Ministry to the Next Level

Compiled by Chris Adams
Foreword by Esther Burroughs

LifeWay Press
Nashville, Tennessee

ISBN 0-7673-3116-8
Dewey Decimal Classification Number: 248.843
Subject Heading: CHURCH WORK WITH WOMEN\WOMEN'S MINISTRY

This book is the text for course LS-0034 in the subject area Women's Enrichment
in the Christian Growth Study Plan.

Unless otherwise noted, Scripture quotations are from the Holy Bible,
New International Version, copyright © 1973, 1978, 1984
by International Bible Society.

Scripture quotations identified NASB are from the *New American Standard Bible*.
© The Lockman Foundation, 1960, 1962,
1963, 1968, 1971, 1972, 1973, 1975, 1977. Used by permission.

Scripture quotations identified NKJV are from the *New King James Version*.
Copyright © 1979, 1980, 1982, Thomas Nelson, Inc. Publishers. Used by permission.

Scripture quotations identified KJV are from the *King James Version*.

Scripture quotations identified THE MESSAGE are from THE MESSAGE,
Copyright © 1993, 1994, 1995. Used by permission of NavPress Publishing Group.

Betty Hassler, Editor
Paula Savage, Art Director
Pam Shepherd, Assistant Editor
Rhonda Porter Delph, Manuscript Assistant
Chris Adams, Women's Enrichment Ministry/Ministers' Wives Specialist

Printed in the United States of America

LifeWay Press
One LifeWay Plaza
Nashville, Tennessee 37234-0175

Contents

Meet the Writers

Chris Adams–Chris has served at LifeWay Christian Resources in Nashville, Tennessee since 1994. She now is the Women's Enrichment Ministry/Ministers' Wives Specialist. Chris compiled this resource, *Transformed Lives: Taking Women's Ministry to the Next Level* and *Women Reaching Women: Beginning and Building a Growing Women's Enrichment Ministry*.

Esther Burroughs–Esther is Director of Esther Burroughs Ministries, "Treasures of the Heart," a speaking and writing ministry. Previously she served in the Evangelism Department, North American Mission Board, Atlanta, Georgia.

John Franklin–John is a Pastoral Ministries Specialist in Church Ministry Leadership at LifeWay Christian Resources in Nashville, Tennessee. Prior to coming to LifeWay, John served as minister of prayer at First Baptist Church, Woodstock, Georgia.

Penny Glaesman–Penny graduated from New Orleans Baptist Theological Seminary with a degree in Pastoral Ministries. Previously she served on staff as Minister to Women and Bible Study Leader.

Johnnie Haines–Johnnie is a Christian motivational speaker and Director of Women's Ministry at Trinity Baptist Church in Southaven, Mississippi. Prior to that she served as Director of Women's Ministries at Metropolitan Baptist Church, Houston, Texas.

Betty Hassler–Betty is Biblical Instructional Specialist in Leadership and Adult Publishing at LifeWay Christian Resources. She also edits adult materials.

Paula Hemphill–Paula is a popular speaker and conference leader for women's events throughout the United States. She is the wife of Ken Hemphill, National Strategist of Empowering Kingdom Growth. Paula and her husband have recently moved from Texas to Nashville, Tennessee.

Rhonda Harrington Kelley–Rhonda, President's wife at New Orleans Baptist Theological Seminary, serves as Associate Director of Innovative Evangelism and Adjunct Professor at the seminary, while coordinating and teaching the Women's Ministry Certificate Program classes.

Carol Kuykendall–Carol is Director of Communications at MOPS International, Inc. She is also a speaker and the author of numerous books including *A Mother's Footprints of Faith* and co-author with Elisa Morgan of many MOPS releases including *What Every Mom Needs*.

Martha Lawley–With hearts for smaller churches, Martha and her husband Roger are active in First Southern Baptist Church in Worland, Wyoming. Martha leads women's Bible studies and serves with her church's Women's Ministry team. Martha also leads women's conferences and retreats nationwide; she is a Women's Ministry trainer and a contributing author for LifeWay Church Resources.

Linda Lesniewski–Linda is the Women's Minister at Green Acres Baptist Church in Tyler, Texas. Linda is author of *A Little Book About a Big God* and is working on a new book which will be published in the Spring of 2005, tentatively titled *Women at the Cross*.

Anne Graham Lotz–Anne, founder of AnGel Ministries in 1988 and daughter of Billy and Ruth Graham, travels across the world as a featured speaker. She is author of *The Vision of His Glory* and *God's Story*.

Elizabeth Luter–Elizabeth, a pastor's wife, is Coordinator of Women's Ministry at Franklin Avenue Baptist Church, New Orleans, Louisiana. Prior to organizing the women's ministry program, she organized the Womans Missionary Union and served as president and coordinator.

Jaye Martin–Jaye leads HeartCall Women's Evangelism and is the Family Evangelism Associate at the North American Mission Board of the Southern Baptist Convention. Prior to this call, Jaye served as Minister of Evangelism, Women and Prayer at First Baptist Church, Houston, Texas.

Dale McCleskey–Dale is editor in chief in Leadership and Adult Publishing at LifeWay Christian Resources. He also edits adult discipleship, family life, and women's ministry materials.

Elisa Morgan–Elisa is the president and CEO of MOPS International, a Christian organization based in Denver, Colorado, designed to nurture mothers of preschoolers through almost 3,000 groups in local churches. She hosts a daily radio program, "Mom Sense," which is broadcast nationwide, and is a speaker and author of such releases as *Real Moms, What Every Mom Needs,* and the *Mom's Devotional Bible*.

Shirley Moses–Shirley is Women's Ministry Team Advisor for Hagerman Baptist Church in Sherman, Texas. She is founder of Women's Ministry connection, a networking ministry in the North Texas area, and Beyond the Call Ministry.

Joseph Northcut–Joseph is the former Team Leader for Field Service in the Discipleship and Family Adult Department at LifeWay Christian Resources.

Laura Savage–Laura fromerly served as Ministry Consultant for Women at the national Woman's Missionary Union in Birmingham, Alabama. She is now a professor in the field of women's studies and communication in a university in Romania.

Janet Thompson–Janet is founder and director of About His Work Ministries (AHW). As an author and speaker on topics relevant to today's Christian women, Janet has been "About His Work" as a lay minister, starting and leading Woman to Woman Mentoring Ministry at Saddleback Church in Lake Forest, California. Janet is also the author of *Woman to Woman Mentoring: How to Start, Grow, and Maintain a Mentoring Ministry,* published by LifeWay Press.

David Tiller–David is the Senior Organizational Development Specialist for LifeWay Christian Stores. He is responsible for developing and conducting seminars in management, communication, customer service, sales, merchandising, and computer software for employees in the corporate office.

Jacqualine C. Truitt–Jacque, founder and owner of PRO-ACT in Pasadena, Texas, is a licensed professional counselor and a licensed marriage and family therapist. She is also a Nationally Certified Counselor. Jacque has been in practice for over 15 years. Jacque and her husband David have been married 35 years and have led mariage workshops across the nation.

Foreword

by Esther Burroughs

*J*esus said, "I am come that they might have life, and that they might have it more abundantly" (John 10:10, KJV). The One who made this promise also said: "I am the way, and the truth, and the life. No one comes to the Father except through me" (John 14:6, NIV). Everywhere Jesus went, He brought truth and hope. We are women of hope because we know the person, Truth.

After leading out in the effort to introduce and establish women's ministry in the local church, I am so pleased women's ministry leadership has prepared this book to assist women leaders in moving to the next level ... to mature spiritually while living out a servant lifestyle.

This book offers excellent practical help. I am particularly pleased with the order of its chapters, which defines the priority of women's ministry: prayer and Bible study. There is no more important path for women to follow than that which includes a consistent prayer life and in-depth Bible study.

In my own life, I define prayer and Bible study as worship. Through worship we discover our individual spiritual gifts that reveal our uniqueness in the body of Christ—a critical issue for women. It is only after we embrace our acceptance in Christ that we can define our singular, particular role in the body of Christ. For example, once I've accepted my unique gift in the body and know what I have to offer, I am free to accept my sisters' gifts in the church body. How freeing to embrace our individual giftedness even as we celebrate our sister's gifts, knowing that together we make the body more like Christ.

If women are concerned only with the results of their individual gifts, the body may begin to look too much like one person and not enough like Christ. If we over-commit, we rob others of places to serve in the church. As women leaders, we want to help position women in the Son, teaching them how to draw strength and wisdom from God's Word—not our words. There is a big difference.

As you lead women in your church, encourage them to imitate Christ in their unique ministries. Remember: as we work in various church ministries, we are field hands, laborers together, as Paul said, working in Christ's kingdom, knowing He brings the harvest. The harvest comes ultimately at the end of the age—not the end of an event! Maintain an eternal focus in your ministry, always thinking of the bigger picture, the "kingdom of God."

As we worship and adore Him, because He calls us to Himself, we will develop a thirst for even more of Him. And out of that worship, we are called to serve our world. I call it "stooping in grace" to minister to many types of people:

- Hurting women;
- Single moms;
- Homeless families;
- Unreached language groups;
- Mothers of prodigals;
- Terminally ill persons and caregivers;
- Professional women in the workplace;
- Fulltime homemakers;
- Those with addictive lifestyle behaviors;
- New church members and seekers;
- The lost.

On His way to the cross, Jesus assembled a ragtag army of motley characters, and, today, He continues to call ordinary persons–like you and me–to Himself. Why? Because He has chosen to work through us! In my book, *Splash the Living Water*, I say: "Jesus turned daily interruptions into life-giving encounters." He shared the abundant life with the Samaritan woman while introducing her to the Living Water. She then turned from her sinful life to embark on a soul-winning life.

We must follow the Savior's leadership principles as we face the great challenge of leading women.

- Jesus died for women.
- Jesus healed women.
- Jesus empowered women.
- Jesus taught women.
- Jesus loves women.

My prayer is that God will use this book to equip and empower women … to call out new leaders … to disciple women … to challenge them to become the fragrance of Christ. Imagine a God who pours into us the enticing fragrance of salvation and then draws others to Himself through His fragrance in us. This is your challenge as a leader! Are you ready?

Introduction

by Chris Adams

In looking toward producing another women's ministry leadership resource, my first reaction was, "Oh, not another book!" Writing is not one of my favorite things to do. But helping leaders continue to develop ministry to and with women *is* one of my favorite activities and is the task to which God has called me. I find so much joy in working with leaders across the country who truly have a heart to reach and disciple women for Christ.

If you have not read *Women Reaching Women: Beginning and Building a Growing Women's Enrichment Ministry*, I recommend that you read it first. Once you've implemented the principles it offers, you are ready for "the next level." *Transformed Lives* will help lay a firm biblical foundation for your women's ministry.

The reason for this book is two-fold:

- Leaders continue to ask questions about issues not addressed in *Women Reaching Women*. A need for continued leadership development remains.
- My heart's desire is to see women continue to grow so they can find their place in His kingdom's service. Our prayer is that under God's direction, this book will help leaders equip women to reach out and minister to others.

I have often said, "there's no formula for women's ministry." Each church is unique. Without prayer, discernment, and the Holy Spirit's leadership, no ministry will be as effective as He desires. Each leader's priority must be relationships, not methods. First is your relationship to Christ: if you as a leader are not spending time daily with Him in prayer, meditation, and Bible study, you will not discern where He is at work among the women in your church and community. Second is your relationship to others. Is your first concern program or ministry?

Terry Hershey identifies the differences between programs and ministry:

- Programs focus on techniques—ministry focuses on people.
- Programs look for numbers—ministry sees changed lives.
- Programs need quick answers—ministry understands grace in uncertainty.
- Programs see the course—ministry sees the hearts.[1]

The bottom line is that transformational discipleship leads women into a life that reflects Christ through their thoughts, words, and actions. As we reach out to women that should be our primary goal. As you read and study this resource, I pray God will draw you to the ideas He desires for you to implement in your church. As you move forward through the Holy Spirit's leadership, women's lives will be changed, and our world will be changed … one woman at a time!

---

[1]Terry Hershey, *Young Adult Ministry* (Loveland, CO: Group Publishing Inc., 1986), 70.

Prayer

Foundational Strategy for Effective Ministry

by John Franklin

I've never known anyone planning a new ministry who aimed at mediocrity or failure. I've never heard anyone say: "You know, if I start off with just a few people and never do much, that's fine with me. I don't mind spending all my time and energy for nothing. In fact, if I just attain the level of status quo, I'll be excited."

Most leaders dream of continuous growth and a powerful impact upon the lives of all involved. Unfortunately, not every ministry succeeds. Sometimes those that do succeed outwardly, fail to produce life changes inwardly in the participants.

If you are beginning a new women's ministry, building an existing ministry, or initiating a new aspect of your ministry, these are the questions you must ask: *What is the foundation I must lay above all others? What is the key that unlocks God's door to power?* Only then can you be confident your ministry will succeed.

Many who believe they know the answer to these questions point to God's activity in calling His people to prayer. Currently, American Christianity is experiencing an unprecedented revival of interest in prayer. Book studies, Bible studies, discipleship courses, programs, prayer rooms, and prayerwalking represent just some of the activities riding this growing crest of interest in prayer.

Many confidently proclaim that the medicine of prayer has been the missing cure that will heal the abysmal moral condition of America and impotent church life. The overlooked key is the people of God on their knees, and whoever would be successful in ministry must pray.

As of this writing, my job assignment is to help churches begin or strengthen prayer ministries. You might suppose, then, that I would be very excited by this emphasis on prayer. Actually, it has become a cause of great concern to me. I am disturbed because in the Bible, prayer was not the foundation; rather, it laid the foundation. Getting the cart before the horse, as the saying goes, creates all kinds of misconceptions that lead to disastrous results.

My goal in this chapter is to deal with five misconceptions about

> What is the foundation I must lay above all others? What is the key that unlocks God's door to power?

9

prayer in our day, then biblically prove what the foundation really is. Having done that, I will write about prayer's indispensable role in leading others in a love relationship with God.

Five Subtle Misconceptions

1. *Prayer insures successful ministries*–In other words, prayer is the insurance policy that these ministries will be blessed. Certainly no people have ever experienced God's power without prayer, but the Scripture bears witness that many have prayed without life-changing results. Consider the Jews of Jeremiah and Ezekiel's day who prayed and fasted, yet perished. Consider the Pharisees of Jesus' day who diligently prayed, yet the Romans destroyed Jerusalem. Both Scripture accounts affirm that God's mighty hand never moved on their behalf. Thus, praying does not guarantee success. Something greater than prayer remains.

2. *The more I pray, the more God answers; or the more prayer, the more power.* While these statements may be true, it is also true that many people have sought God for extensive periods of time with no results. God hears because we are on His agenda, not because of our effort or sacrifice. A national prayer leader once said that the issue is not to get people to pray more, but rather to help them have a vision from God. In the Bible all prayer flowed out of an understanding of what God is up to. Praying in the wrong direction or for the wrong thing, no matter how earnestly, has no more power than no prayer at all. Staying focused on God's person and purposes helps us to avoid the pitfall of misdirected, fruitless praying. Something greater than prayer remains.

   > Staying focused on God's person and purposes helps us to avoid the pitfall of misdirected, fruitless praying.

3. *God answers prayer.* In the Bible God never separates the request from the condition of the heart of the one praying. Who you are and what you are asking have direct correlation with each other. God doesn't answer the prayer so much as He answers the pray-er. James 5:16 doesn't read "prayer avails much." Instead it reads, "The effectual, fervent prayer of a *righteous* (italics mine) man avails much" (NKJV). A righteous woman is one who walks in a love relationship with God and follows His agenda and purposes. Therefore, you cannot implement a program, devise a strategy, or promote a campaign, however noble, and expect God to bless it unless you and the people in your ministry are connected to Him. Something greater than prayer remains.

4. *Prayer changes things.* No, God changes things. If prayer changed things, then many world religions would have incredible spiritual impact. Instead, God remains sovereign. He alone determines what happens, not our prayers. Something greater than prayer remains.

10

5. *There is power in prayer.* The power is in God. Anyone who believes that prayer has power might also substitute the activity of prayer for an encounter with God. The goal is not merely to pray. The goal is to pray, allowing the prayer to create the opportunity for an encounter with God. Something greater than prayer remains.

The Key to Success in Ministry

So, what is the key that is greater than prayer? The key, the foundation of success in ministry, is a deepening love relationship with God. A successful ministry is a by-product of intimacy with God. The more you talk with God, study His Word, nurture a love relationship with Him, and are obedient to Him, the more God gives you.

Contrasting our service and God's self-sufficiency reveals this truth. God doesn't need us to accomplish His work. If He did, He would in some sense be dependent on us. The Scripture says, "He is not served by human hands, as if he needed anything" (Acts 17:25). In reality, God would have less trouble if He just used the angels to accomplish His plan. They respond immediately. Since God doesn't need anyone, His only motive is His desire for a love relationship with us.

In beginning and growing women's ministries, God is looking for women who will love Him totally. Because the love relationship pleases God, He invites women to be where He is, and He honors the love relationship by accomplishing His work through those women. If at any time they stray from the love relationship, God immediately moves to bring them back into a right relationship with Himself.

Warning: To an activity-oriented people there is great temptation to bypass the love relationship and use prayer as a means to success. First Corinthians 13 admonishes us that service for God motivated by anything other than love is not recognized! God seeks a love relationship first. The Ephesian church of Revelation received a strict warning about substituting activity (even if the activity is good and desired by God) for relationship (see Rev. 2:1-7).

So, practically speaking, how do you nurture a deepening relationship with God, especially in your role as leader? What are the key principles you must practice? How can the quality of your relationship with God grow and improve? Consider the following list. Although not exhaustive, these elements are essential.

1. *Step out in faith.* Have you ever been amazed at those whom the Bible identified as saints? Many of those described in Hebrews 11 did not have very good track records, at least not by our standards. For

> The key, the foundation of success in ministry, is a deepening love relationship with God.

example, Jacob was extremely manipulative, deceptive, and self-centered. Rahab was a prostitute. Samson lacked self-control with women. How could these be included alongside such stellar examples as Enoch, Joseph, or Samuel? If both groups are considered saints, a standard greater than performance must exist.

The common denominator shared by both groups is that when God spoke, they believed Him and obeyed instantly. Faith pleases God. In fact, without faith, it is impossible to please God. As a leader you should expect that God will give you tasks that require faith. Otherwise, when circumstances are difficult or a challenge looms impossible, you may ask God to intervene. You may be tempted to pray, "Oh God, please do something to lighten the load." God will respond: "I'm the One who led you to this point. Now I want you to exercise faith so that I can display my glory."

The biblical principle is simple. Walking by faith creates the opportunity for God to do something supernatural. Everyone watching your life will recognize that God did it, and He will receive the glory for it. So be prepared. If you're serious about growing in intimacy with God, you can be sure He will ask you to step out in faith and trust Him for "impossible" things in your ministry. However, be certain you know it is God leading you to step out in faith. Don't test God by devising your own plan. If it's your idea and not His, you will fall.

If you're serious about growing in intimacy with God, you can be sure He will ask you to step out in faith and trust Him for "impossible" things in your ministry.

2. *Put God first.* The very first Commandment warns that nothing shall be before God. God tolerates no competitors. He demands preeminence over our families, our checkbooks, our careers—everything. And He will test you to learn which you'd rather have—your ministry, success, the praise of others—or Him.

3. *Seek His interests.* All the great saints had the ability to see from God's perspective what He wanted, and they were zealous for His sake. When Jesus overturned the money tables in the temple and denounced those who turned His Father's house into a market, Scripture records that the disciples remembered that "Zeal for your house will consume me" (John 2:17). Moses pleaded with God to refrain from destroying the Israelites. Why? Because Moses was worried that God's name would be dishonored among the heathen. God will constantly examine your prayer life to see if it seeks His perspectives and interests.

4. *Love holiness.* God is holy. He hates wickedness and loves righteousness. Any deepening relationship with God will be marked by the removal of those sins and failings that so easily beset us. God blesses integrity more than intelligence, skill, wisdom or experience.

5. *Be willing to change for Him.* The life of every Bible person who followed God was marked by change. The changes varied from career, to geographical location, to belief and practice of faith, to methodology or organization, to family relationships, and to character. In ministry, you may need to reorganize or restructure to be more effective; you may have to change or modify your leadership style. Remember—changes always fall in line with what is necessary to accomplish God's assignment for you.

6. *Focus on serving others first.* You show love to Jesus when you serve His children. In John 21, Jesus asked Peter to show his love for Him by feeding His sheep. God always looked for shepherds to edify and strengthen the flock (see Ezek. 37 or 1 Pet. 5). God is not nearly as concerned with the number of people involved in your ministry as He is with whether or not you love the number He gives you, regardless of their actions.

7. *Practice these principles and pursue Him with passion and intensity.* Haphazard, nonchalant, and inconsistent practice of these disciplines will not produce intimacy. Consistency in practicing these disciplines determines closeness. All the saints who enjoyed great favor with God exercised these disciplines which lead to godliness.

Your job as leader is to nurture your daily walk with God. While this book deals with the skills and ideas necessary to leadership, your success in ministry ultimately comes from the quality of your relationship with God. God never allows us to overlook or bypass the love relationship.

When a life is characterized by love for Him and demonstrated by the previous qualities, prayer will be rich and deep. When we cease to grow in the areas that please God and turn away from the love relationship, it is evident in our prayer life. We experience a dryness in prayer, no apparent answers, or even a dull routine.

Leading Women in a Love Relationship with God Through Prayer

In the previous section I explained that the foundation for success in ministry is a deepening love relationship with God, not prayer. However, nothing creates a better environment for growth in a love relationship than prayer. This fact explains why those who pray experience power from God in their ministries. Therefore, to experience the power of God in women's ministry, prayer is vital—both in your life and in the lives of others. How do you motivate women to seek God in prayer?

God is not nearly as concerned with the number of people involved in your ministry as He is with whether or not you love the number He gives you, regardless of their actions.

Nothing creates a better environment for growth in a love relationship with God than prayer.

Before You Pray

We are often told that to build an effective prayer ministry we must simply pray. Four other ingredients are necessary for the prayer leader.

- *Build relationships with the women.* Whenever God or the great saints of the Bible sought to lead others, they first built relationships. For example, Jesus' call to Peter, James, John, and Andrew on the Sea of Galilee was preceded by spending time with them at the Jordan River (see John 1:35-51). Paul and Barnabas spent time praying and planning together before they embarked on their first missionary journey. Leading others to build a love relationship with God cannot be separated from the quality of relationship you build with them.

    As a leader, invest your primary one-on-one time with those women you've chosen to help you lead. Jesus built relationships with all people, but He deliberately and purposefully spent time alone with His disciples, His leaders. Long-term growth in a ministry is assured when you invest in your leadership.

- *Motivate.* People do not seek God on their own because of sin (see Rom. 3:9-11). Even after experiencing salvation, Christians must renew themselves day-by-day or love and passion will grow cold. In the Bible God set apart as leaders those who were skilled in challenging and motivating the people to seek God continually. Prayer can become perfunctory without inspiration. Pray for God to lead you as you lead others to a deeper prayer relationship with Him.

- *Model and create opportunities.* Prayer is more caught than taught. Model the importance of prayer by praying as you begin all meetings. Take the time to pray during decision-making, when you hear of pressing needs, and as you are led by the Holy Spirit. Give individuals every chance to hear and observe you and other prayer warriors in your church. Look for opportunities to mobilize women in the church to pray. Schedule special times of emphasis around churchwide events, particular crises, or the national day of prayer. Public prayer modeling will impact private prayer lives because most people imitate what they see instead of experimenting to develop their own style.

- *Teach women to recognize when God is speaking.* In order for women to experience a dynamic love relationship with God, prayer must be a dialogue. Learning the art of listening is just that—a learned skill. Unless a Christian is taught to recognize how God speaks,

Public prayer modeling will impact private prayer lives because most people imitate what they see instead of experimenting to develop their own style.

she will never enjoy an abundant relationship with Him. Therefore, as a leader, teach formally as well as informally ways to know when God is speaking. When an individual is connected to God, the motivation to pray becomes an internalized desire.

When an individual is connected to God, the motivation to pray becomes an internalized desire.

When You Pray

Praying as a group has some distinctives that must be recognized.

1. *The necessity of corporate prayer*—Most of the time Jesus taught on prayer using the plural: "Where two or three are gathered together in My name" (Matt. 18:20, NKJV). "Whatever things you [plural] ask in prayer, believing, you [plural] will receive" (Matt. 21:22, NKJV). "When you [plural] pray, say 'Our Father' (Luke 11:2, NKJV). "Ask, and you [plural] will receive" (John 16:24, NKJV). In fact, the only time He addressed individual prayer was when He spoke of "going into your closet." Unfortunately, American individualism fights against this biblical mandate. However, the Book of Acts clearly records that whenever God moved mightily—whether at Pentecost, handling threats, commissioning the first deacons, or securing Peter's release from prison—it was done in the context of a praying group. These examples clearly affirm that Jesus expects corporate prayer to be the foundational strategy in prayer for advancing the kingdom.

Jesus expects corporate prayer to be the foundational strategy in prayer for advancing the kingdom.

2. *The perspective of a prayer group*—Some differences exist between the way one prays alone and the way a group prays. As a leader you must present a model for group praying. Otherwise group members will pray as individuals rather than as a team. The following three concepts apply uniquely to group praying.

    • A prayer group comes to understand the will of God corporately. The Holy Spirit rarely gives any one person the total picture of what He desires. Instead, as the group prays He will touch the hearts of members so that the picture becomes clear to the group.

    • No one monopolizes the prayer time. Long prayers by one member hinders the Holy Spirit as He works in the group.

    • The depth of a prayer group develops over time and is determined by unity of purpose for God and relationships within the group. Groups that bond around these two elements tend to have more authority before the throne of God.

3. *How the Holy Spirit communicates with the church during the prayer meeting*— There are definite evidences as the Holy Spirit moves in prayer. Learning to recognize these patterns creates an understanding of God's plan and the desired response.

You can be certain
God is working in
prayer when there is a
growing consensus
among the believers.

- Creating unity–One of the great ministries of the Holy Spirit among believers is to create oneness. An encounter with God among a group of believers connected with God results in the majority of members arriving at the same conclusion. You can be certain God is working in prayer when there is a growing consensus among the believers.
- Creating understanding/insights through Scripture–Giving group members Scripture is one way the Holy Spirit indicates His mind and leads the church in the direction He desires. The Spirit may bring solutions to mind, an awareness of necessary actions, or an understanding of what God is doing.
- Creating insight/understanding through testimony–Testimony usually occurs before the prayer time, but may spill over into the organized prayer group. God may touch individual hearts with reminders of ways He has worked in their lives.
- Placing a burden on church members' hearts–Be sensitive to someone who suddenly is deeply impressed and cries out to God with fervency. The Holy Spirit may touch the rest of the congregation's heart to share the burden.
- The spirit of the prayer–Occasionally a person may pray and it seems as if they are swept up to a different level. A deep awareness of God's presence may pervade the group.
- Supplication–The Holy Spirit often helps a Christian beseech the mercy of God. Tears, groanings, pleading, and/or begging for God's mercy may accompany this type of prayer. It often occurs when praying for the lost or a backslidden Christian under conviction of sin.
- Peace/confirmation/assurance of heart–Romans 8:16 says, "the Spirit Himself bears witness with our spirit" (NKJV). Often those who pray experience an assurance of God's answer or an unexplainable knowledge that He has taken care of the situation. The Holy Spirit communicates that He has heard the prayer and will take care of the situation.

What God has to say is far more important than what we have to say. Train women to listen for what God is trying to communicate to His people during prayer. Below are some proper ways to respond to God when He reveals Himself in the ways listed previously.

1. *What if you received an insight?*–Suppose you are participating in a prayer meeting and suddenly you understand a Scripture passage, the meaning of a testimony, or how to pray more specifically for a

16

situation. What should you do? Immediately voice the insight. The Holy Spirit will use that to reveal His will to others. Sometimes you may understand only part of God's will, but as you pray aloud that portion, someone else may understand the rest. The Holy Spirit uses one or more minds to bring understanding and reveal His will.

2. *What do you do if you are burdened or have the spirit of prayer or supplication?*–Simply pour your heart out before God; however, do not attempt to manufacture this burdened spirit. Lengthy prayers squelch the group unless the prayers are inspired by God.

3. *What if someone expresses a burden?*–It is good for other members of the body to surround that person and encourage her by praying with and for her. If it is a burden from God, then other members need to pray as God touches them.

4. *What if someone is broken by awareness of sin?* Allow her to pray. Often the Holy Spirit wants to deal with additional people and the prayer may allow God to work in other's lives. (Gently stop this type of prayer if the pray-er begins to call names.)

5. *What if you receive assurance/peace/confirmation?*–The Holy Spirit is informing you that He is going to answer that prayer. At that very moment the intercessor should praise God even before the results become evident. *Warning:* You cannot manufacture this experience. God reveals Himself in this way occasionally, but not always. When it is the Holy Spirit giving peace, you will know that based on your personal relationship with God.

The Format for Extended Prayer

1. Talking (5-10 min.)–It's important for group members to connect with one another and to focus. Keep this time brief. Initially, most prayer group members tend to talk more than they pray.

2. Getting focused (5-10 min.)–The quality of prayer depends on whether or not members are connected with God. In order to connect with God, minds must first be focused on His person, His purposes, or His ways. Without focusing, people tend to pray about the most recent situation on their minds. Focusing can occur in several ways. The following elements may prove helpful as you take time to focus.

   • *Reading Scripture*–Read aloud God's promises in the Bible or relevant Scripture passages that address God's current activity in your ministry.

   • *Praising God in song*–Music has a wonderful way of helping the heart to focus on God, His truth, or His attributes.

The quality of prayer depends on whether or not members are connected with God. In order to connect with God, minds must first be focused on His person, His purposes or His ways.

17

- *Sharing testimony of answered prayer*–Often the Holy Spirit will electrify the group through testimonies of God's work and blessings.
- *Conducting a heart evaluation*–Sometimes we need to evaluate the condition of our hearts before we meet God. Read aloud Ephesians 4:20–5:7, then allow members time to reflect on their relationship with God.

3. Praising God and confession (10-15 min.)–Praise safeguards our hearts. It reminds us to want God more than the things we request. Express gratefulness and adoration for Who and what God is. As we focus on Him, we become aware of our shortcomings, leading to confession.

4. Petition and intercession (10-15 min.)–When we focus on God, we are more likely to understand things from God's perspective and pray according to His will.

5. Responding to God after the prayer time (10-15 min.)–Since prayer involves listening, lead the group to process whether or not God spoke. Suggestions for this processing period follow.

After You Pray

Admittedly, God doesn't speak every time a group prays, but a time of processing ensures that when God does speak, members will know how to respond. If God doesn't speak frequently, there's a problem and you should ask God to reveal it.

- *Talk about what the group sensed.* Sometimes it's abundantly clear as you pray what God wants. Other times you only discover God's desires after thinking and meditating. Look for unity. If unity is not evident, guide the group to continue watching and praying.
- *Ask: How should we respond?* Do we need to make any changes? Determining change keeps your ministry in step with God. The goal of a love relationship is not to hear God speak. The goal is to learn why He's speaking so we can obey and serve Him. Lead the group to practice action motivated from love.
- *What do you do if the Holy Spirit laid a burden on someone's heart?* If He lays a burden on someone's heart, it is so that His people may become involved and respond to Him. For example, if a woman suddenly experiences a burden for a lost family in her neighborhood, then the Holy Spirit may be alerting her that He is working in the life of that family to bring them to Christ. The group may want to invite the family to dinner at a member's

If He lays a burden on someone's heart, it is so that His people may become involved and respond to Him.

house, look for ways to befriend their children, invite them to a marriage seminar, and so on. The goal is to look for ways to join God in the work He is already doing.

A Final Word

When evaluating the effectiveness of your prayer ministry, gauge the hearts of those involved for passion and obedience more than frequency and method. God's number one assignment for any leader is to shepherd the hearts of the people.

Therefore, when the group prays, always look for what God is saying, as well as whether or not the love relationship of the women is still vibrant. How often people pray, praying for the right thing, or involvement in church ministries or Bible study doesn't determine the quality of a love relationship with God. Better gauges are passion, intensity, desire for God, conversation topics, free-time activities, willingness to change, and ultimately an obedient response to all God desires. These are qualities a leader should encourage. If the heart remains faithful to God, the behavior will follow.

For Smaller Churches
by Martha Lawley

Good news for smaller churches: the size of the church or women's ministry has no bearing on the power available through prayer. God has promised that "where two or three come together in my name, there am I with them" (Matt. 18:20).

Each of the seven key principles of developing a love relationship with God begin first in an individual. A large group is not required to adopt any of these habits. Prayer is a necessary element in any size ministry.

God's measure of success is intentionally different from that of the world. Success is growth in an individual's love relationship with God. Smaller churches have all the necessary resources to experience God's success. Prayer is one of the most under utilized, yet fully available resources Christians have.

Some smaller churches are actually further along in the process of prayer than some larger churches. As these smaller churches have recognized their limited resources and been forced to depend upon God to meet daily needs, prayer was not an option, but a necessity. God has already provided all that you need to begin a prayer ministry!

Prayer is a necessary element in any size ministry.

Prayer

Beginning a Prayer Ministry and Prayer Groups

by Johnnie Haines

Women's ministry is made up of many components. Bible study, fellowship, missions, worship, ministry, evangelism, discipleship, and recreation provide a well-rounded ministry. One activity ties each of these components together as well as empowering their results–prayer. Prayer is "spiritual breathing," bringing life to every other part of the ministry. If you want to see God open His Word and apply it to women's lives, have them pray for wisdom and understanding. If you want to build unity in your ministry, have women pray for one another. Prayer changes hearts, lives, and attitudes among God's women. Prayer is literally the key to the heart of God.

Prayer is "spiritual breathing," bringing life to every other part of the ministry.

Chris Adams, Women's Enrichment Ministry Specialist at LifeWay Christian Resources, says that prayer should be the very first step of every meeting, decision-making discussion, and problem-solving session within a ministry. As you lead women to pray, you will be amazed at the problems that will be avoided as you grow together in faith.

In this chapter, I will offer some suggestions for you to tailor-make a prayer ministry for your church. The wonderful thing about prayer is that it doesn't matter what size ministry you have or how organized it is. Prayer works! Where two or more are gathered, He promises to be in their midst (see Matt. 18:20).

Reasons Women's Groups Should Pray

- God commanded that we should pray. It is not just a "fringe benefit" of the Christian life.
- Prayer paves the way for God to meet our needs and for us to recognize Him as the source of our provision.
- Answered prayer builds the body of believers and encourages them to pray even more.
- Prayer puts God on the throne of our lives.
- Prayer teaches us to seek His face, not His hand of blessing.
- Prayer sensitizes your group to sin and prepares women to meet and defeat temptation.

20

What Prayer Will Do for Your Group

- Prayer refocuses the perspective of the group to eternal things.
- Prayer quiets fears and calms nerves and feelings.
- Prayer transfers your burdens from your shoulders to His.
- Prayer upholds others before Christ. When the answers come, no doubt will exist about Who has been at work.
- Prayer empowers believers to serve.
- Prayer can sensitize an entire group to God's will and work.

Knowing What to Pray For

I am always surprised when women comment that they really don't know what to say when they pray. Prayer is conversation with God. It is just "real" talk between two friends—your heavenly Father and you. There is no magic formula or correct way to pray.

John 15:7 assures us that if we are abiding in Jesus, whatever we ask, He will do. Abiding in Him allows us to literally walk so close to Him that we already know what He wants us to pray for. Once we know God's will, we can ask with bold confidence, with certain knowledge that He will hear and act upon our request (see 1 John 5:14-15). What can we count on being within His will?

- God wants us to grow spiritually. He wants to equip us in every good thing (see Heb. 13:20-21). You can pray in perfect accord for God to provide the time and clear your schedule for Bible study and prayer.
- God desires that we continually encourage one another (see Heb. 10:19-25). Our intercessory prayers strengthen those for whom we pray.
- God longs to see souls added to His kingdom (see Matt. 28:18-20). I can assure you that if you are praying about these things you are going to be praying within God's will!

Personal Prayer Time

Before praying in a group, practice the discipline of personal prayer. Some women become discouraged by hearing the amount of time one of the "giants of faith" spend in prayer. They do not realize that prayer is a learned skill. The disciples asked Jesus to "teach [them] to pray" (Luke 11:1). Spend time in the Word studying godly examples of how the saints of old prayed and then follow their lead.

In my younger days as a Christian I struggled with staying interested in prayer. It was a pursuit that seemed too "quiet" for my personality. I would

> Prayer is "real" talk between two friends—your Heavenly Father and you.

> Prayer is a learned skill.

begin praying with the best intentions, but my mind would wander so badly that I forgot what I was saying. Often I began to pray about a situation and would catch myself trying to figure out a solution myself, totally forgetting that I was asking the King of kings for His help! (I'm certain there were days He sat in His heavenly realm, watching His "sanctified Seiko™," waiting for me to get back on task.) I discovered two methods which helped me to use my prayer time wisely.

Journaling

God began to lead me through a process of recording my prayers, solving much of my "attention deficit" problem. I have journaled my prayers in some form for more than 10 years. God taught me many things through this process. I believe writing your prayers is important because:

- It allows you to document answers to prayer. When was the last time you remember God answering a specific prayer? Will you remember it this time next month? You will if you write it down.
- It will grow your faith. You can be sure that God has led you in the past, so you can trust Him to guide you today. Keep track of the spiritual activity in your life so that you will not forget what God is doing.
- It allows you to see divine purpose in decisions and circumstances. Through journaling, I can stay the course, no matter the cost, if I know that my Lord led me there.
- It provides perspective. What may have seemed like a big issue at the time probably will be of little consequence a year later.
- Journaling helps us see the order and the sequence of God's activity in our lives. We have an orderly God!

Using ACTS

In my personal prayer time, I use the ACTS format (Adoration, Confession, Thanksgiving, and Supplication).

Adoration is another word for *praise*. Praise acknowledges and celebrates the person of God. It focuses on His character and His attributes. Adoration is not the time for thanking Him for blessings that have come from His hands or for asking for other blessings. This is the time set aside to remind you that you are about to worship the King of kings and Lord of lords! Revelation 4:11 reveals that we were created to worship Him.

The second aspect of prayer is *confession*. "For all have sinned and fall short of the glory of God" (Rom. 3:23). Confession is a two-part discipline. It is first and foremost agreeing with God about the sin, and

Keep track of the spiritual activity in your life so that you will not forget what God is doing.

secondly, it is turning away from the sinful behavior or attitude. No matter how long we've been out of fellowship or how disgusting our sin might be, God stands ready to forgive and restore us.

The third aspect—*thanksgiving*—reflects our attitudes more than anything else. Say "thank you" for everything. Thank God for the blessings, provisions, people, and insights into His will you have received. Then for an "extra" challenge, thank Him for those things in your life that are difficult, challenging, or trying. Remember: He is molding you to look a little more like Him.

Then enter the *supplication* portion of your prayer time. Pray fervently for others that they may come to know and do God's will. Pray fervently for yourself. God knows your needs, weaknesses, and fears better than yourself. This is the time to pray for strengthening in your daily walk.

You will never learn to pray unless you begin to pray. Prayer needs very few resources and no budget! You need only to have an open Bible and an open heart to enjoy a successful personal prayer ministry. If you have not been regular in your prayer habits, I encourage you to begin this lifelong pursuit that will change your life!

Group Prayers

Now that we have looked at personal prayer, let's consider corporate prayer. Before any advance plans are made for your women's ministry, begin with prayer. On every women's council or leadership team include a prayer coordinator who keeps members on their knees. She also should coordinate the prayer group's meetings during the coming year.

As leadership, pray together about what God would have you accomplish for Him in the next 12 months and beyond. Be diligent to clear the schedule so that you can pray unhurriedly. Be still and quiet long enough to really "hear" from God (see Ps. 46:10). Remember: God has divine appointments for each of His children. Don't miss yours! Anytime you enter a place of prayer with a humble, willing, and sincere heart, He will provide and prepare the way before you. You will find it exciting to complete the vision He has for your women's group!

As the year continues, begin every leadership meeting with prayer. If the leaders do not pray, the groups are not likely to pray. If prayer is not a priority for you, it will be difficult to make it a priority for others.

If prayer is not a priority for you, it will be difficult to make it a priority for others.

Handling Prayer Requests in Small Groups

The focus of some groups will be solely on prayer. Although other groups will focus on Bible study, fitness, or missions, each group should include some time spent in prayer. Without well-defined perimeters, one can easily turn a small-group Bible study into a prayer group. Before a prayer request or comment is shared, train women to pass it through four "approval" gates. Sometimes the least said, the better.

- Is it true?
- Is it confidential?
- Is it kind?
- Is it necessary?

The following suggestions work well for handling prayer requests in the group. Perhaps you can build upon one of these ideas to match the temperament of your group.

- Take the first or last 10 minutes of the small-group time to share requests while each member makes her own list. Establish time guidelines for requests so that members have equal but reasonable time for sharing. The guidelines could include: (1) Make requests in 10 words or less; (2) Pray only for immediate family or friends (you might change the perimeter of concerns each meeting); (3) Pray not only for physical healing but also for spiritual needs and growth points in people's lives. (4) Then ask specific persons to lift these requests to the Lord, thus keeping control of the time.

- Many groups spend a great deal of time talking about prayer but very little time really praying. Spend more time praying than talking about it.

Spend more time praying than talking about it.

- One person can volunteer to record the requests for the entire group on a prepared form (see below). The form can be updated and mailed to everyone after the meeting.

Date	Request	Update	Note Sent
1/5/98	Sue's daughter undergoing surgery 1/7	Surgery Successful	1/7/98
1/5/98	Robin's husband lost job 1/27/98	interview 2/15/98 accepted job	2/15/98

Although it can be a little more work, this form is very effective for several reasons. It allows you to record and see the answers God is providing. This system informs those who might

be absent from the group and encourages them to pray also. We are all guilty of praying without expecting answers. Teach women to pray expectantly.

- Another system is to arrive with your prayer request in written form. Again, establish guidelines concerning the length of the requests as well as the boundaries for persons and requests. Instruct group members to place requests in a designated container and then allow the small-group leader or prayer leader to take them home. The leader sorts the requests and begins a prayer chain, calling each of the people involved.

Occasionally during a group study, someone may voice an urgent need or concern. Stop right then and take it to the Lord in prayer. Then proceed with your study. Taking the time to stop and pray assures that person of your support.

Types of Prayer Groups

There are several types of prayer groups that can enhance and uplift the other aspects of your women's ministry.

1. *Early Prayer Groups*—An early prayer group can function as intercessors on behalf of the entire ministry. Each week before the women gather in small groups, intercessors can pray for the meetings. The leader of the early group compiles requests from the small-group leaders and from those who have indicated prayer requests in other ways. A quiet meeting place assures the group can pray undisturbed—quiet enough to "hear" from God and secluded enough *not* to "hear" anyone else! By the time women arrive, God will already be at work.

2. *Prayer Chains*—Prayer chains are effective in several different ways. Each small group can have its own prayer chain, or prayer chains can be volunteers from different small groups. Any combination is workable. The better acquainted you are with the people for whom you are praying, the more likely you are to pray faithfully. Whatever the group composition, these same suggestions apply:

   - Require a time commitment. Encourage prayer chain participants to commit to the chain for the duration of the group study. It is disheartening to be the caller in line either right before or right after someone who has lost interest or has dropped out of the chain.

   - If participants hear a recorded phone message, encourage them to leave only their name and number and then proceed to call the next person on the list. Do not leave requests of a sensitive

The better acquainted you are with the people for whom you are praying, the more likely you are to pray faithfully.

25

and confidential nature on an answering machine.

- Always share the prayer requests exactly as given. Do not comment or express personal opinions on the situations.
- Share answers to prayers as soon as they become known.
- Plan for the last person on the list to call the first person on the list and verify that the request circulated through the chain.

3. *Prayer Partners*—The experience of being prayer partners will bless those who choose to participate. These may be selected by drawing names out of a bowl, or asking persons to turn to the left or right and pray with the one sitting beside them. If you know the women in your group well, consider assigning partners who have a common need or shared experience. The partners then set a regular day and hour to meet at designated intervals for a specific amount of time and pray for each other's needs. The benefit of prayer partners is the opportunity to build camaraderie between two women. Encouragement and mentoring is a bonus result of this type of prayer ministry.

> The benefit of prayer partners is the opportunity to build camaraderie between two women.

4. *Bountiful Blessings*—Bountiful blessings groups are prayer groups that meet for a specific short-term purpose. They can be a source of great blessings for individuals experiencing major trials or crises. Blessings groups might gather to pray someone through a session of chemotherapy. Another group might pray for someone anticipating a life-changing move. Still another group might pray specifically for the mother of a rebellious child and the resulting circumstances. These groups meet weekly anywhere from four to six weeks.

Here is a sample prayer letter received by members of a bountiful blessing group.

"Thank you for committing to pray for Becky and her family each week. We are praying for God's perfect will as Becky goes through this time of cancer treatment. But, more than that, we are praying that God will be glorified in all of our lives as we boldly approach the throne with our needs and watch God work.

"Prayer is the best that we can do; yet we sometimes feel that it is the least we can do. Experts can make diagnoses, prognoses, prescribe medicines and dictate care, but only God can heal. As we pray each week, we are coming before the only "Expert" who can make a difference!

"As we pray requesting 'bountiful blessings' for Becky, I know that we will also receive 'bountiful blessings' because we will learn more about the absolute power of our God."

Each week when the group meets, the person for whom the group is praying provides a verse of Scripture (perhaps a personal favorite or a verse that relates to her specific need) to claim that week, as well as praises and requests for the following week. Here is a sample form:

Week of _____

Scripture for this week: _____

Please pray for: _____

We praise You for: _____

The group meets for a short time, focusing their prayers on the designated person. Groups may meet after worship services or before or after the Bible study sessions. A Bountiful Blessings group is very intense and has proven life-changing for those involved.

5. *Mom's Prayer Group*—Encourage mothers to pray for their children. For example, mothers can gather based on their children's age group, spiritual standing (unsaved, wayward), or special needs (emotional or physical healing). A mom's prayer group is a wonderful relationship-builder within the ministry as mothers unite to express love and concern for their children.

Moms In Touch International operates an effective prayer program in several cities. Mothers gather in selected area locations to pray for specific schools, faculty, administration and the children who attend.

Sarah Maddox and Patti Webb have written a book entitled *A Mother's Garden of Prayer.*[1] Its purpose is to teach mothers how to pray Scripture for their children in a wide variety of situations.

6. *Lost Sheep Group*—Many women grew up without the benefits provided in a loving Christian home. My heart is broken anew every year as I meet women who have been praying faithfully for years for their unsaved spouses, parents, and children.

At the beginning of each year, I invite women to pray faithfully and persistently for the unsaved in our extended families. This invitation encourages everyone in the ministry to become involved in praying on their own for the lost, preferably at a designated time each week. A Lost Sheep group can focus their prayers around this concern. If you implement this idea you will have the joy of celebrating the victory in each family as one-by-one individuals come to know the Lord.

7. *Special Events Group*—Every special event should have a prayer team actively involved in every detail of the planning. Prior to the event start time, conduct a mandatory prayer time with the entire committee in the facility where the event will take place. Consider taking a prayer-walk through every room to be used during the event. In each of the smaller rooms, pray that God will speak individually to each woman present. In the large meeting room, pray that hearts will be knit together and turned toward the Father. I have prayed over every chair, instrument, and microphone! I have also personally signed every printed program for an event while praying for each woman who would receive it. Enlist the efforts of every committee member to offer suggestions for prayer. A godly perspective ensures a godly result.

A friend sent me a poem that perfectly illustrates this conviction. Her church was planning a Daughter's Tea, named so because every woman is a daughter! It was written from the heart of Debbie Stuart, a women's ministry leader from Willowpoint Baptist Church in Shreveport, Louisiana. I am privileged to share it with you.

The Father's Tea

This simple bag of flavored tea,
Serves as a reminder for you and me
To earnestly prepare for our Daughter's Tea
Through special prayer on bended knee.
His plan, it's true we cannot see.
By faith in our hearts we will believe
His presence is with us on our journey
His plan and purpose is our destiny.
The Lord can use this "Daughter's Tea:
To usher women into His company,
And bring to hearts such serenity
And change our lives for all eternity!
It will all be over eventually
Then we can rest so peacefully,
With eyes fixed toward the heavenlies
We'll sit with the Father and have some tea!

This poem was duplicated, attached to tea bags, and distributed to church members as a reminder to pray for the event.

God Wants to Bless Your Ministry

The desires of our hearts can be like concert tickets bought and reserved at the "will call" window of our lives. Sometimes the desire is right, the provision is made, but we fail to "call" for it. God is waiting just outside many of our circumstances—waiting for us to invite Him inside. Of course, God can and does shower us with blessings that we do not ask for. But Scripture encourages us to ask: "Ask and it will be given to you; seek and you will find; knock and the door will be opened to you. For everyone who asks receives; he who seeks finds; and to him who knocks, the door will be opened" (Matt. 7:7-8).

We serve the God who is the great "I AM" not the "I WAS." He wants to do an incredible work in your life and in the life of your women's ministry. I encourage you to involve yourself and your women in prayer. Prayer will inspire, empower, and totally change your women's ministry as it changes the women involved.

> The desires of our hearts can be like concert tickets bought and reserved at the "will call" window of our lives. Sometimes the desire is right, the provision is made, but we fail to "call" for it.

---

[1] Sarah O. Maddox and Patti Webb, *A Mother's Garden of Prayer* (Nashville: Broadman & Holman, 1999).

For Smaller Churches
by Martha Lawley

If your women's ministry is not large enough for its own prayer coordinator or separate prayer group, incorporate purposeful prayer into everything you do with the women of your church. This approach is an effective way to begin establishing a foundation for a more structured prayer ministry. You will model prayer and reinforce the importance of praying.

If you choose to begin a prayer group, remember that a prayer group can be any size. There is no direct relationship between the size of the group and the effectiveness of prayer. A small prayer group dedicated to seeking God's will is the best way to begin the process of identifying the needs God want your women's ministry to address.

Many LifeWay resources are available to enrich our prayer lives. These tools can be especially useful in smaller churches where trained staff is limited. They range from six-week studies such as, *In God's Presence: Your Daily Guide to a Meaningful Prayer Life,* by T. W. Hunt and Claude V. King, to more in-depth prayer studies, such as *Disciple's Prayer Life: Walking in Fellowship with God,* by T. W. Hunt and Catherine Walker (see p. 221).

How to Study the Bible

by Anne Graham Lotz

(*Editor's note:* In order to lead or administer Bible study groups, you must first develop and practice personal Bible study skills. The following material has been taken from the Bible Study Workshop led by Anne Graham Lotz in her study, *The Vision of His Glory.* See page 221 to order this study.)

Effective daily Bible study will occur if you:
- Set aside a regular place for private devotions.
- Set aside a regular time for private devotions.
- Pray before beginning the day's assignment, asking God to speak to you through His Word.
- Write out your answers for each step in sequence.
- Make the time to be still and listen, reflecting thoughtfully on your response in the final step.
- Don't rush. It may take you several days of prayerful meditation on a given passage to discover meaningful lessons and hear God speaking to you. The object is not to get through the material, but to develop your personal relationship with God.

The Bible Study Workshop has a single purpose: to present an approach that will help you know God in a personal relationship through His Word. The Bible study approach you will be introduced to will help you communicate with God through the Bible.

What You Need for Bible Study
- ❑ Bible
- ❑ Notebook
- ❑ Pen or pencil
- ❑ Time
- ❑ Prayerful, open attitude

Steps to Bible Study

Step 1: Look in God's Word.

Begin by reading the designated passage of Scripture.

Step 2: What does the passage say?

When you have finished reading the passage, make a verse-by-verse list of the outstanding facts. Don't get caught up in the details, just pinpoint the most obvious facts. Ask yourself: "Who is speaking? What is the subject? Where is it taking place? When did it happen?" As you make your list, try not to paraphrase, but use actual words from the passage itself.

Step 3: What does the passage mean?

After reading the passage and listing the facts, look for a lesson to learn from each fact. Ask yourself: "What are the people doing that I should be doing? Is there a command I should obey? A promise I should claim? A warning I should heed? An example I should follow?" Focus on spiritual lessons.

Step 4: What does the passage mean to me?

The most meaningful step is step 4; but you can't do step 4 until you complete the first 3 steps. Take the lessons you identified in step 3 and put them in the form of a question you could ask yourself, your spouse, your child, your friend, your neighbor, or your coworker. As you write the questions, listen for God to communicate to you personally through His Word.

Step 5: Live in response.

Pinpoint what God is saying to you from this passage. How will you respond? Write what you will do now about what God has said to you. You might like to date it as a means not only of keeping a spiritual journal, but also of holding yourself accountable to following through in obedience.

Exercise: Mark 9:2-9

Work through Mark 9:2-9 on the next two pages using the approach just presented. A completed example follows on pages 33-35. The exercise will be more beneficial if you do not refer to the completed example until you work through the exercise on your own. Then, look at the example. Track each verse carefully through all five steps so you can see how the facts are developed into lessons which then unfold into personal questions.

Step 1: Look in God's Word.
Begin by reading Mark 9:2-9.

Step 2: What does the passage say?
When you have finished reading the passage, make a verse-by-verse list of the outstanding facts. Don't get caught up in the details, just pinpoint the most obvious facts. Ask yourself: "Who is speaking? What is the subject? Where is it taking place? When did it happen?" As you make your list, try not to paraphrase, but use actual words from the passage itself.

Step 3: What does the passage mean?
After reading the passage and listing the facts, look for a lesson to learn from each fact. Ask yourself: "What are the people doing that I should be doing? Is there a command I should obey? A promise I should claim? A warning I should heed? An example I should follow?" Focus on spiritual lessons.

Step 4: What does the passage mean to me?

The most meaningful step is step 4; but you can't do step 4 until you complete the first three steps. Take the lessons you identified in step 3 and put them in the form of a question you could ask yourself, your spouse, your child, your friend, your neighbor, or your coworker. As you write the questions, listen for God to communicate to you personally through His Word.

Step 5: Live in response.

Pinpoint what God is saying to you from this passage. How will you respond? Write what you will do now about what God has said to you. You might like to date it as a means not only of keeping a spiritual journal, but also of holding yourself accountable to following through in obedience.

Completed Example of Mark 9:2-9

Step 1: Look in God's Word.

Begin by reading the passage of Scripture. Underline, circle, or otherwise mark text if it will aid your study.

Step 2: What does the Scripture say?

Make a verse-by-verse list of the most outstanding, obvious facts. Don't paraphrase; be literal as you list the facts.

2a   Jesus took three disciples alone up a mountain.

2b-3 He was transfigured before them with clothes dazzling white.

4   Moses and Elijah appeared with Jesus.

5   Peter said three shelters should be put up.

6   He didn't know what to say.

7   A voice spoke from the cloud saying to listen to Jesus.

8   Suddenly they saw no one except Jesus.

9   They came down from the mountain.

Step 3: What does the Scripture mean?

Identify a lesson to learn from each fact. Focus on spiritual lessons.

2a   Jesus wants to be alone with us.

2b-3 There are times we have to be alone with Jesus in order to have a vision of His glory.

4   The vision of His glory will be the focus of believers in eternity.

5   Instead of worshipping Christ, some who call themselves Christians want to build earthly monuments to His Name.

6   Sometimes our emotions prompt us to speak when we should be silent.

7   We are commanded by God to listen to what Jesus says.

8   When everything else fades away, including our visions and dreams of glory, our focus should still be on Jesus.

9   We eventually have to come down from the mountain.

Step 4: What does the Scripture mean to me?

Rewrite the lessons from step 3 in the form of questions. Be personal as you formulate your questions.

2a   When do I make time to be alone with Jesus?

2b-3 What fresh vision of Jesus am I lacking because I don't spend time alone with Him each day?

4   How drastically will I have to adjust my focus from what it is today to what it will be one day in eternity?

5   What earthly monument–a ministry, a church, a denomination, a reputation–am I seeking to build instead of genuine worship of Christ?

6   When have I spoken out when I should have been silent in worship?

7   Having glimpsed the vision of His glory, how obedient am I to God's command to listen to the voice of His beloved Son?

8   Where is my focus?

9   What can I take from this experience back into my everyday life?

Step 5: Live in response.

Pinpoint what God is saying to you from this passage. How will you respond? Write down today's date and what you will do now about what He has said.

March 1, 2000: I will begin today to make time each day to get alone with Jesus, read my Bible, and listen to His voice.

Personal Word from Chris Adams:

As a woman's ministry leader, you are a role-model to the women in your ministry. You set the tone by your attitudes, words, and actions. The most important aspect of your role as leader is your own personal relationship with Christ. All the methods in the world will not compensate for lack of an intimate relationship with Him. Your leadership should flow out of that relationship.

I sincerely hope this chapter on personal Bible study skills will strengthen your desire to meet God in His Word daily and will help you as you participate in and/or lead women's Bible studies.

Bible Study

How to Lead a Bible Study

by Dale McCleskey

As a women's ministry leader, you may find yourself enlisting leaders for small-group Bible studies. If you were asked to provide a job description for Bible study leaders, could you? The following information will help you understand types of Bible studies, characteristics of effective leaders, and their responsibilities. The following chapter, "Administrating Bible Studies," will help you if you administer more than one group.

Bible Study Groups

Resources for Bible study groups are designed for three different types of group experience.

Resources for Bible study groups are designed for three different types of group experience:

1. *Video driven.* A video-driven study cannot be conducted without the video. The content of the course is in the video. The member book serves as a viewer guide for the video and additional, supplemental, or support material for the video. An example of a video-driven study is *The Vision of His Glory* by Anne Graham Lotz.

2. *Print driven.* A print-driven study can be conducted without a video, even if one is provided. In this case, the video is supplemental, or support material, for the printed study. Print-driven studies include *Life Lessons from Women in the Bible* by Rhonda Kelley and *In My Father's House: Women Relating to God as Father* by Mary Kassian.

3. *Hybrid.* A hybrid study contains both print and video and can be studied in several ways: print only, video only, or a combination of print and video. Obviously, the latter would be the most complete form of the content and would involve the learner in a more complete experience. Examples of hybrid studies are *A Heart Like His* and *Breaking Free*, both by Beth Moore.

Bible Study Groups Involve Both Individual and Group Study

Individual study. Each participant needs a copy of the member book, which contains reading assignments and activities designed to reinforce and apply learning. The member book is divided into an introduction and several weeks of content. Many resources divide every week's material into five daily lessons, each requiring from 20-45 minutes to complete. Other resources are divided into chapters that members read at their own pace through the week. Participants complete the daily reading and the learning activities at home in preparation for the weekly group sessions.

Group sessions. Participants meet once each week for a one- to two-hour group session that guides them to discuss and apply what they have learned during their daily, individual study. The small-group sessions encourage accountability and allow members to benefit from the insights of other participants as they process the material they have studied during the week. The small groups also help build relationships as participants share prayer concerns and pray together. If the study includes video, members watch weekly video presentations, followed by discussion and/or additional truths and challenges.

Bible studies are ideal for a weekday or a weeknight study or during the church's Discipleship Training period. If they meet during a 50-minute to one-hour time period preceding other regular church activities, group leaders must adapt lesson plans that call for an hour-and-a-half- or two-hour sessions. Group leaders must allow time for mothers to leave their children in child-care facilities before the session begins. At the end of the session, they must allow adequate time for mothers to pick up children before the start of another church activity.

If the group meets on some schedule other than weekly or bi-weekly, consider using an aid to encourage daily Bible study. One LifeWay resource—*Day by Day in God's Kingdom*—is a discipleship journal built around six Christian disciplines. It allows disciples to record their spiritual journeys as they study other courses. Another possibility is *Whispers of Hope* by Beth Moore, a devotional guide for 70 days (see page 221).

Choosing Leaders

If you use the model of a large group that breaks into smaller groups, you will need to enlist both a large-group Bible study leader and small-group leaders. The large-group Bible study leader is not a teacher but an organizer, coordinator, and facilitator. The large-group leader shows the video. Participants complete the corresponding video response sheet at the end of each week's material in their member books as they view the video.

The small-group leader should be someone who is interested in exploring the crucial truths of the course being studied and who desires to help others grow in intimacy with God. A long list of qualifications and years of teaching experience are not required. A heart prepared by God—being available and teachable—is more important. Paramount to this leader's

The small-group leader should be someone who desires to help others grow in intimacy with God.

success is a strong commitment to study of the course and a faithful fulfillment of the basic responsibilities of group leadership.

Most Bible studies have one leader, usually called a facilitator. The facilitator is responsible for convening the group and conducting the session. You will need to enlist a leader for every 8 to 12 people. Facilitators are responsible for taking prayer requests, leading a prayer time, and guiding participants to discuss each week's material in the member book.

The personal and spiritual qualifications you need to look for in facilitators include:
- a heart committed to exploring biblical truth and the desire to lead others in the same pursuit;
- a commitment to complete the work the particular study requires;
- faithfulness to each weekly meeting and to preparing thoroughly for each meeting;
- a commitment to fulfill the basic responsibilities required of the particular study or course;
- a dedication to prayer and to caring for group members.

If you enlist leaders with these qualifications and commitments, your Bible study ministry will make a positive impact on your church and community.

Facilitating Small-Group Discussion

Group discussion helps members make meaningful application to their daily lives.

One purpose of the group discussion each week is to help members make meaningful application to their daily lives. Facilitators guide discussions of each week's content. Share the following guidelines with facilitators to make these discussion times effective in challenging participants spiritually and promoting life change.

Guidelines for Small-Group Facilitators
- Arrange the chairs in the meeting room in a circle or a semicircle so that participants can see one another. Seating should not physically exclude anyone.
- Greet members as they arrive and start the meeting on time. Allow five minutes for participants to share prayer requests; then pray or ask a participant to pray. Make notes when prayer requests are shared. Encourage members to pray for one another during the week. If someone is experiencing difficult circumstances, mail a note or call between sessions.
- Lead the discussion, adapting the suggested lesson plan in the

38

leader guide to the needs of the group. Emphasize that only participants who wish to respond should do so; no one is required to share responses. Do not force the discussion questions on members. Adapt and change the suggestions in leader materials as necessary. Be flexible if members wish to spend more time on one group of questions or if they raise specific issues. Be sensitive to members' particular needs as the discussion progresses. Remember that your job is not to teach the material but to encourage and lead participants in sharing their insights about the work they have done during the week and in applying the content to their spiritual journeys.

- Be personally involved without relinquishing leadership. Your role as facilitator is that of a fellow disciple—one who shares the same struggles the other participants have in their spiritual lives. You need to be emotionally vulnerable and willing to share some of your own feelings and responses. However, you must also recognize that someone must lead the group and direct the discussion at all times. Be flexible but do not allow the discussion to veer off on a tangent. Keep the focus on the week's content and its application.

- Try to create a relaxed atmosphere that will help every member feel a sense of belonging. Use first names. Do not rush the discussion.

- Pray for the Holy Spirit's leadership; then allow Him freedom to direct the session as He wills. His movement may be evident in tears of joy or conviction, emotional or spiritual brokenness, or the thrill of a newfound insight. Be sensitive to signs of God's work in a person's life and follow up by asking the person to share. Give participants the opportunity to testify to what God is doing. Often the testimony may help another person with a similar issue.

- Be sure that you do not talk too much as facilitator. Do not be afraid of periods of silence.

- Be an encourager. Show a caring, loving spirit. Communicate acceptance and concern. Especially if your group includes non-Christians, you need to create an atmosphere that communicates, "I accept you as you are." Accepting participants does not necessarily mean that you agree with their values or choices. You can love a person without agreeing with that person.

- Listen intently and aggressively. When someone shares some-

Your role as facilitator is that of a fellow disciple—one who shares the same struggles the other participants have in their spiritual lives.

If someone is unsaved, follow the Holy Spirit's leadership to know the right time to talk with the person privately to lead her to Christ.

thing personal or painful, lean toward her. Use facial expressions to show concern. Nod your head.

- Be ready to address special needs that members may reveal. If someone is unsaved, follow the Holy Spirit's leadership to know the right time to talk with the person privately to lead her to Christ. If a participant reveals emotional pain or family problems, assure her of the group's concern and support, and pause briefly to pray with the person. Then offer to meet with her later to help her find additional help if needed.

- Set boundaries. Do not permit a group member to act in a verbally abusive way toward another member. Do not force group members to do or say anything. Try gently nudging a group member to a point of discovery and growth instead of pushing her to a conclusion for which she is not ready.

- End the discussion period on time. A few minutes before the time to end the discussion period, help the person speaking reach a point of closure. If someone is not finished, affirm the importance of what the person is saying. Offer to continue the discussion next week and ask that member to introduce the topic at the beginning of the next meeting. Or you may need to spend time privately with the person if the topic does not relate to the entire group. Finally, remind group members to pray for one another during the week.

Actions to Take After the Session

Encourage group leaders to evaluate every session. Ask them to take the following actions each week:

1. While the session is still fresh on your mind, immediately record concerns or impressions to pray for any group member. Remember to pray for these concerns throughout the week.
2. Evaluate the session by asking yourself the following questions. Record your answers in your journal.
   - Was I adequately prepared for today's session?
   - Did I begin and end on time? If not, how can I use the time more wisely next session?
   - Does anyone need extra encouragement this week? Note whether or not a card or a phone call is appropriate. Then remember to follow-up on each one.
   - What was my overall impression of the session?
3. Read the next session guide in order to prepare for the next session.

Coping with Problems in the Small Group

As you enlist group leaders, prepare them for the fact that no matter how meaningful the study and how effective the leadership, difficulties can arise in any group. Share with those you enlist the following common problems of groups and suggest ways for dealing with them:

Absenteeism. Absentees miss a potentially life-changing experience and diminish others' learning. Contact the absentee, communicate your concern, and encourage her to make up the work. Otherwise, a participant will quickly get further behind and likely drop out.

Not completing at-home assignments. In courses requiring individual daily study, emphasize in the introductory session that a significant course requirement is doing daily study, including completion of the learning activities. Anyone who is not willing to make this commitment should not participate in the study. If someone continually refuses to complete the assignments, meet with her and suggest that she withdraw and participate at a time when she can devote herself adequately to the study.

Disagreement with the content. Some debate in a group is productive. Remember that the Scriptures should always be the final source of authority. If debate becomes counterproductive, suggest that you and the participant discuss the matter later so other members can participate in the present discussion.

"Be patient, bearing with one another in love. Make every effort to keep the unity of the Spirit through the bond of peace."
Ephesians 4:2-3

Do not feel threatened if someone expects you to be an authority and to answer all of her questions. Emphasize your role as the facilitator of the discussion, pointing out that participants are to learn from one another and that you are not an authority on the subject. Suggest that a volunteer research the question during the week and report at the next meeting if the person insists that an answer is important to her.

A participant who dominates the group. Ways a person may dominate a group are—
- claiming a major portion of each discussion period to talk about her issues;
- repeatedly waiting until the last 10 minutes of a meeting to introduce an emotionally charged story or problem;
- attempting to block other group members' sharing;
- judging others' behavior or confessions;
- challenging your leadership in a hostile way;
- criticizing other group members' motives or feelings.

As the facilitator, make sure every person has an opportunity to share. Discourage dominating members by calling on others, by asking someone to speak who has not yet responded, or by focusing directly on someone else. If these methods do not work, talk privately with the dominating person and enlist the person's support in involving everyone in future discussions.

When a person is going into too much detail and is losing the attention of the group, you will usually notice that the group has disconnected. Direct the sharing back on course by discreetly interrupting the person and by restating the point she is trying to make: "So what you are saying is …." Another method is to interrupt and restate the question you asked originally: "And Liz, what did you learn about God's love through that experience?" Even if the speaker is somewhat unsettled by this response, she should respond by restating the response more succinctly.

Many people need to break free from behaviors that have their roots in childhood traumas or painful experiences. Thus, some group members may feel a need to talk about the details of their painful experiences. Such discussion can very well damage or destroy the group. Survivors of trauma do need to talk about their pain, but such emotional processing is not the purpose of a Bible study. Refrain from attempts to turn the group into a therapy session.

The idea that you can help someone is very seductive. You may feel great pressure to direct the group into "helping" a hurting member. Please do not give in to the urge. Keep the focus of a Bible study group on truth and application of that truth. If the person needs counseling or a support group, help her find the assistance she needs. Avoid the mistake of allowing the group to lose its focus.

Keep the focus of a Bible study group on truth and application of that truth.

Conclusion

In this chapter you have reviewed several types of Bible-study groups in women's ministry and the qualifications and responsibilities of the group leadership. Now you will be better equipped to enlist, train, administer, supervise and evaluate Bible-study groups. The following chapter will give you additional help in these roles.

Bible Study

Administrating Bible Studies

by Elizabeth Luter and Dale McCleskey

As a women's ministry leader, a primary responsibility will be planning, publicizing, and implementing Bible study groups in your church. All of the resources found in the *Women's Ministry Catalog* published by LifeWay contain leader helps, either in the back of the member book or as a separate leader guide. Although these suggestions include ideas for how to plan and conduct individual courses, they do not provide a vehicle for administering several groups. This chapter is written to help the person who oversees more than one Bible study group and wants to provide the best possible coordination and evaluation.

"Your word is a lamp to my feet and a light for my path."
Psalm 119:105

Responsibilities of the administrator include–
- selecting the studies and their leaders;
- scheduling the studies;
- promoting the studies and coordinating enrollment efforts;
- coordinating and supporting the work of group facilitators;
- ordering and distributing resources;
- maintaining and submitting accurate records of participation each week as Discipleship Training attendance;
- evaluating group facilitators, resources and group experiences.

Plan Ahead

The following steps are suggested to assist the person organizing Bible studies.

1. Enlist the support of your pastor. The pastor's endorsement will encourage people to deepen their spiritual lives. Perhaps he will agree to announce from the pulpit this discipleship opportunity.

2. Talk with the potential participants to determine the level of interest in this type of study. Consider distributing questionnaires and survey instruments at women's ministry events. Include names of possible studies or a list of topics from which to choose. Also ask if the study should be offered during the day, in the evening, or both. When scheduling the study, be sensitive to the needs of women who work outside the home.

43

3. Schedule the weeks on the church calender that will allow the greatest participation. Fall and spring studies usually result in more participation than do summer sessions. However, summertime may afford some persons with seasonal careers—such as school teachers—an opportunity to attend an intimate discipleship study.

4. Offer child care if possible. This will increase your attendance and ensure greater weekly participation.

5. Decide the time schedule. Most Bible studies are designed for a minimum of 50 minutes with 2 hours suggested for an in-depth study.

6. After estimating the number of participants, order member books between four and six weeks in advance by writing to LifeWay Church Resources Customer Service, One LifeWay Plaza; Nashville, TN 37234-0113; FAX order to (615) 251-5933; PHONE 1-800-458-2772; EMAIL to CustomerService@lifeway.com; ONLINE at www.lifeway.com; or visit the LifeWay Christian Store serving you. Decide if the church will pay for member books or if participants will pay for their own. Experience has shown that if members pay for their books or a portion of the cost, they are likely to make a more serious commitment to the study. Be sure that scholarships are provided for members who cannot afford to purchase their own books.

7. Reserve small-group meeting rooms for the number of groups you will have. Arrange the meeting rooms to be as intimate as possible. Chairs should be arranged in circles or semicircles. Semicircular rows of chairs are acceptable for a large-group room.

8. Conduct a planning session for the group leaders. Complete the following actions in the meeting.
   • Discuss their responsibilities:
      —greeting and registering participants at the introductory session;
      —calling members assigned to their small groups after the introductory session and encouraging them to complete the daily assignments for week 1;
      —checking small-group members' attendance;
      —taking prayer requests, conducting prayer time at the beginning of the small-group period, praying for participants, and encouraging participants to pray for one another;
      —guiding members to discuss the week's material;
      —promoting fellowship among group members;
      —noting opportunities for follow-up ministry.
   • Discuss registration procedures. If you have several groups

beginning at or near the same time, plan to set up several registration tables with signs indicating the studies to be offered. Assign small-group facilitators to handle registration at their stations. Provide them with a supply of member books, registration cards, pencils, and reusable name tags. They should wear a name tag, greet registrants with enthusiasm, and answer their questions as best they can or promise to find out the answers.

9. Plan to keep accurate records and report attendance to the church office. Regardless of when the study is offered, it is a Discipleship Training study and should be reported as Discipleship Training participation on the Annual Church Profile. Another reason to keep accurate participation records is that participants can earn Christian Growth Study Plan diplomas for completing the study.

10. Evaluate the group experience. Supply an evaluation form at the final group session or mail attendees an evaluation form with a self-addressed stamped envelope. No one should be asked to sign the form. A separate evaluation form can be prepared for the group leader. In addition, solicit comments as you see group members at other women's ministries functions. Keep evaluation forms together in a file by the name of the study as a ready reference if you choose to offer the study again at a later time. Be sure you have addressed all of the concerns indicated on the evaluation forms.

11. Keep in touch with group leaders throughout the group experience; offer support and encouragement. Be a ready listener if a leader is experiencing a frustration; offer advice only when it is asked for!

12. Pray, and keep praying that God will involve the members He desires and that He will validate this study with His presence and activity!

Provide Variety in Bible Study

Obviously not all women have the same Bible study needs. An effective women's ministry must offer enough variety in content, leadership style, and schedule to meet the needs of participants. Seek to address all levels of spiritual maturity and learning styles. One type of presentation for all participants is rarely adequate. Consider the following types of diversity you can provide:

Seek to address all levels of spiritual maturity and learning styles.

1. Provide Diversity in Levels of Bible Study–New or immature Christians may feel incapable of participating in in-depth Bible studies. On the other hand, anything less than an in-depth study for an intermediate to mature believer may create frustration and result in a lack of interest.

2. Plan for Variety in Length—A mature believer can usually complete a 10- to 12-week study. However, immature to intermediate believers may be depleted after six weeks or less.

3. Provide Diversity in Teachers—For reasons of maturity, personality, and simple preferences, one style of teaching can never meet the needs of every believer. An effective Bible-study ministry requires several gifted teachers with a unique capability to challenge and interest a variety of learners.

4. Vary Meeting Times/Days—Consider offering several different studies— night and day. This approach is challenging and taxing, yet necessary to maintain an effective ministry.

5. Vary Beginning and Ending Times—Open-ended studies are important so that newcomers can enter at any point during the study. However, most studies are written in such a way that picking up the resource half-way through the course can be difficult. If you stagger the studies so that new studies begin frequently, newcomers can be assimilated without having to wait 8 to 12 weeks. Studies that begin and end on a certain date motivate most attendees. Time limits also allow members to move from study to study.

Determine Subject Matter

Providing interesting and challenging subject matters presents a great challenge. Resources must be evaluated to determine the level of spiritual maturity to which they appeal. Never label any individual's level of spiritual maturity, but for planning purposes you can think in terms of entry-level, intermediate, and advanced Bible study. As you plan, you will want to provide opportunities to reach and minister to each type of learner. An inability to direct women to their proper group-level classes leads to ineffective ministry.

Most women's ministries have insufficient staff to adequately evaluate resources. Consider asking a spiritually mature church member, perhaps a retiree or widow, with the appropriate discernment and skills to evaluate potential resources in her spare time. A shy person may find this to be a service ministry; it may even open the door to reaching someone who has been inactive in your women's ministry.

Promote the Studies

Target persons in your community who are interested in Bible study. Church bulletins, newsletters, handouts, posters, fliers at Mothers' Day Out, announcements in worship services and in Sunday School classes, phone calls, and word of mouth are excellent and inexpensive ways to promote the study. Sometimes local radio and television stations announce upcoming events free of charge.

To assist you in promoting the study, many LifeWay videos include promotional segments. You will find both a segment designed for use inside the church and one for use in a broadcast format. Use the in-church promo in a worship service, in a women's Bible study class, or in other locations where women regularly gather during the week. You have permission to duplicate this segment if you wish to create a loop tape that plays continually. Be sure to have someone prepared to announce the date, time, and place of the introductory session and to invite persons to attend. If the tape is left to play unattended, place a sign beside the monitor that lists the date, time, and place of the introductory session.

The second promotional segment is a 30-second commercial that can be used on a local television station or cable channel. A blank screen for the last few seconds has been left so that you can have the television station or cable company insert your personal invitation on the screen. Again, you have permission to duplicate this commercial as needed. If you would like a broadcast-quality copy of either the longer promotional segment or the television commercial, you may order one for the cost of the tape, plus labor, by calling (615) 251-2882. Allow between two and three weeks for duplication and delivery.

Launch the Studies

If you have several studies beginning at or about the same time, conduct a well-promoted meeting at which you present an overview of all resources and scheduled studies. This meeting can be a part of another women's ministry event. Allow women the opportunity to choose a study that particularly interests them or addresses a need. Then at the individual introductory meetings of each Bible study include a more extensive overview of the topic or resource, providing yet one final opportunity for women to affirm their study choice before the group closes or before purchasing materials.

Additional Practices for Healthy Bible-Study Groups

As an ongoing part of Bible-study ministry, you will need to train all leaders to practice the following disciplines:
1. Wean Group Members from Stagnant Comfort Zones—At some point in their spiritual journeys, all believers need a challenge. Certain group environments and familiar people can create comfort zones that

stagnate their growth. While we must be cautious in pushing someone beyond her learning level, we can be equally destructive by failing to motivate her to seek new horizons. Most of us are hesitant to stretch beyond our own self-perception, but a good teacher/leader, with proper discernment, will see beyond her student's potential and create the challenge. Transitional resources are important to help learners stretch beyond their comfort zones.

2. Practice Accountability—Challenging women to be accountable to God for what they learn is another necessary task. Train leaders to develop accountability partners rather than enlisting one group member to check up on the entire group. If someone knows a fellow group member is nurturing her success and growth, she will strive to please that person. Accountability is a necessary bridge in the learning process; it provides incentive and makes the journey more effective for all those involved.

3. Develop Spiritual Gifts—Teach leaders to observe and make note of their students' individual gifts. The ability to incorporate these gifts into the learning process will motivate and encourage continual participation. Women like to feel needed. We have a sincere desire to share our abilities. When gifts are utilized in the appropriate place, women experience a sense of satisfaction and are encouraged to continue the process.

4. Celebrate Graduations—Everyone enjoys the excitement and recognition of successful accomplishment. Closure of some sort is necessary for each ministry or study opportunity. This indicates the end of one task and suggests new horizons for service ahead. While certificates are always acceptable, personal remembrances, however inexpensive, marking the date and time are special reminders of the journey. Completion celebrations that include a variance from the normal group procedure will create a sense of excitement and anticipation.

5. Cultivate Unity in the Ministry—Although you may have a variety of study groups meeting during the same time period, provide opportunities for joint fellowships to maintain a sense of unity. Encourage groups to challenge one another. Make a special point to affirm new believers in their sincere zeal and excitement for God. This will also encourage mature believers who sometimes become sluggish in their joy. A reminder of God's goodness will rejuvenate their spirits and eliminate separatism.

6. Make Room for Failure—Allow groups and individuals the freedom to fail. If previously set goals are unreached, motivate participants to

persevere. Model a "can-do" attitude that reflects the flexibility to make changes at a moment's notice. Failure does not have to be devastating with fortitude and sheer determination.

Note the following words from Beth Moore about administrating a women's Bible study ministry:

Because of my love for in-depth Bible study, I've tried to make it my business to know what works and what doesn't in a ladies Bible-based study. Through the years I've asked many women what they liked or did not like about the way their Bible studies were conducted. I've also offered countless evaluations at the conclusion of those which I have taught. I believe women are looking for the following characteristics in the administration of their group Bible studies:

- Women want organization! Women have very little time in our busy culture. When they give the precious resource of their personal time, it is undoubtedly at the sacrifice of something else. They want to participate in a well-planned program and use their time wisely.

- Women who register for in-depth Bible study want the greater emphasis to remain on the Bible study. In other words, during discussion time, they are more interested in what God has to say and the response of the women to His Word than they are in haphazard opinions. The effective leader will keep discussions focused on the responses of the women to God's Word.

- Women desire well-respected guidelines rather than stringent restrictions about attendance and confidentiality. An effective leader makes the group aware that if guidelines are respected, there will be no need for restrictions.

- Women want to feel connected to their small group. They want to meet other members. They want to know they are missed when they are absent. And they want to know they are an addition to the group when they are present.

If you utilize these suggestions, you will be more effective in organizing, administering, and evaluating the Bible studies offered by your women's ministry. At times when you may feel overwhelmed with the details of such a task, recall that the Word of God is the only offensive weapon in the armor of God (see Eph. 6). As we lead women to study and know His Word, we are providing the fertile soil for transformed lives.

> Women want to participate in a well-planned program and use their time wisely.

Bible Study

Small-Group Leadership Skills

by Joseph Northcut

Women need meaningful relationships. Without feeling connected to others, women often do not reach their full-potential—becoming more Christlike and being transformed. When a small group of women gathers to study and discuss God's Word, pray together, and help one another apply what they've learned, they discover a new power and strength for living their lives. The Holy Spirit carefully molds them into a beautiful example of community. Deep, life-changing growth always occurs in the context of relationships.

Small groups are effective tools to help Christian women carry out the Great Commission. Jesus did not call us just to evangelize the world. He called us to make disciples. Small groups provide a safe place for individuals to tear down walls and discover answers—answers that lead to transformed lives. In his book *Leading Life-Changing Small Groups*, Bill Donahue states:

> "Small groups were an integral part of the early church. They were small enough to allow individual members to minister to one another, use their spiritual gifts, and be discipled in the teachings of Christ. In addition, they were vibrant and life-giving communities where evangelism could take place as unchurched people watched a loving and compassionate community in action. Small groups not only built up the church but were vehicles for reaching a lost world for Christ."[1]

Facilitating a Small Group

If you are a small-group leader, your role is facilitator, not teacher or lecturer. According to *Webster's,* the word *facilitate* means "to make easier." Applied to the task of discipling, it means to help persons develop by clearing away obstacles that impede growth. It describes how Jesus led and taught His disciples.

Creating a Proper Small-Group Environment

The primary goal of a small group is for each member to feel accepted

Small groups provide a safe place for individuals to tear down walls and discover answers— answers that lead to transformed lives.

and able to share openly her thoughts and ideas. As a facilitator, strive to create an atmosphere of warmth and acceptance by being positive and encouraging. A small group can become a "home base" to its members, a place of love and honest sharing.

A small group can become a "home base" to its members, a place of love and honest sharing.

The proper environment–or climate of the group–is critical to small-group success. You may have little if any knowledge of group members' situations and experiences before the first group meeting. As facilitator, your first task is to create a relaxed atmosphere that promotes a sense of belonging and is conducive to sharing and learning. The following are ideas for creating a suitable environment.

- *Be aware of your own eye and body language.* Eye contact can dissuade or encourage someone to talk. Body language reveals interest and enthusiasm or boredom and irritability. Remain alert to group members' eye contact and body language to determine if the discussion is helpful and of interest to them or if the conversation is off track and members are losing interest.

- *Be accepting of tears and emotions.* Often, facilitators will place a box of tissues in the center of the circle to indicate that tears are allowed here! Women can then reach for a tissue without someone in the group having to fish for one in her purse. When tears occur, don't shift the focus or reject the person or the tears. Instead, comfort them by saying, "It's OK. It's healthy to cry."

- *Accentuate the positive.* Use these encouraging statements: "That's an interesting point." "Thank you for sharing." As you express appreciation for participation, women will feel affirmed and accepted.

- *Allow women personal space.* Some group members may feel uncomfortable sharing personal thoughts when discussion turns to individual application or when the topics involve sensitive issues. Be discerning in this situation.

- *Befriend group members.* Free time or breaks during the group meeting can be uncomfortable for those who are new to the group. Introduce them to others and demonstrate a personal interest. Get to know your group members–their needs, interests, and strengths. Meet members where they are.

Preparing to Lead

1. *Pray! Pray! Pray!* The best preparation will be time spent in prayer. Before you invite people to join your group, pray daily that God will lead the group members He wants to attend, that He will unify them,

and that He will empower you to lead and encourage them. Ask the Holy Spirit to guide you in working with each member. God's Word through the Holy Spirit achieves its transforming effect on people.

2. *Determine group size.* Keeping the group small provides each member opportunity to interact in the group discussion. When a group exceeds 12 persons, a few will dominate and/or sub-groups will emerge.

3. *Select an appropriate place to meet.* Choose a room with movable furniture so that members may participate in a variety of learning methods. A circular seating arrangement is best for eye contact and maximum participation.

4. *Arrive early.* Whether you are meeting at church, in your home, or in someone else's home, allow ample time to arrange the room and prepare for the study (distribute handouts, display visuals, arrange teaching aids, and so forth). Arrange equipment (such as a flip chart, marker board, overhead projector, or television monitor) in positions that allow all members to easily see and hear. Complete these tasks before the first group member arrives.

5. *Arrange the seating.* Give consideration to the following factors.
   - Be sure members can see one another and you can see them. Be sure members can turn with little difficulty to see each other's faces. Remember, group members communicate with facial and bodily expressions as well as with the voice. The backs of people's heads don't say much!
   - To avoid glare, face chairs or seating away from large windows and close the curtains when possible.
   - Turn chairs away from the entrance to the room. Latecomers may feel embarrassed if they face other members while entering.
   - Select for yourself a straight-back chair in which to sit. This posture communicates openness and alertness. A cushioned chair often causes a leader to appear too relaxed.

Leading the First Session

1. *Greet members individually as they arrive.* Catch up on personal news.

2. *Allow members to choose their own seats.* This small but important detail ensures members will feel comfortable in the group.

3. *Establish the Bible as your authority.* As the facilitator of a group, the Bible is the group's authority and the Holy Spirit is the Teacher.

4. *Define the purpose of the group.* Whether a prayer group, Bible study group, support group, or another type of group, participants need clear guidelines as to why you are meeting. Some women will turn a Bible

study into a prayer group or vice versa unless you as leader remain true to your purpose and intervene.

5. *Establish and clarify expectations.* Members have certain expectations for one another and for the facilitator as they journey together. Discuss the following expectations during your first group session:

- Privacy. Many groups practice a confidentiality covenant that states that information shared within the group is respected as confidential and not shared outside the group. A good rule of thumb is never tell someone else's story.

- Starting and ending times. Keeping commitments is critical if you as facilitator wish to gain the confidence of group members. Starting and ending the session on time is a key commitment. Here are a few suggestions for approaching a group member who is habitually late:

    (a) Pull her aside and talk in a friendly, nonconfrontive manner.

    (b) Without making her feel guilty, explain the distraction of late arrivers.

    (c) Determine the reason she is constantly late.

    (d) Adjust the starting time if possible and convenient.

    (e) Demonstrate concern and a Christlike attitude.

- Attendance. Regular attendance is important not only to individual learning, but also to group members who depend on one another for support, encouragement, and good ideas.

- Homework. Curriculum groups (book studies) are planned on the assumption that members have read the material and completed the exercises and activities prior to the group meeting. During each group session members are asked to share, on a voluntary basis, their responses to the learning activities. Members benefit from comparing what they have learned between sessions with the responses of others in the group. If some in the group have not completed the activities, they become "takers" and not "givers" to the group. In addition, they will be unprepared to share their own feelings with the group. As facilitator, model the expectation by completing all the assignments yourself. Be prepared to talk with individuals outside the session if it becomes obvious assignments are not being completed.

- Voluntary participation. Emphasize that you will not ask anyone to share personal information. Encourage members to share their feelings, attitudes, insights, and experiences as they feel comfortable to do so. Trust the group process. Members are capable of contributing to the group. Encourage members to talk directly to one another rather than through you.

6. *Explain the small-group process.* Review the format you will use for each session so that members know what to expect. If you are using a curriculum, clarify the connection between homework assignments from the study materials and their use in the group sessions. Teach members how to use the study materials.

7. *Provide structure to the group.* Guide discussion (or prayer), guide them through any obstacles (members who monopolize, members in crisis, and so forth), make assignments for the next session (when appropriate), and draw discussion to a close. Do not hesitate to influence the discussion when things are headed off track. You might say: "This is a very interesting discussion, but I think we've strayed from our original topic. Maybe we could discuss this topic another time."

8. *Be flexible.* As facilitator, be prepared to change or rearrange your lesson plan in order to maximize what may be happening with members as they experience the group. At times you may need to discard your plans to meet members' needs and interests.

9. *Close the group by reaffirming a pertinent truth or fact.* Leave the group with one important truth or idea for application. Let the group know you are available even though the group meeting is coming to a close.

Leading Discussion

The following are helpful hints for leading a small-group discussion:

1. *Avoid dominating and controlling the group.* The facilitator's role is to draw out other people and encourage them to share. The optimal group situation is one in which members address one another directly with pertinent questions and feedback.

   Share your own opinions and feelings to stimulate discussion when others are reluctant. You will be modeling the role. When discussion is free-flowing, wait until others have shared and adequate time remains for your comments.

2. *Encourage group participation.* If only a few women respond, say, "Let's hear from some of you who have not yet had the opportunity to share." Eye contact can encourage members to talk (but do not stare). If you sense that a group member truly would like to share but is hesitant, ask her. "Trudy, I sense that you would like to share. Is that the case?" Refrain from putting anyone on the spot by calling on them by name. "Suzanne, what do you think?" rarely endears you to that

person! A silent person may be listening and receiving, but unable to verbalize her ideas at that point.

3. *Ask simple and clear questions.* Is your question complicated or confusing? Can it be easily understood and remembered? Ask one question at a time. Asking two questions at once confuses the issue and one or both questions may not be properly addressed.

Some questions can be answered with a yes or no, some with only a few words. Closed-questions have an accepted answer and thus inhibit free discussion. Open-ended questions often begin with the words *what, how,* or *why.* They allow group members to respond with feelings and ideas that are important to them (for example, "What do you think about ... ?" or "How do you feel about ... ?"). Open-ended questions challenge group members to think and avoid a bias.

4. *Deal with difficult questions honestly.* Be willing to say: "I don't know. Does anyone else have input?" Admit your own humanity and imperfections. Members are more likely to share with a fellow struggler than with someone who gives the impression she knows all the answers. If the answer can be found, ask someone to look it up before the next session or offer to do so yourself.

5. *Keep discussion Bible-centered.* Members may disagree on a particular interpretation. It's OK to say, "Here's what I believe." "We may agree to disagree." But as facilitator, don't let "anything go." Refer back to the Scripture or to comments made by the study leader.

6. *If you allow tangents, make them work for you.* At times, tangents (something off the target of the study) can be good. Watch group members closely, making eye contact, to determine if the tangent seems to be a common concern. If a tangent motivates participation, good! Monitor the time involved and, if necessary, redirect the conversation at the appropriate time.

7. *Take advantage of silence.* When waiting for a response, 10 seconds can feel like 10 minutes to the facilitator. But group members may not feel the same. A good question requires time to think and respond. Facilitators who are uncomfortable with silence may have a tendency to provide the answer or ask another question. Refrain from answering your own question. A few silent moments allows the group time for insight and thought. However, if prolonged, silence may indicate participants do not understand the question. After a reasonable time, use a different approach and restate the question.

8. *Don't force conversation.* If group members have sufficiently discussed the relevant issues, conclude the group or go on to the next topic.

9. *Don't allow a particularly verbal person to monopolize group discussion.* Most small groups include at least one member who talks more than the others. Although not intending to offend, she may at times be inappropriate and disruptive. When asking a question or waiting for a response, avoid making eye contact with this person. Make eye contact with others, instead. Ask for new opinions. Say something like: "Some of us have contributed many ideas. Let's allow some other group members to share." Appreciate the individual who is dominating and move to someone else. In extreme cases, you may have to speak privately with the "monopolizer." Ask for her cooperation in getting others to participate.

Equipping and Training Others as Small-Group Leaders

Your key to ministry success is NEVER DO MINISTRY ALONE!

Your key to ministry success is NEVER DO MINISTRY ALONE! Equipping and training is an ongoing process and must be tailored to each individual leader.

Finding Potential Small-Group Leaders

1. *Pray.* Ask God to lead you to the right people.
2. *Make a personal commitment to equip people.*
3. *Know who you are looking for.* Select qualified people who are:
   - Growing Christians who take seriously the lordship of Christ.
   - Active church members who support other church ministries and corporate worship services.
   - Teachable in their spirits.
   - Passionate about and have a heart for ministry.
4. *Develop a personal relationship with those you are considering.*
   - Find their *hearts* before you ask for their *hands.*
   - Discover their motivations.

Enlisting Small-Group Leaders

1. *Share your vision for this ministry.* If they cannot see where you are leading them, they will not remain committed over the long term.
2. *Ask for a commitment.*
   - Ask only after you have shared your dream and vision.
   - Ask early—timing is important. Don't wait until the last minute.
   - Ask in person.
   - Ask with already high expectations that "stretch." In other words, get them out of their comfort zones so they will grow.
3. *Communicate the high priority you place on their ministry.* Help them to feel

that what they are doing is significant in God's kingdom and in the life and ministry of your church.

Supervising Small-Group Leaders

1. *Set goals for growth.*
   - Clearly state the goals.
   - Make the goals appropriate, attainable, and measurable.
   - State the goals in writing.
2. *Communicate the fundamentals of the task.* Communicate responsibilities and the functions involved.
3. *Train them using the following five-step process.*
   - Model—You lead a group with them in attendance.
   - Mentor—Together you co-lead or share leadership.
   - Monitor—They lead a group and you participate.
   - Motivate—They lead a group and you are in the background encouraging them.
   - Multiply—They lead a group and model for someone else.
4. *Empower them with the "Big Three."*
   - Responsibility—Once you have given them responsibility, don't take it from them by offering too much assistance or direction.
   - Authority—Allow them to be in charge of their groups. Don't allow group members to come to you with questions or suggestions unless you also involve the leader in the discussion.
   - Accountability—Lead them to be accountable for what happens in the groups and for achieving the purpose for the groups.
5. *Provide tools, training, resources, and support.*
6. *Check on leaders in a systematic manner.* Inspect what you expect!
7. *Stay with them in their process until they sense success.*
8. *Provide ongoing equipping and training opportunities.*[2]

Take the Long Look

Effective small groups do not materialize overnight. Your small-group leadership skills will improve as you continue leading groups. In turn, leaders you enlist will benefit from your modeling effective leadership. As women become familiar with the small-group process, they will model the role for newcomers to their groups.

Generally, groups do not begin to bond until the second or third week. Do not force the process by which members become comfortable with one another. Too intimate sharing in the first couple of sessions can frighten or inhibit women who are not accustomed to intimate sharing.

Just as anything of
value must be
cultivated and
nurtured, your small
groups deserve your
best attention and
care.

Just as anything of value must be cultivated and nurtured, your small groups deserve your best attention and care. They will produce much joy and growth in your women's ministry.

---

[1] Bill Donahue, *Leading Life-Changing Small Groups* (Grand Rapids, Mi.: Zondervan Publishing House, 1996), 26.
[2] Notes from "Equipping the Laity" Ministry Conference, INJOY, Inc., John Maxwell, presentor, July 1995, First Baptist Church, Springdale, Arkansas.

For Smaller Churches
by Martha Lawley

The principals of leadership for those in smaller churches are the same as for those in larger churches. Remember: Christ was the model of godly leadership and He lead a group of 12. Some suggestions concerning leadership in smaller churches, in reality, apply to all leaders. Learning to help and encourage individuals to succeed in their relationships with God and others is an essential ingredient for effective, godly leadership.

In a smaller church it is particularly important to see each woman as a unique resource and to commit to helping her "fan the flames" of her gift(s). It is in her best interest that this is done first and foremost, resulting in producing women who are more equipped for service within women's ministry programs. This investment in the lives of women is well worth the experience. I pray we do not neglect the responsibility we have as leaders to help each woman find her special place.

Just because your church operates in small groups by virtue of its size does not necessarily mean you are proficient in small group skills. This chapter provides invaluable information on understanding, developing, and practicing the skills necessary to maximize the small group experience. The helpful hints for leading a small group will be useful in evaluating your existing groups and can be implemented in any size church.

The basic steps to equip and train others in small group ministry described in this chapter are applicable to any size church. These suggestions require little or no financial resources to implement.

Spiritual Gifts

Biblical Basis for Gifts

by Paula Hemphill

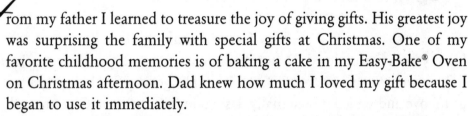

From my father I learned to treasure the joy of giving gifts. His greatest joy was surprising the family with special gifts at Christmas. One of my favorite childhood memories is of baking a cake in my Easy-Bake® Oven on Christmas afternoon. Dad knew how much I loved my gift because I began to use it immediately.

Tragically, many gifts fail to produce joy because they go unused or are unappreciated. How many gifts do you have that remain in their original boxes, never enjoyed because the giver didn't choose the gift with you in mind? Perhaps the instructions were too difficult or the gift's purpose was not clear. Whatever the reason, a gift ignored is a gift wasted.

The Bible provides the basis for understanding God's gifts to His children. When we use the principles in God's Word as our standard, we can evaluate ourselves honestly and gain the confidence we need to discern and use our gifts as God intended.

Our task in women's enrichment ministry is to help women find and establish their self-worth in a personal relationship with Christ, identify their spiritual gifts, and use those gifts in service. As this process occurs, each woman will mature and the body of Christ will be blessed.

Good Words from Our Good Father

The Bible is the story of God's love gifts to His children. The story begins with the gifts of creation when God declared His work to be "very good" (Gen. 1:31). Later in the Old Testament, God gave the gift of the Holy Spirit to equip specific individuals to speak for Him and to serve the Israelites (see Judg. 3:10, 6:34). The story continues as God gave His love gift–Jesus–to our lost and dying world! With the coming of Jesus came a new promise: after the resurrection, God would send the gift of the Holy Spirit to indwell and fill every believer (see John 14:16-17).

Since the Day of Pentecost, the Spirit has given gifts to each of the Father's children. These spiritual gifts are actually gifts of grace, custom designed to bring joy while being used to serve the body of Christ (see 1 Cor. 12:7). The gifts can only be understood and appreciated within the

"All scripture is inspired by God and profitable for teaching, for reproof, for correction, for training in righteousness; that the man of God may be adequate, equipped for every good work."
2 Timothy 3:16-17 (NASB)

59

context of a personal relationship with the Giver and in the family relationships of His body, the church.

The Father's gifts are:

- based on a love relationship.
- given through the Holy Spirit's work in us.
- custom designed for each individual.
- given to prepare us for our unique service to the Master.
- given to bless and build the body of Christ.

God's Good Goal

Have you ever wondered what we will do in heaven? The Bible teaches that we will worship and serve God. With His good gifts He is preparing us to love and serve Him eternally. Using our gifts to serve God on earth is our internship for heaven! If this is true, why do only 20 percent of Christians do 80 percent of the work in the local church? Why do so few do so much and so many do so little? Are you asking the same questions as you evaluate your church and your women's enrichment ministry?

In the early 1980s my husband Ken was called to pastor First Baptist Church, Norfolk, Virginia. As the church grew, its needs grew. God began to teach us how to help new believers find and use their spiritual gifts in the life of the body of Christ—the church.

When we asked church members why they didn't serve, they usually gave one of two reasons for their reluctance to minister. They responded, "I'm not worthy" or "I'm not able." The first answer reveals a lack of self-worth and a failure to properly understand our inherent value based on Christ's sacrifice for us and God's affirming statements of our worth as His children. It also demonstrates that forgiveness is not a reality in the person's life. No one is worthy without the sin covering provided by Jesus' blood. My worthiness flows from my love relationship with the Savior. Gratitude for God's goodness always leads to service.

The second response, "I'm not able," demonstrates a lack of understanding of spiritual gifts and their purpose for the body of Christ. It is also a sign of self-dependence rather than surrender to the in-working power of God's Spirit. In the flesh, I am not able, but the Bible assures me that in Christ I can do all things (see John 15:5; Phil. 4:13). Panic sets in when we are unprepared. Teaching, loving correction, and training strengthen confidence.

We pray for God to educate and motivate His gifted body, His children! Not 20, not 80, but 100 percent of the church must be involved for maximum blessing. All believers are members of His body, but we identify with a local church family. The health of the church family life, many call it "body-life," is directly related to the participation of every gifted child. God loves and gives. His children love and serve. The body grows. God is glorified!

The health of the church family life is directly related to the participation of every gifted child.

Good Gifts in Creation

God, our Heavenly Father, reveals Himself as Creator and Giver of life. As Creator, God gives us a miraculous physical body, a mind that thinks and reasons, and natural abilities and talents. We are "fearfully and wonderfully made" (Ps. 139:14), and we can affirm that God's works are wonderful. Do you find it difficult to thank God for your body or for your mind? Most women can find something about themselves that they don't like and would choose to alter.

As loving parents of three daughters, Ken and I confirm that each of our daughters is beautiful just as the Lord formed her and a unique individual. We want them to believe and act on what we already affirm. That is what God, our loving Heavenly Father wants each of us to believe. We are His children and He loves us. We can say with the psalmist: "I thank you, High God—you're breathtaking! Body and soul, I am marvelously made! I worship in adoration—what a creation!" (Ps. 139:14, *The Message*) Praising God helps us to overcome negative thoughts. Praise acknowledges that His work is good and that we are His workmanship—magnificent treasures.

Good Gifts in Re-creation

Sin distorts the perfect creation of God, and many women bear the scars of past failure and abuse left by sin's curse. The miracle of re-creation or "new birth," transforms the pain of the past and gives power in the present and hope for the future. In John 3:16 we read that because God loves, He gave His own Son. The ultimate motivation for God's greatest gift was His love for you and for me. Just as with any other gift, God's love gift must be received and embraced. "For by grace you have been saved through faith; and that not of yourselves, it is a gift of God; not as a result of works, that no one should boast" (Eph. 2:8-9, NASB).

The richness of the Father's grace gift cost Christ His life. God generously and graciously gives the gift of forgiveness and the gift of salvation through the willing sacrifice of our Lord Jesus Christ. When we respond in faith to the gift of God's Son, we are re-created, born again into God's forever family. After adopting us into His eternal family, our Father gifts us with a lavish inheritance in Christ. He confirms the inheritance with

When we use His gifts, we give the Father pleasure and joy. We also allow His body, the church, to work effectively and efficiently.

the family seal, the gift of the Holy Spirit. These marvelous truths set forth in Ephesians 1 provide the basis for new life in Christ.

There is more! Through the Holy Spirit, God gives special gifts to each of His children—gifts of grace that allow us to serve Him and to serve in His body, the church. These gifts, *charismata* in Greek, are "manifestations of grace." When we use His gifts, we give the Father pleasure and joy. We also allow His body, the church, to work effectively and efficiently. The gifts preclude any pride or boasting by the one who receives the gifts. The emphasis is on the Giver—the Trinity: Father, Son, and Holy Spirit—not on the gift (see 1 Cor. 12:4). The proper response to God's graciousness is an attitude of thanksgiving and gratitude that results in service to the body of Christ and praise to the Father.

One Woman's Surprising Story

The life of Mary Magdalene is a wonderful example of salvation and deliverance leading to service. In Luke 8:1-3 as Jesus and His disciples preached from city to city, they enjoyed the support of "some women." Mary Magdalene, Joanna, Susanna, and "many others" had experienced Jesus' healing touch. They had been delivered from the evil spirits and diseases that bound them. These women had been forgiven much—and they loved much. Their love led them to follow Jesus from Galilee and to serve Him by ministering to His and the disciples' needs.

These women formed the first women's enrichment ministry, the first woman's missionary movement, the first women's evangelism team! What can we learn from them and their gifted service to Jesus? These women were set free to serve. This devoted band of women used their diverse gifts to minister to Jesus, and they gave generously to support the preaching of the gospel. They came from different economic and social strata of society, but their personal relationships with Jesus broke down the cultural barriers between them.

Mary Magdalene had a dark personal history; she had been controlled by seven demons, the full compliment of evil. She would have been considered hopelessly lost by her generation—not your top candidate for missionary service. Do you know a woman who could be considered unreachable? No one is too hard for God to reach. If you had asked Mary about her availability for service, she would probably have felt unworthy and unable. But Jesus changed her! Jesus saved Mary Magdalene and adopted her into His family. When Jesus freed Mary from evil, He opened the door for her to serve Him immediately, using her gifts to extend the redemptive work of the gospel.

Mary Magdalene was sealed into fellowship with the women who followed Jesus. They appeared together at the foot of the cross, in the garden at the tomb of the Savior, at the resurrection, and in prayer in the upper room (see Matt. 27:55-56; Mark 15:40-41; 16:1-2; Acts 1:13-14). In ministry, in grief, in joy, and in intercession, these women found support in new family relationships with the followers of Jesus.

Good Gifts for Body—Life

In Matthew 16, after Peter's confession that Jesus is the Christ, the Son of the Living God, Jesus made the first mention in the New Testament of the "church." Jesus declared that He would establish a new community, a family of faith. He called this new community the *ecclesia*, "a called out people," or His church.

Later in the New Testament, the apostle Paul wrote to the new believers in Corinth, in Ephesus, and in Rome, and described the church as Christ's body—a living, growing organism dependent on the proper function of each individual part. Every individual is significant and necessary to the health of the body. There is strength in the unity of the parts working as a complete, integrated unit.

When the lost world observes the unity and love expressed within the body of Christ and the cooperative working of the members, they see the power of God at work and they can believe in God. As each part of the body fully realizes its God-given potential, the body grows. Each individual is gifted for the effective work of God's redemptive plan.

Peter wrote that "His divine power has given to us all things that pertain to life and godliness, through the knowledge of Him who called us by glory and virtue" (2 Pet. 1:3, NKJV). God gives us everything we need. Have you ever prayed for a healthy church, a "no-need church"? If God has given the Christian "all things," why are so few believers using their rich inheritance for the common mission we share in His body, the church? The answer may lie in a confusion about spiritual gifts and how their proper use builds healthy church family relationships.

Too many churches have developed into dysfunctional family systems. Individual members are wounded by bickering factions and power struggles within the church family; their self-esteem is damaged, leaving them feeling useless and unappreciated. The tragic result is that many Christians try to go it alone as "lone ranger" Christians, avoiding the local church. Others may join a fellowship but stay on the fringes, refusing to use their gifts in the ministry of the body. In either case, the whole family suffers and the work of God is hindered.

"I do not ask in behalf of these alone, but for those also who believe Me through their word; that they may all be one; even as Thou, Father, art in Me, and I in Thee, that they also may be in Us; that the world may believe that Thou didst send Me."
John 17:20-21 (NASB)

The goal of a healthy family is for the children to mature into responsible adults, starting new families of their own. Likewise, evangelism should lead to birth and growth. The joy and the opportunity for ministry grows with the family, gifts are affirmed, and individuals are appreciated for their uniqueness.[1]

The gift discovery process requires both instruction and example. Working together in mutually caring relationships will often provide the positive affirmation one needs to aid in discovering one's gifted purpose in the body. When necessary, accept the warning and correction as loving reproof that allows you to develop a healthy personal identity. The more a church family provides the context for positive instruction and feedback, the less demand there will be for corrective teaching.

Good Words of Correction
Instructions on Spiritual Gifts in 1 Corinthians

The apostle Paul served as a missionary church planter in the Mediterranean world. After preaching in Corinth for 18 months and seeing many come to Christ, Paul began to minister in Ephesus (see Acts 18:1-17). After receiving disturbing reports from some of his co-workers in Corinth, Paul wrote letters to the Corinthian church. This church was fractured by power struggles and bickering. At the core of its many disputes was a distorted understanding of the Holy Spirit's work and an elitist mentality concerning spiritual gifts.

Paul addressed the Corinthians as "my beloved children" and stated that he had become their "father through the gospel" (1 Cor. 4:14-15, NASB). Paul's understanding of family relationships in the church led him to correct the Corinthians for their lack of maturity and helped him to establish sound teachings on the issues disturbing the fellowship. His reproof had one goal: to take the Corinthians to the next level, to see their church healed and healthy. Paul wanted to see these "babes in Christ" grow up (see 3:1)!

The Corinthian church behaved like a dysfunctional family. Blatant immorality and unresolved legal battles between members splintered their fellowship. Selfishness and self-centered actions destroyed the spirit of the Lord's Supper. Boasting in the prowess of their favorite spiritual leaders characterized the church. Does this sound familiar?

Many Christians are afraid to study spiritual gifts because they are confused and intimidated by those who claim spiritual superiority based on their experiences or gifts. Some have seen inconsistency in the moral behavior of those claiming to be "spiritual." Confusion about the work

of the Holy Spirit and His connection to the gifts prevents many believers from fully appreciating the power and in-filling supplied by the Comforter.

In the opening verses of 1 Corinthians, Paul established a foundation for his teaching on spiritual gifts by giving the Corinthians solid principles to help them rebuild healthy families. Healthy families begin with healthy individuals. Paul, their spiritual father, wanted these "children" to have strong self-esteem based on their identities in Christ, individually and corporately.

Six Keys for a Healthy Self-Concept

- *Sanctified*—In Christ, I am washed clean, set apart by God for His special purpose and His use. As I surrender to His miraculous atoning work through the Holy Spirit, I place my life at His disposal (see 1 Cor. 6:11).
- *Saint*—God calls me a "saint," literally meaning "holy one." I am pure and blameless based on the cleansing power of Christ's blood, not by any merit of my own (see 1:2,8).
- *Single-minded*—God has given me the "mind of Christ," allowing me to know the things freely given to me by God. As each believer thinks like Jesus, disagreements dissolve and harmonious thinking builds unity (see 1:10; 2:12,16).
- *Spirit-filled*—The Spirit of God lives in me, filling me with the richness of Christ's life. Every believer is a sacred dwelling place for the Spirit (see 3:16; 6:19; 12:3).
- *Spirit-gifted*—The Holy Spirit gives me an individualized gift or gifts, especially designed for me and my task in the church family. No one is left out! Gifted to serve, I occupy a unique place in the body, prepared by God just for me (see 12:7,11,18).
- *Servant*—God has given me the opportunity to serve Him by serving others within the body of Christ. The assignment I am given is the Master's choice and not my own. To obey is my responsibility; the results are His (see 3:4-17; 4:1-2).

God's Word clearly teaches that each believer is a sanctified saint, a single-minded, Spirit-filled, Spirit-gifted servant. Understanding these truths defuses any arrogance and pride. On the contrary, they should produce an overwhelming humility and gratitude within the child of God.

First Corinthians 12:14 records Paul's response to the Corinthians' questions about spiritual gifts. As you read these chapters, notice Paul's emphasis on diversity in the unity of the body.

"Now there are varieties of gifts, but the same Spirit. And there are varieties of ministries, and the same Lord. And there are varieties of effects, but the same God who works all things in all persons. But to each one is given the manifestation of the Spirit for the common good."
1 Corinthians 12:4-7 (NASB)

The Corinthians believed that miraculous spiritual gifts, such as speaking in tongues and performing miracles, proved the gifted ones were spiritually mature. They believed some gifts were better than others, exalting the gifted person. They zealously sought ecstatic experiences. Their behavior implied the question, "Don't spiritual gifts prove that we are spiritual persons?"[2]

Paul began his answer by redefining and broadening their understanding of the work of the Holy Spirit and spiritual gifts. He clarified the sovereign initiative of the Holy Spirit in relation to their gifts:

- Each member has a gift.
- Each gift has one goal—the common good of the body.
- Each gift is given as the Spirit wills (see 1 Cor. 12:11, NASB).
- No member has all the gifts.
- Many members make up one body.
- Mutual care grows from the unity of the body.

Paul used the imagery of the human body to illustrate his message. Body parts work together to make life possible. Many of these body parts are unseen, and we may not understand or appreciate their necessary functions. What if the whole body were a big ear? How would one see? It sounds silly until we realize that the Corinthians were expecting every member of their "corporate body" to be the same, act the same, perform the same function, and share the same gifts. How handicapped would the human body be if it said to the feet, "I have no need for you"?

Some members may receive less honor or notoriety in the working of the body. To feel you do not belong to your church because you are not like those who appear to be more visible is to deny how God put the church together.[3] A women's Bible study teacher may be more visible than a woman who stuffs envelopes for a retreat mailing but each woman is necessary to the healthy body.

The members are diverse and so are the gifts Paul identified in 1 Corinthians 12:8-10 and 12:28-30. Paul's letters include four gift lists; no two are the same (compare Rom. 12:6-8 and Eph. 4:11). While Paul mentioned the dramatic gifts of speaking in tongues and performing miracles in 1 Corinthians, he did not include them and others in Romans 12 or Ephesians 4. If the four lists are combined, there are approximately 20 gifts, depending on how they are designated. Along with the leadership gifts of apostle, prophet, and teacher, Paul broadened the possible gifts with general categories of "helps, administrations, service, and showing mercy." These general categories give the lists an open-ended quality. These lists are not comprehensive but illustrative.

Paul encouraged the Corinthians to "earnestly desire the greater gifts" (1 Cor. 12:30, NASB), and he showed them what to seek. The greatest gift is the gift of love (see 13:13). While an emphasis on some gifts may create divisions and pride, love binds the body together, nurturing mutual respect and appreciation for every member. Ministry and service without the supernatural love of Christ are self-serving and self-glorifying.

Paul's correctives are needed in our churches today. No one person can do every job. When we take a position God intends for another member, we hinder her involvement and we can burn out from overwork. No one is indispensable, but everyone is necessary. We do not always comprehend the true value of the gifts being used behind the scenes. We need to engage all women so that they can find their places in the body.[4]

Good Words for Practical Training
Paul's Instruction on Spiritual Gifts in Romans 12

There is no sign that the church in Rome experienced the conflicts related to spiritual gifts suffered by the Corinthians. After laying out the basis for the Christian life in the first 11 chapters of the letter, Paul made a transition to application. How does a Christian live the salvation life every day? Victorious living is possible as we apply solid biblical teaching through an active participation in the gifted body where God has placed us. These principles summarize the biblical basis for understanding and using spiritual gifts.

Six Principles for Victorious Living:
- *The yielded body*—Sacrifice is an act of the will. Giving our physical beings to God is an act of surrender and worship. God wants our availability more than ability.
- *The transformed mind*—Thoughts affect actions. Our life choices change as we allow Christ to give us new and renewed minds. Victorious Christians choose to capture each thought and bring it into obedience with Christ's thinking and teaching (see 2 Cor. 10:5). God's Word is the source for renewed thinking.
- *Universal giftedness*—Each Christian has the gift of God's grace and God has given each unique but different spiritual gifts. No one is left out!
- *Unity in diversity*—Praise God you are part of one body in Christ. Like the master craftsman, God weaves our unique gifts into one masterpiece, His church. Remember: Jesus prayed that we would experience this unity as we love one another supernaturally.

"Hope does not disappoint, because the love of God has been poured out within our hearts through the Holy Spirit who was given to us."
Romans 5:5 (NASB)

- *Interdependence*—The fact that we have different functions within the body means we need one another. We function together for a common goal—to glorify our Father and to bring Him pleasure.

- *Energetic exercise*—Use it or lose it! Just as muscles atrophy when not used and exercised, so God's gifts atrophy when we fail to use them to edify His body. The body-life suffers when one member is a couch potato. Get out there and exercise God's grace gifts—you and the body will be healthier.

What a wonderful message to women today. In the body, we find fulfillment through using the spiritual gifts each of us possess. The open door of service and ministry builds a healthy self-image and builds the body. As leaders in women's enrichment ministry, will we open the door and invite other women into service for the Master, preparing them for heavenly service?

[1] Ken Hemphill, *Mirror, Mirror on the Wall-Discovering Your True Self Through Spiritual Gifts* (Nashville: Broadman & Holman, 1992), 27.
[2] Ibid., 48.
[3] C. Gene Wilkes, *Jesus on Leadership* (Nashville: LifeWay, 1996), 37.
[4] Ibid.

For Smaller Churches
by Martha Lawley

What a joy for the smaller church to discover God's perfect provision within its own members! Leaders should provide a positive environment for members to understand what the Bible teaches about spiritual gifts and assist members in discovering and using their gifts within the body.

Leaders should set the example of biblical service in accordance with their unique gifts. Each woman on your leadership team should know and be willing to share with others what her spiritual gift(s) is and how God is using the gift(s). Then, lead members of your women's ministry to claim their giftedness.

Sometimes a smaller church may more clearly recognize the need for everyone to be involved in service. This recognition is a great place to begin allowing God to work through spiritual gifts teaching and training. Resist the temptation to fill jobs just to get tasks accomplished. Allow God to work through the process of gift discovery and implementation.

Spiritual Gifts

Gifts Discovery

by Paula Hemphill

Webster's Dictionary defines the word *adventure* as "an exciting or remarkable experience." Discovery is the process of "revealing or uncovering." You wouldn't be reading this chapter if you didn't have a desire to discover how God has uniquely gifted you as His child.

The Christian adventure of gift discovery is a life-long process as the believer walks with Christ in the indwelling power of the Holy Spirit. Other Christians can help in your gift discovery as they encourage you and affirm your service. Trying a variety of jobs can lead you to discern the areas in which you experience joy in ministry and are effective in helping the church grow stronger.

The prospect of finding your God-created purpose implies that once the gift is discovered, you will use it as intended by the Giver. The desire to know what you have been given is connected to your willingness to serve God by exercising your gift or gifts to bless Him and build His church, His body. It may be necessary for you to move out of your comfort zone to attempt service in new areas of ministry.

> *"We have not received the spirit of the world but the Spirit who is from God, that we may understand what God has freely given us."*
> 1 Corinthians 2:12

Distinguishing Between Gifts, Talents, and Traits

Gift discovery can be confusing. How do you distinguish between birth gifts, personality traits, and spiritual gifts? Are they interconnected? When God created you, He gave you birth gifts, or talents, and a distinct personality. As you grew and matured, you began to identify those talents and to develop them as you received training and the affirmation of parents and teachers. Maybe you had a variety of interests, but you noticed strengths in specific areas. You made choices to invest time and energy in the use and the discipline of your talents, improving your abilities.

As you surrender your physical and emotional being to God, your birth talents can be transformed by God's power and used for service in the church, to give God glory. The born-again musician may surrender her voice to the Lord and experience the empowering of the Spirit as she sings. Her vocal cords, and everything necessary to sing become tools for edifying the church. Her facial expression and movements can radiate the presence of the Holy Spirit. God integrates her physical and emotional being with the spiritual gifts of ministry and service.

When you are born again by the Spirit of God, you are given a spiritual gift or gifts at the new birth, just as you were given talents and interests when God created you physically. The Holy Spirit wants to reveal your spiritual gifts and to help you find fulfillment in serving Christ.

The First Prerequisite

The first prerequisite for knowing your spiritual gifts is knowing God through a personal relationship with Jesus Christ. Occasionally, unsaved people join a church and volunteer to use their talents to serve. Efforts to serve God in the flesh can lead to frustration for the non-Christian and to conflicts within the church.

In her book, *Lose the Halo, Keep the Wings,* Virginia Wilson shares how she led people to Christ and served as a pastor's wife before she had a personal relationship with Christ. She knew what to do and how to do it from years of exposure to Christian culture. She wanted to help people. She knew about Jesus, but she didn't know the Savior.[1] What a difference! Confronted by her sin and her own efforts and self-righteousness, Virginia repented and asked Jesus to forgive her and to come to live within her heart. After she came to know the Lord, Virginia began to use her gifts of mercy to minister to women through her writing and mentoring.

Problems come when Christians serve God in the flesh, in a state of carnality. The carnal Christian attempts supernatural service with natural resources. She fails to depend on the infilling of the Spirit to energize her gifts. Unconfessed sin and disobedience to the Holy Spirit hinder gift discovery. The confession of sin, the cleansing of the Spirit, and the constant filling of the Spirit allows a believer to experience the supernatural power and presence of God. She becomes a channel of blessing to the body of Christ by the activation of her spiritual gifts for ministry.

Stop now and ask yourself the following questions. Answer honestly, giving yourself time to process the answer.

- When did you come to know Christ as your personal Savior? Where? Can you identify with Virginia Wilson?
- As a Christian, is anything hindering the flow of the Holy Spirit in your life and your gift discovery? Have you tried to impress others with your "spirituality," resulting in spiritual pride and self-gratification? Do you experience jealousy and dissatisfaction if you compare yourself to other women? Have you failed to glorify God in your body?

The first prerequisite for knowing your spiritual gifts is knowing God through a personal relationship with Jesus Christ.

When you are born again, you become a spiritual person, and the Holy Spirit makes all things new (see 2 Cor. 5:17). The indwelling Holy Spirit belongs to every believer! Your body becomes the "temple of the Holy Spirit, who is in you, whom you have received from God" (1 Cor. 6:19). The indwelling Spirit will never leave you nor forsake you, but the infilling of the Holy Spirit is conditional and continual. Every Christian is commanded to "be filled with the Spirit" (Eph. 5:18).

Make a conscious commitment to present the members of your body to Christ. This is an act of worship (see Rom.12:1). The whole idea is to surrender your hands, feet, brain, tongue, whatever part, to the control of the Spirit. Jesus is faithful to the promises in 1 John 1:9. If you confess, He will cleanse you and you will become a conduit for His power to touch others for Christ.

The Blessing of One Obedient Life

Beth Moore is a great example of how God uses our life experiences, the painful crossroads in our life-map, as building blocks for ministry. A popular writer and speaker from Houston, Texas, Beth allows her hurt and pain to become the platform for relating to women. Beth's motive for discovering her gifts was a deep desire for intimacy with the Lord.

Beth testifies that as a child she was remarkably shy and withdrawn. As she began teaching a women's Sunday School class, she presented her body, her mind, and her time to the Lord as a sacrifice. Her spiritual gift of teaching was developed and matured as Beth was found faithful in study and in her walk with the Lord. She says simply, "It basically comes down to the pure discipline of pursuing God every day."[2]

The Holy Spirit demonstrates His power to overcome our "natural bent" and uses our weakness as the platform for supernatural ministry. Beth's adventure in discovering and using her God-given spiritual gifts have provided spiritual nurture and challenge to many women. God wove the threads of her story and her gifts to create a yielded servant.

The Holy Spirit demonstrates His power to overcome our "natural bent" and uses our weakness as the platform for supernatural ministry.

Key points to remember:
- *Realize that God created your talents and personality.* Thank Him that in the new birth His power can transform those birth gifts for service. Your passions and interests can direct you to areas of need and opportunity.
- *God does not work in our lives by compartmentalizing our talents and gifts.* He created us as integrated beings: body, soul, and spirit.

Our spiritual gifts can compliment and not compete with our birth talents. With God it is not an either/or but a both/and when it comes to using your birth gifts and spiritual gifts to bless others and to praise God.

- *Don't put the Holy Spirit in a "gift box."* Infinitely creative, the Spirit may surprise you by revealing a spiritual gift that transcends your personality and natural talents.
- *As Christians we are filled with the Spirit at our spiritual birth, but we "leak" and require the daily, moment-by-moment infilling of the Holy Spirit to truly discover our spiritual gifts and to use them fruitfully in the edification of the church.*
- *The motive for gift discovery is to know God more intimately.* All spiritual gifts are a reflection of His character and goodness. To understand and appreciate your giftedness is to know more intimately your loving Father.

The Process of Gift Discovery

Have you ever completed a spiritual gift inventory or a personality questionnaire to help you identify your giftedness? Many Christians have been asked to assess their God-given gifts by answering questions, then graphing the responses to develop a gift profile. There are many good resources that take this approach.[3]

Another approach is to allow the Holy Spirit to speak through the Bible, through the affirmation of the church, and through prayer. Personally, I am more convinced and convicted when the Lord speaks to me through His Word. The process of listening to the Holy Spirit begins with prayer and Bible study. Use the ABC's of gift discovery as a listening guide as you begin the adventure of unwrapping God's spiritual gifts.

Use the ABC's of gift discovery as you begin the adventure of unwrapping God's spiritual gifts.

The ABC's of Gift Discovery

1. Ask the Holy Spirit for truth in your innermost being (see Ps. 51:6). The truth can set you free to serve as God has designed you.
   - Ask for the wisdom to understand yourself as God has created you (see Jas. 1:5).
   - Ask for the Spirit to help you understand your spiritual gift(s) (see 1 Cor. 2:10-12).
   - Ask for the faith to accept and use your spiritual gift(s) (see Luke 11:10).
   - Ask for the Spirit to reveal to you the needs of your local body of

believers—the church. Could you be God's gift to the church to meet a specific need in the body?

2. Believe God's Word when it says that YOU are gifted (see 1 Cor. 12:7). Be zealous for the gifts that will edify the church (see 1 Cor. 14:12).

3. Commit to move out of your comfort zone and try new avenues of service. The Holy Spirit can speak loudly through life's painful experiences when you have received comfort through other believers. You can use those times of God's ministry to you as a catapult to ministry to others.

4. Discern through the affirmation of other Christians where God is directing you to serve. Where do you find personal fulfillment in service? What have you done lately that caused others to say, "a job well done"?

5. Examine your motives for seeking God's gifts. Can you pray, "Not my will but thine be done," when it comes to God's invitation to serve Him?

6. Follow the Spirit's leading when He reveals your passion, your burden for a particular area of ministry. Where do you sense God's invitation to join Him?

Spiritual Gifts and Spiritual Mentors: Gifts and Women in the Bible

Read Exodus 31:1-5 in your Bible. The Spirit filled the artisans for the tabernacle building project with the wisdom to complete their tasks in the temple construction. Using their creative gifts and craftsmanship, they served the Lord. What kinds of artistic expressions and workmanship are useful to your church, to the women's enrichment ministry? Can you design graphics for a brochure or compose a presentation on the computer? arrange flowers? sew costumes for a drama or write a script for a skit? Set your imagination free. Do you consider these artistic gifts as potential spiritual gifts when empowered by the Holy Spirit?

Now read the four passages listed below and note the different gifts in each list. Remember: the gift lists are illustrative, not comprehensive. List the gifts in each passage in the margins or on your own paper.

1. 1 Corinthians 12:7-11. Who is given gifts? (v. 7). For what reason are the gifts given? (v. 7). Who distributes the gifts and who decides which gifts are given to each individual? (v. 11).

To understand how some of these gifts can be activated in women's lives today, I find it beneficial to examine the work of the Spirit through the stories of biblical women. As you study the Scripture, ask the Holy Spirit to give you the wisdom to discern your spiritual gift.

- Mary of Nazareth (Luke 1:46-56)—Mary expressed great wisdom in understanding her situation, her grasp of God's activity in history, and in discerning God's character. Are you able to help others apply truths and see God's hand at work?
- Hannah (1 Sam. 2:1-10)—How was God's knowledge acknowledged by Hannah? Do you possess insight and perception, the ability to understand facts and situations?
- The Canaanite Woman (Matt. 15:21-28)—Why did Jesus commend this woman for her faith? Are you optimistic and do you inspire others to have confidence in the Lord?
- Anna (Luke 2:36-38)—Anna had the gift of prophecy, the work of the Holy Spirit to proclaim God's message and to speak inspired words that edify. Are you serious and straightforward in the way you speak truth to others?

2. 1 Corinthians 12:28-30. Does anyone have all of the gifts? Does everyone have the same gifts? Of the gifts listed in this passage, which ones would you identify with a "position" or "office"?

- Priscilla (Acts 18:24-28)—To teach is to explain difficult concepts in a way that is easily understood and to communicate truth and instruction effectively. How did Priscilla and her husband Aquila instruct Apollos? Do you enjoy studying and processing information? Do you like to share what you learn with others? In 1 Corinthians 12:28, Paul used two words that appear only in the New Testament: helps and administrations. Helps is defined as the ability to meet needs, joyously doing for others. Do you have this gift? Do you recognize this gift in other women in your church?

3. Luke 8:2-3. The women mentioned in this verse followed and served Jesus. They were women "behind the scenes," doing whatever was necessary to help the ministry progress. Do you prefer to work in unseen jobs, out of the public eye? "Administrations" refers to the ability to steer in the right direction, as in steering a ship. Do you have the ability to inspire other women to cooperate on a project? Can you organize well and generate teamwork?

- Deborah (Judg. 4:4-14; 5:1-11)—A multi-gifted woman, Deborah was a prophetess, a judge, and a leader in Israel. With the gifts of organization and administration and the discipline to delegate, Deborah served alongside Barak and the people volunteered. What

can you learn from her about godly leadership? Was she a risk-taker?

4. Ephesians 4:11-12. Why did God give leaders to the church? What is their purpose? Who are they preparing for service?

- The Samaritan Woman (John 4:1-30,39-42)—This woman practiced the gift of evangelism. She was compelled to communicate the gospel. By effectively sharing her testimony, others were drawn to the Savior. Do you have a burden for the lost and the unreached people of the world?

5. Romans 12: 6-8.

- Martha (John 12:1-8)—Martha is serving, using her gift of ministry. Do you love to cook? Do you take meals to church members and enjoy doing things for others?

- Mary (John 12:1-8)—Generously and joyously giving, sacrificing for the Lord's needs, Mary lavished her gift with no expectations except to please Jesus. Do you have the joy of giving? Are you a good steward of your resources? Are you sensitive to the needs of others?

- Elizabeth (Luke 1:39-45)—Exhortation encourages and comforts those in our sphere of influence. Elizabeth counseled and mentored the young mother of Jesus. Are women drawn to you for advice and encouragement?

- Dorcas (Acts 9:36-42)—A woman with the gift of mercy, Dorcas continually ministered to the poor widows of Joppa. With a concern for the hurting in her community, she used her gifts in benevolence ministry. Do you possess a tender sensitivity for those who suffer? Do you enjoy just "being there" for those in pain?

- Key Thought: Most of these women were not "serving" in official church positions. Their gifts were used by the Spirit of God to meet the needs of the body, where and when those needs arose.

- Key Question: Are you waiting for a position or are you willing to activate the gifts within you and serve the Lord as He invites you to minister?

As the Holy Spirit shows you the gifts He has given you, realize that you have a unique, God-designed purpose. God intends for you to find joy and fulfillment in His gifts to you, His precious child. Continue to pray that God will direct your interests and passions into fruitful ministry.

God intends for you to find joy and fulfillment in His gifts to you.

[1] Virginia Wilson, *Lose the Halo, Keep the Wings* (Birmingham: New Hope, 1996), 13-18.
[2] Vicki Selles and Jon Kent Walker, "The Teachable Moments of Beth Moore" *HomeLife*, March 1999, 16.
[3] C. Gene Wilkes, *Jesus on Leadership* (Nashville: LifeWay, 1996), 44-48.

For Smaller Churches
by Martha Lawley

As leaders in the smaller church, we need to carefully examine our motives in involving people in service. The pressure to accomplish tasks is particularly great in the smaller church. The desire to get things done is not wrong. However, it should never be the primary motive for encouraging others to serve.

The goal for you as leaders in your church and women's ministry is to help women discover and fulfill their unique, God-designed purpose. The ABC's of gift discovery found in this chapter provide an excellent framework for any size church seeking to unlock the blessings God has provided through the discovery and use of each member's spiritual gifts.

Each of the biblical women mentioned in this chapter were involved in smaller ministries. The key was not the size of the group they were affiliated with, but rather, each woman's individual obedience to God. These women also illustrate the many diverse gifts that the Spirit gives women.

Spiritual Gifts

Using Gifts in Ministry

by Paula Hemphill

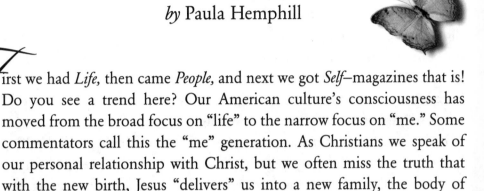

First we had *Life,* then came *People,* and next we got *Self*—magazines that is! Do you see a trend here? Our American culture's consciousness has moved from the broad focus on "life" to the narrow focus on "me." Some commentators call this the "me" generation. As Christians we speak of our personal relationship with Christ, but we often miss the truth that with the new birth, Jesus "delivers" us into a new family, the body of Christ. Through salvation Jesus moves us from loving ourselves selfishly to loving ourselves appropriately, to loving our new family—the church, to loving the world—His world. Loving His world and using our gifts in ministry to His body go hand-in-hand.

God's plan is to engage each individual as a unique part of His body. The parts fit together in an interdependent pattern based on God's design and His strategy to touch the world with the message of Christ's love. What an awesome privilege to join God in His plan to redeem the world!

Our challenge as leaders in women's enrichment ministry is to actually move the "me" generation to the next level in ministry, a level of service appropriate to each woman's maturity in Christ. How do we help women use their spiritual gifts in ministry? The very word *use* implies activity. When we use a muscle by exercising it regularly, it grows stronger and often leaner. We would say it is growing "fit and healthy." The muscle isn't strengthened in isolation from the body. It is an integral part of the whole. If we are going to get the women in our churches fit and healthy spiritually, we will have to help them realize their potential in Christ within His body. The "body-life" will be enhanced and blessed as each individual "exercises" gifts given by the Lord.

"For we are God's workmanship, created in Christ Jesus to do good works, which God prepared in advance for us to do."
Ephesians 2:10

Our Own Personal Trainer

I know how important it is to exercise regularly. My problem is changing my "knowing" into "doing." I lack discipline without motivation. Last summer our daughter Rachael got married. When I thought about fitting into my mother-of-the-bride dress, my desire to get in shape radically changed. I had something important to prepare for and the anticipation affected my attitude toward exercise. To help me follow through with my new commitment to get in shape, I secured a "personal trainer."

The trainer planned the day's exercises, set the weights, and cheered me on. What a difference a little accountability made. I knew that my trainer was watching my progress, keeping tabs on my workout schedule, and monitoring my endurance level. He challenged me to go beyond what I thought I could manage, constantly encouraging me to "keep on keeping on." Some days I would dread going for my workout. After getting to the gym, I found I really enjoyed the exercise. I was encouraged because I followed through with my commitment. The end result wasn't bad either! I felt better about myself and I looked better, too.

Each Christian has a personal trainer–Jesus.

Each Christian has a personal trainer. Jesus, through the indwelling Holy Spirit, is challenging us to do the works God has prepared for us. He has a goal in mind. He is preparing us for a very special wedding–the marriage feast of the bride of Christ, the church. Our workout here on earth is the warm-up for the main event! Jesus is the perfect trainer because He created us, redeemed us, and knows us better than we know ourselves. He also knows the work the Father has prepared for us. Consequently, the Spirit distributes spiritual gifts to allow us to accomplish the work.

In the movie *Chariots of Fire,* the Scottish Olympic runner Eric Liddell was asked by his sister Jenny why he was investing so much time training to race. She felt he was neglecting his ministry as a missionary. Liddell responded: "Jenny, God made me for a purpose–for China, but He also made me fast. When I run I feel His pleasure." Liddell was using his God-given physical ability to glorify God. He worked hard to prepare to use the members of his body to run for God's glory. In the process, Eric Liddell sensed God's presence; Liddell gave his best for his heavenly coach. After winning the gold medal in the 1924 Olympics, Eric Liddell fulfilled his spiritual purpose and served as a missionary in China until his death at the end of World War II. His entire life is a picture of the integrated way God uses our gifts, physical and spiritual, in ministry.[1]

• Using spiritual gifts is a workout, and hard work is often required for results.
• The goal is preparation for an eternity of service.
• The pleasure of God's presence and affirmation is a powerful motivation for using the gifts He has given.

As a leader of women's enrichment ministry in the local church, you have the opportunity to serve with the Lord as an "assistant coach." Your task is to help women use the gifts they discover, motivating them to stretch and progress to the next level in serving God and blessing the "body-life" of your congregation. Many women struggle to get started. As in any workout program, the goal of service must be obvious and measurable. Motivation and encouragement are necessary for success. May God bless you as you apply the following principles with the women in your fellowship.

Prayer Is the Initial Step

When Jesus observed the great needs and the potential harvest of souls, He instructed the disciples to pray for workers to go out into the fields. Compassion for hurting and needy people moved Jesus to pray (see Matt. 9:36-38). What is your response to the many lonely, struggling women in your community?

In 1981, when my husband and I moved to Norfolk, Virginia, I was one of those hurting women. As a pastor's wife, I found it difficult to share with our new congregation my grief over the premature death of our third child. In that booming metropolitan Hampton Roads area, with the largest naval base in the world, there was overwhelming opportunity for our church to reach young military families. Some women approached me about starting a weekday women's Bible study. At that point, the term "women's enrichment ministry" didn't exist in our vocabulary. As the group of 15 women met together, prayed and bonded as a loving family, I found my spiritual gifts stimulated and my emotional wounds healed. Those women became my "sisters in Christ" in every sense of the word.

The first study we worked through as a group was Evelyn Christenson's *What Happens When Women Pray?*[2] As we prayed together, God challenged us to host an evangelistic luncheon for the women of our community. Our prayer group had grown to include 45 women, but we needed many more helpers to ensure success for the luncheon. What did we do as a committee? We prayed for laborers—childcare helpers, kitchen staff, and people to answer the church telephones. At that time, the church employed only one secretary. We watched as God performed miracles in answering specific prayer requests! One hundred and fifty women attended the luncheon and several women accepted Christ.

As you pray for women to be called to service in areas where their gifts will be used most effectively, be open to the possibility that women may resign from one position to move to a new arena of ministry. The average adult changes careers four times. In the church we have a tendency to

What is your response to the many lonely, struggling women in your community?

pigeonhole people. If someone has been an effective worker, we don't want to train a new leader to replace her. As leaders, we may not want to move out of our comfort zones and build new leadership relationships. It's easier to work with a dependable and familiar leader than to stretch and grow with a member who may be new to your fellowship. Pray that the door of opportunity will be open for women to serve where the Holy Spirit and their passions lead them.

Be bold in asking for open doors for ministry. The story of Lydia, a successful first-century businesswoman, is a great example. The apostle Paul began mission work in Europe with a prayer meeting, and Lydia was there. The Holy Spirit opened Lydia's heart as she listened to the message of the gospel. Soon after becoming a Christian, Lydia opened her home, offering gifts of service and hospitality to Paul and his companions (see Acts 16:9-15). Lydia saw a need and asked if she could meet that need.

Be bold in asking for open doors for ministry.

A friend shared with me how God moved her to say yes to an invitation to minister after she had initially said no. As others interceded for God to call the right person for the job, the Lord slowly but surely changed her mind. We can pressure women to use their gifts by applying the classic guilt trip, but effective service will flow when the Holy Spirit's call and conviction come in a woman's heart. Prayer is the jump start for helping women identify and use their spiritual gifts.

- Do you have an active group of intercessors regularly praying for your women's enrichment ministry?
- Is prayer ministry a vital part of your overall church growth strategy?

Preparation Is Crucial

Preparation involves teaching, training, and actual hands-on practicing. Equipping women is an ongoing process, as it is for the entire church body. God gives leaders and teachers the responsibility for the equipping ministry. There are tremendous resources available for in-depth study of spiritual gifts and leadership development. Ken Hemphill's *Serving God: Discovering and Using Your Spiritual Gifts*[3] and C. Gene Wilkes' *Jesus on Leadership*[4] are suggestions for inclusion as you develop a curriculum for women's ministry. Barbara Joiner has recently revised her book, *Yours for the Giving: Spiritual Gifts*[5]. All of these suggested studies include gift assessment guides. We cannot assume that women will understand their giftedness and the biblical principles that lead to a healthy use of gifts. Knowledge and study can dispel the fear and fog factors that create confusion about spiritual gifts.

"As each one has received a special gift, employ it in serving one another, as good stewards of the manifold grace of God."
1 Peter 4:10 (NASB)

A Success Story

First Baptist Norfolk takes preparation for service very seriously. As part of her regular staff responsibilities, Women's Ministry Director Gail Motley also assists new church members in finding their places of service through a required orientation study called "Uniquely You in Christ."[6] After individually working through a variety of questionnaires dealing with spiritual gifts, personality, and personal experience profiles, the new members meet with the pastor and Gail. After the pastor presents the biblical mandate for each member to exercise his/her gifts, he challenges those present to use their spiritual gifts in service. Then Gail walks them through a detailed list of key ministry opportunities. The response to the systematic study and the presentations of the needs of the body has been remarkable. The new members are so enthusiastic about serving the body that long-time church members are requesting the orientation.

Knowledge and study can dispel the fear and fog factors that create confusion about spiritual gifts.

This success story didn't just happen. A tremendous amount of work went into the development of the program now being used. Experimentation revealed weaknesses in previous methods for activating believers for ministry. Ongoing evaluation reveals that positive progress is being made in helping believers move to the next level in using their spiritual gifts.

- Do you have a systematic cycle of study in your church to help women identify their spiritual gifts?
- Have you clearly identified and listed ministry opportunities for women to consider where they can use their gifts?
- Do you encourage women to serve temporarily in a position to allow them to evaluate their effectiveness in that area of ministry?

Practice Tests the Gifts and the User

Practice may not make you perfect, but it often contributes to skill development. Beth Moore wanted to improve her speaking skills, so she joined Toastmasters. Beth had the opportunity to speak every week to a group of businessmen, many of whom were Jewish.[7] Accountability increases the commitment to practice. Allowing a woman to substitute teach or giving her the opportunity to intern in a position permits her to test her gifts.

Testing Can Reveal Strengths and Weaknesses

Our faith can be tested when we are stretched by a new or unfamiliar task.

Disappointment and discouragement can torpedo confidence, hindering future involvement in ministry. Serving in difficult positions can be faith proving when the believer trusts God and utterly depends on God's strength and not her own. Fear of failure and self-doubt prevent many women from using their spiritual gifts. Failure can be a positive force for change and growth.

Try to think of failing forward. The "failure" helps us to see our giftedness more clearly, and it can reveal deficiencies in preparation. Our seeming failures can be transformed into stepping stones when we seek to fulfill God's plan. Instead of being negative, the failure moves us to the next level in understanding where we fit in the body. The key to healthy failure in the testing fires of service is the encouragement of the body and God's Word. All things do "work together for good to those who love God, to those who are called according to his purpose" (Rom. 8:28, NASB).[8]

- Testing has a positive purpose.
- Fail forward; allow your disappointments to propel you to the next level.
- Allow the Lord to use failure and disappointment as stepping stones for His purpose in your life.

Fail forward; allow your disappointments to propel you to the next level.

Coach or Cheerleader?

How does the coach arouse the athlete to maximize a workout? He gives a pep talk! More than that, the coach watches the workout and critiques it. I suggest there are at least three ways for you to cheer others on in using their spiritual gifts. Think of ways you have successfully motivated women to minister.

Affirmation

How important it is for us to speak positively to one another in the life of the church! To affirm one another in Christ is to recognize the good work the Lord is doing and to acknowledge His results in the lives of fellow believers. Often others discern a person's spiritual gifts before the giftee is conscious of the grace of God at work.

Recently two student wives approached me about starting a ministry to women and their families who have lost children through miscarriage or other complications after birth. Both of the women making the request had experienced such a loss and their passion was to comfort others in need. Neither of the women knew that I had a similar life experience. Affirming their desire to serve was a

joy, and watching as they started H.O.P.E. ministry has been exciting. The acrostic stands for "Helping Others Prayerfully Endure." Personal pain transformed into passion, blended with spiritual gifts of mercy, yielded ministry. Affirmation is fuel for the ministry flame, encouraging fruitful service.

- Do you regularly affirm the women who serve with you? Can you think of someone who has affirmed your spiritual gifts?
- Encourage women to serve from their passions and not positions.

Appreciation

Appreciation is similar to affirmation, but different. To express thanks and grateful recognition for blessings is to offer appreciation. As Christians, our hearts are to be constantly conscious of God's good gifts. Our response is to offer thanksgiving and praise to the Lord, the source of everything lovely and precious. When we appreciate others, we need to communicate our thanks to them in word and deed. We often fail to thank those who are closest to us, taking the blessings of relationships for granted.

Colossians 3:12-17 encourages us to treat one another with gentleness, compassion, humility, and patience, reminding us that in Christ we belong to one body. Our behavior is to be complimented with speaking to one another in psalms, hymns, and spiritual songs, "singing with thankfulness in your hearts to God." The words *please* and *thank you* used to be part of polite conversation and proper etiquette; unfortunately, these words are frequently neglected, even in Christian conversation. Have we forgotten our manners in the body of Christ?

"Let us consider how to stimulate one another to love and good deeds." Hebrews 10:24 (NASB).

- How do you say thanks to those who serve with you?
- Expressing appreciation encourages women to strive for excellence, using their gifts effectively.

Assessment

The coach with the best team maximizes every player by assessing strengths and weaknesses and by making appropriate team assignments. In our desire to help women use their spiritual gifts most effectively, we must evaluate their service gently and truthfully. We want to encourage each woman to serve faithfully. Only Christ can judge the ministry for its eternal impact, but within the body we are accountable to one another.

- Do you have a method for evaluating the effectiveness of your women's ministry?

- What problems arise if one committee member fails to finish an assignment?
- How does the principle of interdependence affect our service in the body?

Remember: Body-life at its best is every member using God's grace gifts for the building and blessing of the church, giving God the glory.

---

[1] *Chariots of Fire,* Warner, 1981.

[2] Evelyn Christenson's, *What Happens When Women Pray?* (Colorado Springs, CO.: Chariot Victor Publishers, 1992).

[3] Ken Hemphill, *Serving God: Discovering and Using Your Spiritual Gifts* (Nashville: Sunday School Board of the Southern Baptist Convention, 1995).

[4] C. Gene Wilkes, *Jesus on Leadership* (Nashville: LifeWay, 1996).

[5] Barbara Joiner, *Yours for the Giving: Spiritual Gifts* (Birmingham: Woman's Missionary Union, 1986).

[6] John S. Powers and Mels Carbonell, *Uniquely You in Christ* (available from Leadership Institute of America, Blue Ridge, GA., 1998).

[7] Vicki Selles and Jon Kent Walker, "The Teachable Moments of Beth Moore," *HomeLife,* March 1999, 17.

[8] Sheila West, *Beyond Chaos: Stress Relief for the Working Woman* (Colorado Springs: Navpress, 1991), 52.

For Smaller Churches
by Martha Lawley

In a smaller church where resources for teaching and training may be limited, consider inviting someone to come and assist with spiritual gifts training. Consider working with other churches in your community, association or state convention to provide joint training for women from several churches. Another possibility is a church-wide training event in your own church.

Effectively assimilating new members into service according to their unique gifts is particularly important in smaller churches. Make this an intentional process. Teaching and training in the area of spiritual gifts is an essential part of the process of assimilating new members into the church. For more help on assimilating new members into the smaller church, refer to the chapter on new members, pages 51-60.

Leading Women to Serve

Outreach

by Elizabeth Luter and Betty Hassler

On the third Monday of every month the Friendship Baptist Church's women's study group met for dinner, a devotional and a missions project. Usually the project was collecting canned food, used clothing, or money for the benevolence fund. Group members traded responsibilities for hosting the meeting and leading the devotionals.

Tonight the usually chatty group was seething with anger. Rumor had it that somebody in the church had called them a clique! Imagine that? It was untrue–of course. They were always open to new members. Wasn't their meeting time and place always printed in the church bulletin? Why, last year Karen had brought her nurse friend who worked the night shift in maternity. She eventually joined the church. A clique? Nothing could be farther from the truth!

They had discussed trying to add new members several times, especially when Maggie dropped out after the twins were born and Verna moved to Arizona. But, you know, a living room will only hold so many people.

The group had thought about starting a second group on another night or during the day. But no one wanted to leave the Monday night group to start one. Certainly, having *two* groups to attend was a little much to expect of anyone.

It was a perplexing problem, all right. But tonight they needed to plan their annual retreat, so they dropped the subject. Maybe next month outreach would make the agenda.

Motivating Women to Reach Out

Many women's ministry leaders identify outreach as the $64,000 question: *Why is it so difficult to get women to care about others who do not have the friendship and support they enjoy on a regular basis?* Among the reasons, these seem paramount.

1. *We all enjoy our comfort zones.* Meeting new people and assimilating them into our groups takes effort. In a sense, the group has to almost start over every time a new person joins to rebuild to a point of sharing and intimacy.

> Why is it so difficult to get women to care about others who do not have the friendship and support they enjoy on a regular basis?

In fact, those who study small groups say that is exactly what happens. A new group member causes a group to revert to stage 1, the exploring stage, where members are assessing one another and wondering how vulnerable they can be. A stage 3 group that enjoys a high level of confidentiality will move backward to stage 1 reluctantly.

Adding new groups, rather than adding new people to existing groups, is one way of encouraging growth without disrupting established groups.

2. *We still have our sin nature alongside our new nature in Christ!* We are not born caring about anyone but ourselves. Growing in love for others is one of our most challenging tasks as we seek to become Christlike. We joke about the "me generation" and those who approach church like a cafeteria line, looking for what fills their cup instead of looking for opportunities for service. Ouch! We all feel the sting of our selfishness.

> Women's ministries leaders must hold up the ideal of service as the point of the arrow we are striving to reach in our programming and ministries.

Women's ministry leaders must hold up the ideal of service as the point of the arrow we are striving to reach in our programming and ministries. Information that is not applied in service becomes a "resounding gong or a clanging cymbal" if love does not motivate action (1 Cor. 13:1).

3. *Outreach sounds like "... and another thing" we add to already overpacked schedules.* Women may feel that being asked to invite and nurture others adds a heap of guilt and another responsibility to overcommitted lifestyles.

Teaching the "as you go" concept from Matthew 28:19-20 helps women realize that God places them around people who need to be reached without their adding an activity to their lifestyles. Jesus reached people as He walked from place to place because He was sensitive to those around Him and always available to the Father when He sensed a need or an opportunity.

Communicate the message that God has "divine encounters" waiting for each of us to discover day-by-day. We will have a difficult time engaging the world around us if our eyes are focused only on ourselves. We must challenge women at every opportunity to observe the needs around them and use what God has taught them to make a difference in His world as they respond to those needs.

Developing an Outreach Focus

Most women's ministry leaders will at some point face criticism for wanting to expand the number of women reached. "She's just building a personal following," "She just wants to take over the church," or "She's never satisfied, no matter what we do" may reflect the feelings of some who are content with "our little group."

How can we dispel the notion that we are building our own kingdoms? By consistently living and telling the message that we are helping to build God's kingdom.

A Kingdom Mentality

Ministry growth doesn't happen until we focus on kingdom work. Women's ministry is not *our* ministry. It is *His* ministry. We can never claim it as our own without pride reigning in our hearts. The only reason we should be leading out in this ministry is because God has called us to lead.

Our focus must begin and continue to be, "Where is God at work and asking me to join Him?" If this is our focus, we will not be attempting to build a prideful ministry based just on numbers or how it would make the leader "look good."

In Gene Mims' book, *Kingdom Principles for Church Growth,* he describes the 1.5.4 Principle:

1–driving force for church growth: The Great Commission

5–essential functions for church growth:

Evangelism

Discipleship

Ministry

Fellowship

Worship

4–results:

Numerical Growth

Spiritual Growth

Ministries Expansion

Missions Advance[1]

Mims says: "One of the greatest dangers we face today in church growth is making methods supreme. Methods used in the fastest growing church in your area may not work in your church, but God's principles of church growth will work in every church."[2]

What will a kingdom mentality do for your women's ministry? Women will begin to grow, reach out to others, and become involved in God's service when all of the above elements are present in our women's ministries and in their individual lives. God works through us supernaturally to accomplish His kingdom's purposes in reaching more for Christ and

> Our focus must begin and continue to be, "Where is God at work and asking me to join Him?"

helping them to grow spiritually, so they in turn are reaching others for Christ. We get to play a small part in His scheme of things as we allow God to use us to help women become all God wants them to be—perfect (mature) in Christ.

We encourage a kingdom mentality by modeling concern for outreach, by leading out in outreach ministries, and by communicating a kingdom mentality at every opportunity. Engage your prayer groups as intercessors. Pray for a kingdom mentality that looks beyond the enrollment of your present women's ministries.

"We proclaim him, admonishing and teaching everyone with all wisdom, so that we may present everyone perfect in Christ."
Colossians 1:28

Building Inclusive Groups for Outreach

Churches used to be a reflection of their neighborhoods, where "birds of a feather flocked together." In today's culture, women of all ages and socio-economic backgrounds may attend the same church. Because of available transportation, people are willing to travel great distances to meet their spiritual needs. Now that diversity is the norm, women may feel polarized in various church ministries according to whether or not they feel acceptance and status.

Women who do not feel welcomed and included—whether because of circumstances, self-esteem issues, or background—may find it difficult to join or commit to women's ministries and have a tendency to shy away. As a result, we must cultivate methods that will attract all types of women to participate in women's ministry. Spiritual growth is enhanced and inevitable within a carefully planned and structured women's ministry. For some women to feel alienated from such a positive experience is indeed offensive to the cause of Christ.

As you seek to be inclusive in outreach, consider whether or not you are only organized according to traditional groupings. Often, women are discouraged from outreach because the person they want to invite to their group doesn't fit the profile. If she is in a mom's group and her friend has no children, she will obviously feel squelched in offering an invitation. A younger woman may hesitate to invite a lonely neighbor because she is older than the other women in her group.

In today's society it is necessary to group according to non-traditional as well as traditional patterns—such as life experiences. Effective ministry today must delve deeper to discover and nurture women's most personal needs.

For example, yesterday's target groups were determined by age. Today a woman in her 40s may be a first-time mother, a mother of teenagers, or a grandmother. Age no longer is a predictor of lifestyle.

Another traditional grouping pattern is marital status. Although many women profit from such groups, grouping only by marital status may be perceived as an artificial barrier to the women of the church getting to know all their sisters in Christ.

Another artificial barrier may be work status—whether in the home or in the marketplace. Stay-at-home moms often enjoy hearing about the workplace and vice versa. We build bonds of love as we seek to put ourselves in someone else's shoes. We may have a perspective to share simply because we are emotionally distanced from that environment.

The point is simple: Do not let your group structure limit opportunities for inclusion. Build the atmosphere of inclusion by seeking to expand your vision to allow groups to form and grow according to life needs and friendships.

Build the atmosphere of inclusion by seeking to expand your vision to allow groups to form according to life needs and friendships.

Targeting People Groups for Outreach

As we look around our churches and communities for women who would profit from women's ministries, lead women to consider these target groups.

Different Denominational Backgrounds—Churches today are made up of a cross section of denominations and belief heritages. Consider offering studies that address "What Christians Believe" as opposed to doctrinal and denominational differences. Studies such as these facilitate a smoother transition into the church for persons from differing backgrounds. Attempting to understand the traditions of the church may hinder new believers from the process of focusing on their new life in Christ.

As time goes on, inquirer classes will become a necessity rather than an option. In preparation for that time, leadership must choose resources that offer understanding and interpretation rather than controversy to this target group.

Carnal/ Infant Believers—Although challenging, this group represents a substantial number of today's believers. Ministry to carnal and infant believers taxes the person discipling. At this stage complacency and comfort are difficult to combat. Through encouragement and nurturing we can lead them to discover the fullness of abundant living.

The Younger Generation—This generation of believers is easily bored and very mobile. An emphasis on salvation and short-term discipleship studies are necessary subject offerings for this group. (See "Three Generations in the Here and Now" in *Women Reaching Women*, p 18).

Often a "lite diet" of spiritual truth without heavy study responsibilities helps to reach the 20-somethings who are unchurched and/or unreached. A friendship breakfast on Saturday mornings or a meeting held in a restaurant meeting room may seem less intimidating.

Socialites (The Up and Out)–What are some ways that we can entice this group to become involved? Often their participation in activities other than worship service is limited to banquets and annual church-day functions. We must discover needs that may differ from those who are less advantaged but are nevertheless important to address if we are going to minister to persons with wealth and/or position.

This group may face circumstances (divorce, spouse's death, job change, downsizing, financial crises, or substance abuse) that result in a severe loss of self-esteem. Leaders and members of women's ministry must nurture their self-worth through the knowledge and Spirit of God.

Those with a Dysfunctional Past–When we accept Christ as Savior we take on a new nature. Our present does not have to simply be a reflection of our past. Small-group settings that offer opportunity for participants to share testimonies of God's grace can encourage women to participate and benefit from the nurturing that can lead to restoration. However, for a previously ostracized person, the safe feeling of having someone to care may create a sense of dependency. Be careful to keep this dependency short-term, remembering that the goal is healthy interdependence.

Economically Deprived–Those who participate in our ministries who may not have adequate daily sustenance can feel too humiliated to ask for help. Swap meets (designated meeting times for women to bring excess clothing, home products, and children's toys and clothes) alleviates the problem of persons feeling singled out for help. Look for ways their gifts can be utilized. No one likes being perceived as only a taker; help them to become givers of time, talents, and abilities.

Intellectuals–New and challenging ways to study resources, (such as the Internet and other software applications), serve as a catalyst to participation by this group. Web sites and email partnerships in ministry are tools for stimulating interest. Use this avenue as an effective means to keep in touch, distribute meeting dates, and issue invitations.

Builders (Senior Adult Women)–Senior women are a valuable asset to your women's ministry. They possess a wealth of life experience and survival techniques for adjusting to life's hardships. When invited to share their rich resources with a younger generation of believers, they may feel intimidated and inadequate. Consider creating a mentoring ministry (see the chapter on mentoring, pages 95-104). In this arena, seniors may feel more comfortable in sharing their wealth of knowledge and experience as well as suggestions for living godly values.

Unchurched—The life experiences of some women do not include any church activity or any past affiliation with a local church body. Our first responsibility to the unchurched is to present Jesus and His gift of saving grace. However, new believers require nurturing. Avoid "churchy" language that does not communicate, such as "walking the aisle" or "growing in sanctification." Make your meetings user-friendly by thinking through anything that would be a barrier. Instead of saying, "Meet in Fellowship Hall" say "Meet in the large room below the sanctuary.

Breaking Down Walls

Many unreached women may hide behind walls that keep you out. Some walls are thicker than others. Our assignment is to penetrate—and even break down—the walls of indifference, resistance, or inadequacy that keep them from being reached.

Choose and encourage leaders who demonstrate an inviting spirit. Challenge everyone to offer a hug and extend a hand to fellow worshippers, both inside and outside the church setting. Wage a massive campaign to prove yourself friendly. Wear "Smile" buttons, "Jesus Loves You" lapel pins, or other creative displays. Enlist those who have a gift of hospitality to cultivate an atmosphere of friendliness within your ministry.

A women's ministry welcoming committee that greets Sunday worshippers is another effective outreach tool. This activity offers an area of service for those with limited time or experience. Consider having greeters present bookmarks which list meeting dates, times, and an invitation to participate in women's ministry activities.

At the beginning of each new study, suggest attendees choose someone sitting nearby to be their buddy. Encourage "buddies" to swap phone numbers and to follow-up when one or the other is absent and to encourage each other in group work. The buddy system provides both old and new members the opportunity to interact. The system also encourages new friendships and may lead to a prayer partnership or an accountability ministry.

Offer seminars geared to common women's health issues, such as menstruation and menopause. Encourage a question/answer format where women are encouraged to share similar fears and concerns. In addition, offer seminars that deal with common life experiences, such as establishing independence from parents, caring for aging parents, and financial planning that cuts across age, marital status, and working status.

Uniting quarterly with men's ministry will foster a proper prospective on male/female issues. Panel discussions, dramatizations portraying

> Our assignment is to penetrate—and even break down—the walls of indifference, resistance, or inadequacy.

reconciliation of men and women, and discussions related to restoration of family values will generate interest and provide opportunities to minister on a broader scale. Carefully planned and publicized sessions may draw the attention of city leaders, family members, or inquisitive, unchurched coworkers.

Meet one or more times each year with other women's groups in the church (missions, music, and so forth) to present ministry descriptions and purposes. Invite unreached women so that they may be aware of all areas of service. While separate agendas are necessary, working together yields greater results.

In addition to these suggestions for breaking down walls of indifference, resistance, or inadequacy, consider the "wall" of boredom with traditional programming. If meetings begin and end in the same way each week or month, attendees may withdraw from regular meetings. The element of surprise is beneficial in keeping and holding the interest of newcomers. Consider changing the order of service and adding unique and creative touches to everyday methods.

Most women enjoy a lively atmosphere. Change the setting of regular meetings and use seasonal influences, church event ideas, or personal creativity to enhance the decor. Along with your speaking and teaching sessions, incorporate a coffee house, praise concert, or swap meet. Utilize as many gifts and talents of the newcomers as possible in an effort to heighten everyone's sense of importance and contribution.

A consistent worship tempo during meetings may lead to boredom as well. Praise choruses, contemporary music, and upbeat testimonies shared by triumphant believers will increase the "worship temperature." Motivational speakers with honest life messages are rewarding and usually benefit Christians in various stages of spiritual growth. Evaluate the responsiveness of participants, either visually or verbally. A written response card prepared ahead of time might be helpful. Adjust meeting situations accordingly, in order to maintain a consistent level of responsiveness and appreciation.

As leaders, pray for the ability to incorporate women from all walks of life. If we have limited experience with women outside our church, we can seek out women in our ministries with the gifts of hospitality and encouragement. As newcomers develop relationships and feel comfortable, they will share their experience with others. Remember–they will serve others with the type of service they have received and seen modeled. The upside is that this process adds new links to the chain. The way we nurture each link will determine the strength of our chain.

Those we reach will serve others with the type of service they have received and seen modeled.

92

In the past, we evaluated our success by the effectiveness of the methods we used. We must continue to network from church to church and city to city, to keep abreast of changes and update our methods. Women's ministry faces a new era, and adjustments must be radical and rapid. Technology will influence our methods for outreach and service in the future. In order to broaden our effectiveness, it is essential that women from different backgrounds and demographics are reached and motivated to serve.

[1] Gene Mims, *Kingdom Principles for Church Growth* (Nashville: Convention Press, 1994).
[2] Ibid., 6.

For Smaller Churches
by Martha Lawley

Sometimes being part of a smaller church can be an advantage when it comes to getting women involved. In smaller churches, women find it harder to justify their lack of involvement with the "someone else will do it" excuse.

Often, the best time to promote an outreach-focused event is while basking in the glow of a successful in-reach focused event. Women will have a genuine enthusiasm that others will recognize and want to catch. Plan an activity for your existing group to experience together. As that experience is enjoyed, the women can begin to recognize the need to "do this more often." This experience can be the perfect time to promote a similar event to which everyone is encouraged to invite at least one friend or neighbor.

Attracting well-known speakers for an outreach event can be a challenge for smaller churches. However, think creatively. God can provide in unexpected ways. For example, do you live in an area that offers recreation or vacation opportunities? If so, consider offering a home or other lodging opportunity for a speaker to use as a family vacation. Other resources include missionaries on furlough, local denominational leaders, or leaders who may be visiting in your area.

Women will attend and participate in classes and events that they feel meet their needs, including time, location, and child care. In smaller churches, leaders will find it important to begin with a few basic needs and find creative ways to build in flexibility. Encourage women on your leadership team and in your church to think "outside the box." We must

Women's ministry faces a new era, and adjustments must be radical and rapid.

never forget that our God is the only One who ever created something from nothing. If we live in a box, it is because we choose to live there.

The technology available today can be an invaluable tool for smaller churches. If properly used, email and access to Christian Web sites can help women feel less isolated and more in touch with one another and can offer much needed encouragement. Smaller churches can use this tool creatively for outreach each time a new name is added to the email file. New technology provides unique opportunities for meeting the needs of women today because we can enter their homes through the computer at their own convenience. We do not have to have everyone together in the same room at the same time. Outreach can literally happen 24-hours-a-day!

Leading Women to Serve

Mentoring

by Janet Thompson

"Lord, I do not know why You have chosen me to begin a women's mentoring ministry at my church. I really do not know where to find the time or resources to begin. It seems like such a big job, but Lord, if this is truly what You want me to do, I surrender myself to You.

"Use me, Lord, and help me always to remember that this is Your ministry, not mine. Please place in my path those who will encourage and support me, and women who are willing to help me begin such a ministry. Please, Holy Spirit, speak to those women who are hungering for mentoring relationships and give them the courage to participate. In Your precious, holy name I pray. Amen."

This was my prayer in 1995 as I set out to launch the Woman-to-Woman Mentoring Ministry at Saddleback Church. I knew of no one at our church who was interested in becoming a mentor or in being mentored, and I certainly had no idea who would help me. All I knew for sure was that the Lord had called me to go and "feed my sheep," (John 21:17, KJV) and I had said OK!

God has continued to use my response to that call to mentor hundreds of "sheep" at Saddleback and thousands of sheep all over the world. How did the Lord take an inexperienced shepherd like myself and gather such a large international flock? I can only respond: through hours of prayer, listening to the Lord, and being obedient to His directions.

What Is a Mentoring Ministry?

Mentoring is role modeling. It is using those "been there, done that" experiences in our lives to help other women through similar circumstances. It is sharing how the Lord helped you through it and offering encouragement and assurance that He is there for the other person, too. Mentoring is coming alongside another woman and teaching her to seek God's Word and the One who has all the answers.

The one being mentored (we call them "mentees") seeks to learn and receive support from a mentor. Mentoring relationships are a two-way experience. At times the mentee will lift and encourage the mentor.

> Mentoring is using those "been there, done that" experiences in our lives to help other women through similar circumstances.

Neither should consider it a hierarchical relationship. However, mentors must take ownership and responsibility for establishing goals and maintaining an ongoing and relevant relationship.

Training for mentors and mentees is an important part of a mentoring ministry. In the paragraphs to follow, you will find a step-by-step approach to setting up a mentoring ministry in your church. For a more complete explanation, with forms to use in your ministry along with training suggestions and a handbook for both the mentors and mentees, order *Woman to Woman: How to Start, Grow, and Maintain a Mentoring Ministry*,[1] available through LifeWay Press (see p. 221).

It is possible to begin a mentoring ministry with only two persons: a mentor and a mentee! Do not become discouraged if there are only a few in the beginning; that is all you need. Starting your ministry small allows you to learn as you grow—the secret to a long-lasting and healthy ministry. As women experience the blessings of mentoring, many will want to give back and serve as a mentor themselves.

Who Should Start and/or Lead a Mentoring Ministry?

Perhaps you feel called to feed His sheep by starting a mentoring ministry at your church; or perhaps you recognize the need but are searching for a leader. You might then be asking: *Who should start and lead our mentoring ministry?* I would answer: A woman who not only feels strongly about the need for mentoring in your church, but also has a passion to see that vision fulfilled. Warning—don't initiate the ministry just because the church needs it or because someone asked you to. Duty or responsibility is not enough—there must be passion and calling.

A leader must know in her heart that this is where the Lord wants her; this is key to getting the ministry off on the right foot and overcoming inevitable setbacks. Without the Lord's direction, hard work and disappointments may cause some to give up. Ministry such as this is a labor of love; enduring passion and call cannot be assigned.

Be open to the possibility that this woman might be a very unlikely candidate. I did not fit the ideal ministry leader profile.

- My interests were not in women's ministry. In fact, I had never attended a women's retreat!
- I had been so busy with my business career that I had cultivated very few women friends.
- I was in a small group at my church, but I had not participated in many church activities. Most people at church did not even know my name.

> The leader must not only feel strongly about the need for mentoring but also have a passion to see that vision fulfilled.

Initially, I did not have a heart for women and their needs. However, as I was obedient to the Lord, He renewed my mind and changed my heart. Now they call me the "mentoring lady," and "the woman who has a heart for women!" I still look over my shoulder to see who they are talking about. Then I look up and praise the Lord for my transformation.

When searching for a leader, pray first for God's guidance and provision. Second, begin networking. Talk about the church's desire to begin a mentoring ministry for women—advertise, describing an opportunity to start a new ministry at your church. Practice patience. Wait and see who the Lord brings forward.

Each woman's call to this ministry will be different. However, the right woman will have a testimony of God leading and preparing her for the position. Pray for discernment to distinguish between those who are self-directed and God-directed.

The leader of a mentoring ministry may or may not be on church staff. *Woman to Woman: How to Start, Grow, and Maintain a Mentoring Ministry* can be used by either a staff or layleader. However, if you are already on staff, it should be easier and faster to access church resources.

Once the leader initiates the mentoring ministry, it's time to implement the foundation steps listed below.

What Are the Foundation Steps?

You may be fortunate to know women who share your interest in a mentoring ministry. If so, the question is, *How do I get them involved?* Or perhaps you are hoping to motivate others to join you in launching the ministry. Either way, the foundation steps are very much the same for encouraging women to come forward and serve as mentors, helpers or administrative team members.

Submitting the Ministry to the Lord's Leadership

Like any church ministry, a mentoring ministry needs to be first and foremost His ministry. Often we become so caught up with planning and recruiting that we forget to depend on the Lord for direction.

The first principle for a successful ministry is to spend focused time in prayer. One of our first sub-ministries in the Woman-to-Woman Mentoring Ministry was a prayer chain. The prayer chain prays daily for all the needs of our ministry. When there is a need for new ministry team members or helpers, we take the specific needs for those positions to the prayer chain. They lift these needs daily to the Lord, as do the other members of the ministry team.

Women in our church are introduced to Woman-to-Woman Mentoring Ministry at orientation coffees. Prior to every orientation coffee, the prayer chain prays that the Lord will provide sufficient mentors and bring the women to the coffee who He wants matched into mentoring relationships.

Share the Vision for the Ministry

The ministry leader must be willing to share her passion for a mentoring ministry. Be prepared to verbalize that passion—often. Your enthusiasm is contagious. When God gives us a vision for ministry, He also gives us the ability to complete it successfully.

Until you can verbalize your motivation, others will have difficulty "catching the dream." The first thing I tell new leaders is to prepare "Your Story." It should be a concise two- or three-minute testimony to generate enthusiasm for the ministry and to keep others and yourself motivated in the future.

In addition to "Your Story," develop a definition of mentoring and the qualifications for a mentor. As you begin advertising and networking the mentoring ministry at your church, people are going to ask: What is mentoring? Who can be a mentor? Be prepared to give short but informative and enthusiastic responses to these questions. Take note of those asking so you can follow up.

Develop a mission statement for the mentoring ministry that clearly states the purpose and focus. Include this mission statement in any advertising or networking efforts and utilize it in establishing ministry guidelines. For example, if you want to limit participation to only women who attend your church, include it in your mission statement. Also state if mentors need to be members of your church.

Enlist Mentors

Establishing an effective mentoring ministry requires women who are willing to step out and invest their lives in other women's spiritual growth.

As a rule, most women feel unqualified and inadequate for the role of mentor, specifically in biblical knowledge. All of us desire spiritual feeding from others. However, establishing an effective mentoring ministry requires women who are willing to step out and invest their lives in other women's spiritual growth.

Humble Christian women may feel it is boastful or presumptuous to assume they are capable of mentoring. Use the definition of mentoring to educate the women of your church. The explanation may be all it takes to help them feel qualified and capable.

Where are the mature Christian women in your church? Are they in a

Bible study group? In spiritual maturity classes offered at your church? Do they attend Wednesday night prayer meetings? Is there a special group for the "young at heart" seniors? Evaluate your church logistics to discover where these women gather, then go to them. Ask to make an announcement at their meetings or to visit and share the vision and concept of the mentoring ministry.

Use Scriptures that instruct one generation to teach the next. Titus 2:1-5 and Psalms 145:4 are familiar verses with this theme. Remind women that these verses do not suggest options. They are specific commands to those of us who know the Lord. Jesus did not save us solely for our own benefit; He meant for our lives to draw others closer to Christ. Paul specifically directed Titus 2:3-5 to all Christian women!

Although we may not always feel like it, God has qualified each of us to invest time in each other's lives. Women who reach out to other women do not have to be graduates of colleges, universities, seminaries, or Bible schools. You may not have a degree from anywhere. However, you do have something that is much more important—life experience!

Mentoring does not require special talents or qualities. All God asks is that we take who we are and give all of it to Him. He in turn equips us to offer ourselves to another in a servant role—that of mentor.

Rebecca Manley Pippert, in her book *Out of the Saltshaker and Into the World,* says: "We must not wait until we are healed first, loved first, and then reach out. We must serve no matter how little we have our act together. It may well be that one of the first steps toward our own healing will come when we reach out to someone else."[2]

A profile card is one way to determine the spiritual maturity of the women you select for mentors. Here are a few key questions: How long have you attended _____ Church? When did you accept Christ? Have you rededicated your life, and if so when? Have you attended any of the discipleship classes offered at _____ Church? When?

Also listed on our profile card are six principles from Saddleback Church's Statement of Faith. We ask potential mentors to indicate if they are in agreement with these beliefs. Another question asks them to consider whether or not there is currently any circumstance or situation in their lives that would interfere with them becoming a mentor.

If a woman is sound in her Christian faith and has walked with the Lord for several years, we encourage her to follow Paul's example. In 1 Corinthians 11:1 Paul confidently told his "mentees": "Follow my example as I follow the example of Christ." Paul said many times that his life was not perfect, but he had his eyes set on Jesus, and if as believers they walked together, they would end up at Jesus' feet.

During the first three years of the Woman-to-Woman Mentoring Ministry in our church, we rejoiced to watch the Lord raise up three generations of mentors. The second year of the ministry, many mentees from the first year were ready to mentor women themselves. Some of these new mentees, mentored by the second-generation mentors, stepped forward the third year and became the third generation of mentors. It is awesome to watch Psalms 145:4 come alive in your church.

Perhaps you are concerned you do not have enough mentors to begin a mentoring ministry in your church. Start with what you have, then watch the Lord multiply the five fish and two loaves to feed the five thousand. Never underestimate the power of the Lord when you follow His clear command for women in Titus 2:3-5. You will observe incredible growth in the women of your church as side-by-side they pray together and encourage one another in their walk with the Lord.

Train

A vital, and often overlooked, part of every mentoring ministry is training. Both the mentors and the mentees should become familiar with the roles and expectations in their relationship. There are a number of ways to accomplish this expectation. In the Woman-to-Woman Mentoring Ministry, we train both mentors and mentees. We base our training on the Woman-to-Woman leader's training material and handbooks used by the mentors and mentees throughout their relationships.

Mentors are more secure when they have guidelines and suggestions to follow regarding their role in the relationships. Likewise, mentees should also understand their vital part in the relationship and set realistic expectations as to what they should and should not expect from their mentors.

Communication is essential. In the Woman-to-Woman Mentoring Ministry, prayer warriors pray daily for mentoring relationships. They contact each mentor and mentee monthly to obtain prayer requests and to see how relationships are progressing. During their period of commitment, prayer warriors meet several times as a group with mentors/mentees.

Midway through the relationship period, the mentors meet together again for additional training. This gathering provides a time to share experiences, ask questions, and receive additional training in ways to nurture and mature their relationships.

Emphasize to potential mentors that training and resources are always available as well as people with whom to pray and consult if they have questions or problems. This information assures women they will not be alone as mentors.

Who Will Train the Trainer?

Teaching and training are key areas that determine the success of both the mentoring relationships and the ministry itself. Consequently, enlist the ministry trainer with careful consideration. She must have a heart for the ministry and convey the core values, purpose, and focus you have outlined in the mission statement and ministry guidelines.

As ministry leader, you may initiate training, but a training coordinator is necessary to an effective ministry, along with training resources and materials. *Woman-to-Woman* leader training materials and mentor and mentee handbooks contain detailed lesson plans and training materials for use by both mentors and mentees throughout their relationships.

Once you've enlisted a ministry trainer, spend some time team teaching. Before delegating all ministry training, observe her teaching style, use of training materials, and handling of difficult questions and situations. When both of you are comfortable, it's time to let her coordinate the training process.

Recruit

Recruiting is an ongoing event! Continually pray for the Lord to bring helpers to the ministry. Whenever and wherever women gather, share information and ways they can participate.

Often women who have not participated in a mentoring relationship volunteer to help. Although it may be tempting to accept their offers, especially if it is an area in need, I recommend you thank them, invite them to attend the orientation coffee, and suggest they participate in a mentoring relationship before serving. A woman who has experienced the mentor/mentee relationship will better appreciate the mission and heart of the ministry and will be a more effective, dedicated and loyal helper.

Our orientation coffee (see page 98) plays an important part in recruiting. When women sign in at the coffee, they receive an "Opportunity to Serve" card that lists all the areas of service in the ministry. We encourage them to share areas of giftedness and areas of interest. Ministry team leaders recruit future helpers from these completed cards. If women indicate they want to help, take them seriously. They may actually feel offended or unworthy if you do not put them to work. I believe if a woman says she wants to help, she means it! I do not hesitate to call her.

When the mentor/mentee relationships have completed their planned time of commitment, we remind each mentor of the next orientation coffee and encourage her to mentor again. We also ask those mentors who feel their mentees are ready to become mentors to encourage them to take the next step by practicing what they have learned. Even if previous mentors are not continuing in another mentoring relationship, we encourage them to serve in other areas of the ministry that need help.

All those who have participated in mentoring relationships receive our quarterly ministry newsletter. The newsletter includes a section that lists and describes available areas of service. The ministry leader and team leaders use the newsletter to promote their areas of the ministry and ways to serve.

Never make the mistake of thinking you have all the help you need. Women's lives are constantly subject to change: pregnancy, moving, returning to work outside the home, changing ministries, and so forth. Whatever the reasons, some women may only serve for a season. A good back-up list is crucial to an effective ongoing ministry.

"Two are better than one, because they have a good return for their work: If one falls down, his friends can help him up!"
Ecclesiastes 4:9-10

Here are some practical ideas for recruiting:

- *Every time* women from the ministry meet or fellowship provide an "Opportunity to Serve" sign-up sheet and emphasize areas in which you need help.
- If ministry members call or contact you personally to offer to help, record their names, even if you do not have a place of service. Develop a system so that as needs arise, information is immediately available. Follow up, occasionally reminding them that when an opportunity is available, you will contact them.
- Send thank-you notes to those who have served in your ministry.

Provide Job Descriptions
Job descriptions are familiar to most of us as a result of work experiences. In the Woman-to-Woman Mentoring Ministry we refer to our job descriptions as Service Opportunity Descriptions. We give a copy to each volunteer. The description is hers to have on hand for future reference.

Design the Service Opportunity Descriptions to your specific situation and church. Include as much information as possible for the volunteers. Use humor to lighten the responsibility of the task and Scripture to remind them Whom they serve.

When a woman volunteers for a position, give her or mail her the Service Opportunity Description. Follow up to learn if she has questions or if there is any part of the task she cannot fulfill. If not, congratulate her on her new responsibility. However, if she cannot meet all of the

requirements, attempt to place her in another area of service that better suits her schedule and talents.

As you develop an administrative team, delegate to them the responsibility for recruiting and distributing Service Opportunity Descriptions.

Develop an Administrative Team

My pastor, Rick Warren, says: "As your ministry grows bigger, it has to become smaller. If not, your ministry will be like a big snowball that is rolling down the hill, getting bigger and bigger as it picks up more snow while rolling. It will soon be a big ball rolling out of control, until it hits a tree and flies into a million snowflakes."

I know Pastor Rick is right. To ensure longevity in your ministry, develop an administrative team as soon as possible and systematically delegate duties to them. However, it is important to carefully consider and select those women who will serve with you in leadership roles.

I, too, had to learn that principle. At first, when someone offered to help, I was so grateful that I immediately responded: "You would do that? Great! It's yours!" Before I knew it, I had a leadership team of 12 women. I rationalized that Jesus had 12 disciples, so I was following His pattern. However, unlike Jesus, I did not carefully select my disciples. I allowed them to find me. After struggling with dissension and the challenges of keeping everyone informed, I allowed attrition to reduce the group to three. Then I patiently established a system to "raise up leaders."

"In my distress I called to the Lord; I cried to my God for help. From his temple he heard my voice; my cry came before him, into his ears."
Psalm 18:6

I suggest you develop a system that incorporates the following:
- Determine the areas in which you want administrative leadership, such as hospitality, publicity, accounting, prayer chain, prayer warriors, special events, and training.
- Develop an Opportunity to Serve Description for each that includes requirements, responsibilities, and duration of service.
- Pray, asking the Lord to bring women with gifts and talents in the administrative areas you have established.
- Consider the women currently serving in the ministry who have experienced the blessings of a mentoring relationship.
- Publicize your leadership needs, but also approach those women who have successfully served in the ministry.
- Spend some time talking to the women you are considering. Discuss the requirements of the position and ascertain if their gifts, talents, and interests are in that area. Everyone works best using God-given gifts, abilities, and interests.
- Never assign an administrative area responsibility.

- When first considering someone for a position, delegate to her several tasks included in that area of responsibility. Observe her work while each of you determine if the job is "a fit."

Once you have selected your administrative team, meet together at least once a month. Encourage each administrative team leader to develop teams within her area of responsibility and to observe leadership potential within those teams. Out of these leaders, apprentices will develop who, if necessary, could step into an administrative role.

In grateful anticipation, watch and marvel as the Lord feeds His sheep using this team of godly servant women.

---

[1] Janet Thompson, *Woman to Woman: How to Start, Grow, and Maintain a Mentoring Ministry* (Lake Forest: AHW Ministries, 1998), 5.

[2] Rebecca Manley Pippert, *Out of the Saltshaker and Into the World* (Downers Grove, IL: InterVarsity Press, 1999).

For Smaller Churches
by Martha Lawley

A mentoring ministry can be effective in any size church. Measure success not as much by how many women participate (although this is important) as by the growth that is occurring in the lives of participants. Look for growth in spiritual terms: maturity, strengthening of relationships, and better understanding of God and His ways.

In a smaller church, where training resources may be limited, consider inviting someone from a neighboring church with a mentoring program to assist with training. This experience would be another opportunity to work with other churches in your community. Conduct training together or separately using the same training resources.

A church may want to consider partnering with another local church to broaden the base of mentors and mentees. For example, the sponsoring church could provide mentors to a mission congregation. A special relationship of cooperation between the two churches will be required. It is wise to have a contact or liaison person from each church to coordinate and respond to any issues.

In a smaller church, where women wear many different hats, you may be able to use your mentoring partners to work as a team to lead various aspects of your women's ministry. While this may not work for every mentoring partnership, it can be an effective way to further the mentoring process and provide much needed leadership support.

Leading Women to Serve

Evangelism

by Jaye Martin

You know the feeling, the feeling that the Great Commission was written with someone else in mind. The feeling that you didn't get the "gift" of conversing with unbelievers, although Christ is the most important Person in your life. You are not alone! It's OK to be honest.

I remember the first time I contacted someone who visited our church. I hung up when they answered the phone. Thank goodness that was before the days of Caller ID! And the first time I volunteered to counsel during the decision time at a church crusade–I hung way back so I would not have to talk to anyone. When I finally was assigned someone, I was so scared that I didn't say anything. She ended up pouring her heart out and then showing me verses in her Bible. She told me she couldn't wait for the day that she could counsel others as I was doing! What a joke! I told her I was sure she could! I also recall the first time I visited someone at home–I prayed no one would answer the door. I waited all of two seconds before insisting that we not waste our time knocking again (loud enough for them to hear, anyway). No, my friend, you are not alone!

Let's look at ways leaders like you and me can overcome our fears in areas that can make us feel intimidated. Although we could study the examples of several Bible personalities, I have chosen Andrew. You may not consider him a leader, even though he was one of Jesus' disciples–which is exactly why he is a good case study. Often we don't feel like leaders. And yet, we are–and must be. Read on!

The Call to Christ

The passage begins with an introduction to Andrew. Andrew was working at his job, doing what he probably learned to do as a child–fishing. He was an ordinary sort of fellow. But Jesus walked by and changed his life. Jesus offered the words, "Come, follow me…" and Andrew did. No hesitation here. Andrew didn't question Jesus; he just did what Jesus asked him to do. He followed. He accepted Jesus' call.

Can you imagine what might have gone through our minds if we had

"As Jesus walked beside the Sea of Galilee, he saw Simon and his brother Andrew casting a net into the lake, for they were fishermen. 'Come, follow me,' Jesus said, 'and I will make you fishers of men.' At once they left their nets and followed him."
Mark 1:16-18

105

been in Andrew's position? Maybe we would have explained that we were in the middle of planning and executing a major event and that next week would be a better time. Or maybe we might have thought about all the people depending on the fish (or the money from the sale of the fish) that we were bringing home. Our friend Andrew evidently thought none of those things—he simply followed Jesus "at once." No excuses.

What can we learn from Andrew? First of all, we can learn Who to follow. *That's easy*, you might be thinking, *We follow Jesus.* But if we had been there, would it have been so easy? Andrew had many legitimate reasons for remaining at his task. It wasn't easy to follow Jesus then—and it's not easy now. The world offers many distractions. The church can distract us from following Christ if we get caught up in all its programs and activities rather than focusing on Jesus.

Our motive should be to please Christ and to lift Him up in all our programming. "Special Events: Programs or People?" in *Women Reaching Women* (see pages 91-104), provides additional suggestions for prioritizing people's needs above programming needs. Our intent in women's enrichment ministry is to help women come to know Christ and to share Him with others. As leaders, we must decide whom we are following before we lead those following us.

When we will follow Christ, He empowers us to share His Word, His truths—to share Him. We have nothing to fear. It's not so much about what we know as much as it is about Whom we know. We are called to follow Christ, whether we feel like it or not.

Remember, the question is: *Who are you following?*

The Call to Multiply Himself

Andrew was one of two who heard John's testimony and followed Jesus (see John 1:35-39). The first thing Andrew did was to find his brother, Simon Peter, and announce, "'We have found the Messiah,' (that is, the Christ). And he brought him to Jesus. Jesus looked at him and said, 'You are Simon son of John. You will be called Cephas' (which, when translated, is Peter)" (John 1:40-42).

After Andrew answered Christ's call, he received the call to multiply himself: he told his brother about Christ. Andrew could have left his brother behind. After all, Jesus had called only Andrew. And certainly Andrew must have been anxious to respond to his high calling. Instead, his first impulse was to find his brother and tell him about Jesus.

How many times have we recognized that God was calling us to a specific task and wanted to begin immediately? Yet, there was a particular

"For God did not give us a spirit of timidity, but a spirit of power, of love and of self-discipline. So do not be ashamed to testify about our Lord, or ashamed of me his prisoner. But join with me in suffering for the gospel, by the power of God, who has saved us and called us to a holy life—not because of anything we have done but because of his own purpose and grace."

2 Timothy 1:7-9

106

person that seemed to be in the way. Perhaps she was standing at the door when it was time to leave for a women's council meeting. Or possibly she called as you were busy completing an assignment. We need to ask ourselves, *"How are we spending our time?"* There are multitudes of good things we can do with our time, but, in the eternal big picture, what is the most pressing? Andrew understood that his most important task was to introduce his brother to his Savior. As leaders we must learn to recognize, then do the important things.

In our fast-paced world, we have a tendency to think, *Tomorrow is another day; tomorrow I'll tell someone about Jesus.* Through personal experience I've learned we cannot be sure of tomorrow. I once felt compelled to share Jesus with three young college women. Within a year, two were killed and one died of cancer. Another time I responded to a woman's plea for someone to visit her dying husband in the hospital. Several of us made the visit, shared the gospel, and he accepted Christ. Three weeks later he died. I've thanked God many times that I was able to rejoice with the angels. I've also had to ask God's forgiveness for times I've missed the blessing because I believed I was too busy with an urgent task.

How are you spending your time? Do you have time carved out for eternal things—for multiplying yourself and for bringing the lost to Christ? If we do not set aside specific time to witness, it will surely be placed on the back burner. We are called to multiply ourselves whether we feel like it or not. We are called to bring the lost to Christ whether we have time or not.

The question is: *How are you spending your time?*

The Call to Multiply His Power

Andrew was with the other disciples when Jesus commanded them to go into all the world. Yet Jesus said they had been appointed so "that they might be with him." Jesus knew that Andrew and the others needed to spend time with Him in order to accomplish their great task—going into all the world. Jesus called Andrew to multiply God's power, not Andrew's.

I cannot speak for you, but I can speak for me. When I tap into God's power, He transforms me. Multiplying His power is possible only when we spend consistent time with Jesus and allow Him to fill us with His power. Through prayer we receive God's perspective and direction. We'll never reach anyone without God's power at work within us.

The question is, *Who provides your power?"* Is it from your material possessions or your position? Is it from your place of service? When I committed to full-time vocational ministry, God had to teach me that my

"He appointed twelve—designating them apostles—that they might be with him and that he might send them out to preach."
Mark 3:14

"But you will receive power when the Holy Spirit comes on you; and you will be my witnesses in Jerusalem, and in all Judea and Samaria, and to the ends of the earth."

Acts 1:8

power did not depend on how many things I owned or the job I had (or did not have!). Although I must confess, much of my personal significance was based on material things. After beginning my ministry, often I depended on my position at church for self-esteem and significance. God helped me to learn (over and over again) that He is my power. He taught me that I am important because He loves me and because He's called me to serve Him. No title could ever live up to that precious truth—and has not. As leaders, we must receive our power from Him and Him alone.

It's easy to focus on the world's blessings or the church's blessings on us. Do not be misled; as leaders, it is not your position or job that makes you important. It is God alone. Spend time with God as Andrew did (see John 1:39). Prayer leads to power—the power that God bestows to accomplish extraordinary things for the kingdom. As leaders, we must depend on Him, and we must lead others to depend on Him and on His power. God calls us to multiply His power in our lives.

The question is: *Who provides your power?*

The Call to Multiply His Resources

"Another of his disciples, Andrew, Simon Peter's brother, spoke up, 'Here is a boy with five small barley loaves and two small fish, but how far will they go among so many?'"

John 6:8-9

There they were—Jesus, the disciples, and thousands of hungry people. It was Andrew who took what little food he found and brought it to Jesus—a meager five loaves and two small fish. Jesus took all that Andrew had and multiplied it.

Andrew was called to multiply his resources. When I imagine myself in the same situation, I definitely would have responded differently. Can I feed 5,000 men and their families? Let's see. I certainly wouldn't have offered person-to-person service—only buffet style. And then only after the decorations were in place, the proper food ordered and prepared (chicken, of course), and advance reservations had been paid in full! No, I definitely would have missed God's blessing.

Not so with Andrew. Andrew searched for available resources. He discovered a little boy who was willing to share all he had for a greater cause. Andrew brought that little boy and his lunch to Jesus. He already knew that Jesus could do anything. Probably Andrew didn't know exactly what Jesus would do, but he knew that Jesus would do something. Andrew brought what he had to Jesus and allowed Jesus to multiply his resources.

Successful events and ministries that lead people to Christ are costly, but God can make all the difference if we faithfully take existing money and resources to Him. As leaders, our responsibility is to bring all that we have to God and allow Him to multiply our resources.

When I began serving in women's ministry at my church, I believed

God had great plans for us! However, our little budget did not offer much hope that we could carry out those plans. We asked, How can we be obedient to God's vision for our ministry? Then we prayed that He would reveal great things and provide great resources. Little by little, things begin to happen. We needed a computer, and a woman gave money just for that purpose. Women volunteered time, spiritual gifts, and talents. We discovered ways to earn money for the ministry. We observed that when we gave our ministry to God, He multiplied what was available. Women were reached for Christ when we committed our resources to Him.

Don't allow insufficient resources to keep you from sharing the most precious gift of Jesus Christ with those who need Him. Ask God to give you His ideas for your ministry. We are called to multiply His resources so that others may come to know Him in a personal way. We are called to depend on God for ways and means to accomplish that task.

The question is: *How can you accomplish the task with the resources you have?*

The Call to Multiply the Cause

Jesus called Andrew and Peter to come follow Him and He would make them fishers of men. Jesus called them to multiply the cause. Everything they did was a vehicle to share the good news of Jesus Christ. As faithful leaders, our responsibility is to train women to follow Christ and to share Him wherever they go, as they go. We are called to multiply the cause through our ministry to women.

One way to multiply the cause is to share Christ in bold, relational, intentional ways and to train others to do the same. Let's admit it. Most women (and men for that matter) are intimidated by sharing their faith. Yet Jesus clearly tells us that this is a responsibility of all obedient believers. The Great Commission is still the Great Commission!

Learning to share Christ personally with others is the first step. Teaching others to follow Him is the second step. Leaders are required to do both. An effective women's ministry reaches outside the walls of the church and leads women to Christ and to share Christ.

Luke 6:40 is a convicting verse: "A student is not above his teacher, but everyone who is fully trained will be like his teacher." That means your ministry will look like you do. That can be a scary thought! Think of it another way. Close your eyes and conjure up a mental picture of your ministry. What do you see? Often, leaders see pictures of themselves. For example, if your strength is Bible study, you may see women studying God's Word. If your strength is missions, you may see women serving in

"As Jesus was walking beside the Sea of Galilee, he saw two brothers, Simon called Peter and his brother Andrew. They were casting a net into the lake, for they were fishermen. 'Come, follow me,' Jesus said, 'and I will make you fishers of men.'"
Matthew 4:18-19

109

mission opportunities. If your strength is evangelism, chances are that in your mental picture, many will be coming to Christ as a result of your ministry. You must model evangelism if you desire a ministry characterized by evangelism. Whether we are naturally gifted witnesses or intimidated by the very thought of doing so, we are called to discover and implement ways to share the love of Christ with a lost world.

The question is: *Why are you doing what you are doing?*

The Call to Urgency

Andrew heard Jesus' call to urgency. He was there when Jesus told the disciples that the gospel must be preached to all nations. He observed first-hand Jesus' priority for reaching the multitudes—one by one. Loud and clear Andrew heard the assignment—do not waste time on the things of this world. As leaders, we must convey the urgency of spreading the gospel of Christ.

I remember a conference I attended years ago. The theme was "Share Jesus Now." The pastor whose sermon I most remember made this point: sharing is what we love to sing about and do. Jesus is the One about whom we share because He has done so very much for us. Then he said: But the problem is "now." Share Jesus NOW. We just don't feel the urgency. We have lost the cutting edge of the gospel. We have lost the reason He came. We have lost the focus on the "now."

The Bible says it this way: "As God's fellow workers we urge you not to receive God's grace in vain. For he says, 'In the time of my favor I heard you, and in the day of salvation I helped you.' I tell you, now is the time of God's favor, now is the day of salvation" (2 Cor. 6:1-2).

Oh my friend, when are we going to get serious about what God has called each of us to do? Perhaps as you read this chapter you sense the need to lead out in evangelism, yet you don't know how. God never intended us to take on this awesome task alone! He wants to help us. He wants to reach people even more than we do. He knows what to say and when to say it. He just wants to use us to accomplish His great work. You've heard it before; evangelism is sharing the good news in the power of the Holy Spirit and leaving the results to God. We have made it so hard—yet it is so easy! Often in witnessing groups we discuss the fact that Satan has blinded the eyes of unbelievers; yet, the truth is, Satan has blinded believers as well. Make a commitment today to get serious about evangelism.

The question is: *When are you going to get serious about the urgency of the gospel message?*

The Call to Action

So, what do you do when you don't feel called to evangelism and you serve in a leadership position? Remember the following:

Remember Your Call to Christ

Remember *Who* you are following. Decide that no matter what you are doing, you will share Christ when you have the opportunity. Make a commitment to your ministry that in every event you plan, you will include ways to reach unbelievers. Use *HeartTalk Leader* to discover ideas for emphasizing evangelism in your women's ministry. See the list of *HeartTalk* resources at the end of this chapter.

Remember Your Call to Multiply Yourself

Evaluate how you spend your time. Are you taking time to mentor at least one person, to model Christ and the Great Commission? Realign your priorities to include time to influence another's life. It may not mean you have to create another time slot. It may just mean that you bring another alongside. Whether it's planning an event or making a necessary visit, take someone in training with you.

Remember Your Call to Multiply His Power

Reflect on *Who* provides your power. Set aside a time each day to tap into God's power. Spend as much time and energy on your spiritual nurturing as you do your physical nurturing. Give your ministry to God and commit to follow Him in every area. Spend time praying in your council meetings. Encourage your leadership to pray for unsaved women on a daily basis. Identify and discuss ways God has spoken and moved in your meetings and events. Share these results with others.

Remember Your Call to Multiply Your Resources

Evaluate your present resources. Include personal material possessions as well as family and friends. Remember: they are only temporarily in your care and belong to God. Give each one to Him.

Thank God for the women who help you lead—your greatest resource. Thank Him for your church leaders and staff. Present yourselves wholeheartedly to the work of the Lord. Work with your leadership to identify available resources, then commit them to God to use for His glory. Ask God to reveal ways you can accomplish the tasks at hand with the resources you have. If God has given you a vision for something you don't possess, you can be certain He will supply it!

"And the gospel must first be preached to all nations. Whenever you are arrested and brought to trial, do not worry beforehand about what to say. Just say whatever is given you at the time, for it is not you speaking, but the Holy Spirit."
Mark 13:10-11

Remember Your Call to Multiply His Cause

Lead your ministry team to include evangelistic outreach in everything you do. Study the four-week training course for women, *HeartCall: Women Sharing God's Heart.* Consider offering a group for leadership before opening it to other women in the church. Study together the method for sharing Christ, then suggest each leader lead a small-group during the course of the study. Share testimonies from this first study group to promote a new study group and at other women's events.

Remember Your Call to Urgency

Analyze your sense of urgency in sharing the gospel message. Ask yourself a hard question, "When am I going to get serious about sharing the greatest thing that ever happened to me?" Write your commitment and verbalize it during your quiet time. Carry it in your Bible, post it in places to remind you that God will help you keep your commitment.

"Now go; I will help you speak and will teach you what to say."
Exodus 4:12

Emphasize the urgency in meetings with leadership and members. Pray together for God to empower your women to go now in the power of the Holy Spirit. And as God said to Moses, "Now go; I will help you speak and will teach you what to say" (Ex. 4:12).

Evangelism Resources

HeartCall, the women's evangelism area of the North American Mission Board, provides several resources to help you in your call to evangelism. To order these resources call Customer Service Center: 1-800-448-8032.

HeartTalk (ISBN 0840085079, $5 for pkg. of 50)—Evangelism witnessing booklets for women that focus on the necessary steps of salvation. The gospel is shared using symbols of the HeartCall logo.

HeartTalk Leader (ISBN 0840085087, $3.99)—Leader's guide to *HeartTalk* provides helpful hints for using the "HeartTalk" witnessing booklet for decision counseling at women's events and in the local church. It also includes the *HeartCall Church Strategy.*

HeartCall: The Call to Prayer (ISBN 0840085044, $12.99)—Women's 366-day devotional book, focusing on praying for the lost. The book includes a place to list those in need of salvation and prayer.

HeartCall: Women Sharing God's Heart (ISBN 0840085117, $9.99)—This four-week study focuses on Colossians 4:2-6 and teaches women how to pray, how to watch for opportunities to share the gospel, how to make sure both their walk and talk provide godly example, and how to study the Word of God in preparation for answering questions. The workbook includes a leader guide for the four sessions. A five-day, four-week study guide provides a Scripture memory plan for presenting *HeartTalk* as well as a plan for praying for unbelievers.

For Smaller Churches
by Martha Lawley

Every Christian and every church, regardless of size, has received the same command to go and tell others about Jesus. Size is not the issue when it comes to evangelism: Christ has already demonstrated what 12 obedient people can do! The same power to carry out the Great Commission is available to all churches.

The fact that God is the One who multiplies resources is good news for the small church. Have you committed your resources to God? Have you asked God to multiple your resources? God will not receive the glory if we choose to rely only on what we can or cannot do.

Consider joining with other ministries in your church to provide evangelistic opportunities. For example, a churchwide evangelism emphasis and training can be planned by a team which includes the women's ministry leaders. Churchwide Discipleship Training may offer ongoing opportunities for evangelism training for both men and women. A partnership between men's and women's ministries is another way to provide opportunities for evangelism training and involvement.

Cooperation among neighboring churches in the area of evangelism can benefit smaller churches. Combining resources and avoiding unnecessary duplication of effort are effective ways of allowing God to multiply what you have to offer. Whichever approaches fit your situation, women's ministry leadership must actively support, participate, and encourage others to take advantage of these opportunities.

A number of excellent evangelism training materials are available today, such as LifeWay's *Share Jesus Without Fear* by William Fay and Ralph Hodge (see p. 221). A straightforward and practical resource, it helps Christians overcome their fear of sharing with others through a proper understanding of the role of the Holy Spirit in the process of evangelism.

Leading Women to Serve

Missions

by Laura Savage

When I was going through the process of buying my first home, I was reminded that there are three factors to consider: location, location, location. That same idea can be applied to women's ministry. There are three considerations when beginning or growing a women's ministry: purpose, purpose, purpose. Without a purpose—a written, memorized, cross-stitchable purpose—you will find it easy to lose focus and enthusiasm.

One of the best ways to evaluate your ministry's purpose statement is to ask yourself and your leadership team how far it reaches—does it only address the needs of the women in your church? Have you included the needs of women in your community? How does your purpose statement challenge women to look beyond their corner of the world to develop a global vision? The purpose of this chapter is to provide some practical ideas regarding the importance of helping women develop that global vision—to help women discover that the whole world can fit into their hearts—through missions involvement.

The Power of Purpose

"'Hear, O Israel, the Lord our God, the Lord is one. Love the Lord your God with all your heart and with all your soul and with all your mind and with all your strength.' The second is this: Love your neighbor as yourself.' There is no commandment greater than these."
Mark 12:29-31

When Jesus was asked which of the Commandments was most important, His response included loving God and loving people. I believe missions involvement is the fulfillment of the second Commandment: love your neighbor as yourself.

Missions is a vital part of any women's ministry that is seeking to provide a holistic approach to helping women become more Christlike. Missions involvement completes the picture of the maturing Christian woman. Missions involvement begins when a woman chooses to make God's commandment her personal commission to take the gospel around the corner and around the world.

The first three sections of this book describe how the heart, soul, mind, and strength can be developed in a women's ministry through prayer, Bible study, and the use of spiritual gifts. When those four elements of the first Commandment are active and growing in the life of a disciple, the second Commandment will be evident in her life as well. Loving your

114

neighbor as yourself demonstrates that you are fulfilling the first Commandment. Developing your one-on-one relationship with God is essential, but for that relationship to make a difference in the world, it must be lived out in the world.

When a woman discovers her purpose as a Christian and is equipped to fulfill that purpose, she will have a reason to be personally involved in God's plan for the whole world. And God's plan for the whole world is that every person will hear and accept the gospel—the message of an eternal relationship that God offers through faith in the redeeming work of Jesus Christ. Jesus' final words to His followers as He ascended into heaven were "Go and make disciples of all nations" (Matt. 28:18-20. See also Mark 16:15; and Acts 1:8).

"Go and make disciples of all nations."
Matthew 28:18-20

Christian women today participate in that plan when they are involved in the process of telling the whole world about Jesus Christ. And being involved in any aspect of the process is being involved in missions.

The Potential in the Process

There are many ways one can be involved in the process of taking the gospel to the lost. The obvious responsibility of all Christians is to personally share the gospel with others and invite them to accept Jesus Christ. (Refer to pages 105-113 for specific information on evangelism.) But other important parts of the process—other aspects of missions—must also be accomplished:

- Praying for the lost who need to hear the gospel;
- Praying for people who are able to reach the lost in other places;
- Praying for your church and its members to develop an outward focus toward the lost and unchurched—locally and globally;
- Giving financial support to missionaries and missions efforts, both locally and globally;
- Participating in community service projects that provide opportunity to reach the unsaved with the intent of sharing the gospel;
- Supporting missionaries and missions efforts by enlisting as a volunteer on short-term mission projects at home or abroad;
- Developing an awareness of the needs of the lost and of those who minister to them and educating others about those needs;
- Holding one another accountable as Christians to be faithful witnesses in their spheres of influence;
- Challenging and equipping Christians of all ages to participate in God's global missions plan.

The common element in each of these aspects of missions involvement

An exciting, effective, holistic women's enrichment ministry will include a vital missions component.

is the purpose—reaching the lost. It's important and necessary to minister to our Christian sisters and brothers and to grow spiritually through involvement in Christian activities, Bible studies, and fellowship. However, these activities don't fit into the missions category unless their purpose is to reach the lost with the gospel of Jesus Christ. An exciting, effective, holistic women's enrichment ministry will include a vital missions component.

The Practice of a Passion

For women's groups that are already established, consider the following ideas for missions involvement. Whether it is a Bible study group, fellowship time, craft class, or exercise class—most any activity can include a missions component.

- Pray for missionaries with birthdays on the day of your meeting.
- Participate in the national Southern Baptist women's prayer project for Muslim women jointly sponsored by Women's Missionary Union, LifeWay Christian Resources, International Mission Board, and North American Mission Board (see pages 221-222 for contact information).
- Establish a prayer-team partnership with a missionary on the field and obtain prayer requests from her for which your group can commit to pray. (*Prisms* by Stuart Calvert suggests ways to pray for missionaries—available from WMU.)
- Make prayerwalking a frequent activity for your women's ministry. Schedule a specific time and place, then focus on a particular group, situation, or event—or simply pray for the needs you see while walking.
- Periodically invite missionary speakers to share with the group.
- Challenge women to be leaders for children's and youth missions education groups, reminding them they will be preparing the next generation of missionaries and supporters of missions causes. Be sure to provide training for these leaders. (Contact your state Woman's Missionary Union office for more information.)
- Choose a particular meeting and focus on a ministry project. The following are some suggestions: conduct a food drive, tutor at a local school, visit a women's shelter, provide assistance to a soup kitchen, or teach life skills to women in a multi-housing area. Be creative; do something that will encourage women to use the gifts and talents they already possess.

- Ask small groups to identify one activity all members enjoy (such as reading, cooking, sewing, and crafts). Then encourage groups to brainstorm ways they can use this interest to reach out to non-Christians. This small-group activity may spark some ideas for missions projects as well as create new configurations of small groups among women. Reassemble small groups to report ideas and watch the excitement build. Some ideas include:

    Sewing curtains for a women's shelter;

    Reading to hospitalized children;

    Shopping for elderly who live in nearby neighborhoods;

    Teaching parenting classes/Bible study for young mothers;

    Tutoring children and adults in English as a foreign language;

    Teaching computer skills;

    At the next large-group fellowship time, share testimonies of any new ministries and reports of lives that have been changed. Celebrate God's activity among the group!

- Enlist several women in the group to alternate bringing missions information to the group. (Use *Missions Mosaic* magazine from WMU as a resource.) Include newspaper current events to help you pray for the missionaries in the locations of the events.

- Serve a variety of cultural foods at your meetings or luncheons; include tidbits about missionaries serving in those cultural areas.

- Develop prayer triplets. Suggest three women pray together for nine unsaved people they know (each person submits three names).

- Train women in how to use *HeartTalk* tracts and plan a reporting time (see pages 112-113).

- Challenge groups to commit to a missions offering goal, World Hunger offerings, and other special missions-related offerings. To interest younger women, choose and give to a specific project or person. Contact the International Mission Board and North American Mission Board for ideas. Work with Woman's Missionary Union leadership in your church to combine efforts in promoting and collecting missions offerings.

- Challenge women to memorize Scripture for witnessing and encouragement purposes. An aerobics class can work Scripture memory into their routines. Rhythm helps memorization.

- Teach women to compose and verbalize their personal testimonies. Allow time for women to share their victories and struggles in witnessing situations.

- Encourage women to participate in disaster relief training through your state convention.
- Provide missions resources such as *Missions Mosaic* (from WMU), *The Commission* (from IMB), and *On Mission* (from NAMB) to inform women about needs for which they can pray.
- Adopt an unreached people group and commit to pray for this group regularly (contact the IMB).
- Contact WMU to learn more about beginning a Women on Mission organization in your church or on a college campus.

There is no limit to what God can do to reach non-Christians through the women in your church.

Acknowledging Particular Pathways of Life

Why doesn't a woman commit wholeheartedly to something others passionately support?

As a women's ministry leader, your challenge is to create an environment where each woman can discover her unique place in God's mission to reach the whole world—where she can practice her passion. However, you will discover many reasons why a woman doesn't commit wholeheartedly to something that others passionately support.

- She may be overwhelmed with her own life and unable to see how she can fit another responsibility into her schedule.
- She may lack an understanding of the biblical basis for missions; therefore, she has no spiritual connection to the concept.
- She may lack experience.
- She may be unclear about the definition of missions; she may perceive missions as something that happens overseas and, therefore, has no personal connection to it.
- She may associate missions involvement with a previous generation; she may not know anyone in her peer group who is living a missions lifestyle, or she doesn't have a mentor who is gradually introducing her to missions involvement.
- She may assume that her only responsibility regarding missions is contributing financially to special offerings each year.

While some of these reasons for lack of involvement are legitimate at certain times in a woman's life, they can also become excuses. An effective women's ministry leader will challenge women to understand that missions involvement is biblical and is not optional for Christians.

Regardless of how busy a Christian woman is or how limited she feels, she can practice her passion for reaching the lost. And for leaders, it is exciting to watch as women discover possible levels of involvement.

118

For the woman who has never been involved in missions, you must "put a face on missions."

- Invite a peer-age, female missionary to be the special guest at a women's event (tea, retreat, conference, and so forth) to lead a prayer time, Bible study, or topical conference. Don't promote the special guest as a missionary, but allow women to discover she is a missionary. In this way, women see the special guest first as one of them, helping them connect to someone who understands the Great Commission as a personal commitment.
- Invite a woman to observe while you work on your next missions project.
- Ask volunteers to email specific missionaries you already know and ask for prayer requests.
- Ask a woman who likes to read to present a book review using a missionary biography or ask a dramatist to present a monologue.
- Take a missionary friend to lunch and invite a woman not yet involved in missions to join you.
- Take a group of women to a nearby ministry center sponsored by your association or area churches and survey their needs—such as food, craft items, window curtains, clothes, and so forth. Lead women to see how their gifts and talents could help meet those needs. They may need your leadership to organize their efforts.
- Model ways to pray for missionaries on their birthdays.

For the woman who has limited time, provide opportunities for mini-projects and allow flexibility:

- Provide a package of note cards and a specific missionary's name and address. Suggest she write a note once a month.
- Suggest she save pocket change for a designated missions offering. Challenge her to fill a jar or bowl by a certain time.
- Provide informative resources about missions.
- Provide witnessing tracts she can share when she travels, runs errands, carpools, visits doctor's offices, or waits in airports.
- Model ways to be "on mission" during daily tasks. For example: how to witness to other baseball or soccer moms; how to share her faith on an airplane; how to encourage a service provider with Scripture; how to pray for neighbors and coworkers; how to use her own life situations to relate to others about faith issues.
- Inform her of items your group is collecting for a missions project and volunteer to pick up her donation.
- Invite her to be a one-time prayer leader or discussion group

For the woman who has limited time, provide opportunities for mini-projects and allow flexibility.

leader at a missions event or assign her a leadership opportunity that requires minimal preparation.

- Assign a specific missions prayer request to be prayed for at a specific time each week, such as while she's driving to work on Tuesdays or cooking dinner on Thursdays.
- Allow her to complete a simple portion of an ongoing craft missions project that she can work on at home for short periods of time. Affirm her help and contribution.
- Challenge her to map out a prayerwalk or prayerdrive for her exercise route or in routine trips around town.
- Ask her to collect articles from newspapers or news magazines related to your ministry's adopted country of unreached people.
- If she travels as part of her professional work, obtain her travel schedule and pray for opportunities for witnessing at specific times. Follow up to receive updates. Provide her with tracts.
- Give her specific prayer requests from those in your church who are participating in mission trips.
- Suggest ways to involve additional family members in missions projects and/or trips.

For the woman who has limited mobility, help her to feel valued and needed in behind-the-scenes responsibilities.

For the woman who has limited mobility, help her to feel valued and needed in behind-the-scenes responsibilities.

- Ask her to call the prayerlines of both the International and North American Mission Boards and to keep you updated on prayer requests (see page 222).
- Provide your ministry project schedule and ask her to pray during the times you or your group are directly involved.
- Give her a map of your group's prayerwalking route and scheduled walking times. Ask her to pray for your group and for specific opportunities during these specific times.
- Help her to establish a savings/giving plan and to understand how important her gifts are to the cause of missions—regardless of the size of the gift. She can collect pennies, coupon money, and grocery store coin change.
- Now and then take the group meetings to her: involve her in the prayertime, a craft project, or ask her to present a book review or other information.

The Perspective of a Lifestyle Priority

Many churches are blessed with women who are already committed to missions involvement—for some it has been a lifestyle priority for years.

For some older women, missions involvement was once the only avenue for women to be involved in church ministry leadership. That one opportunity was their lifeline to spiritual growth with other women, to leadership skills development, and to a broader knowledge of the world at large.

Today's opportunities for women far exceed anything that was only dreamed of 30 to 50 years ago. Some of today's older women are fearful that a new approach to involving women in ministry will leave out the important missions element. This is always a potential risk with any new type of ministry in a church.

Gather the various generations of women for very specific prayer times and strategic planning times. As a result of this "coming together," you may plan special intergenerational events. What might be perceived as tension or friction between the older and younger generations may simply be a lack of understanding of the preferred learning styles enjoyed by the different age groups.

Consider some of the following ideas for older women to bridge the gap between the younger generations of women and their preferred approaches to learning and involvement.

- Encourage her to become a mentor. Help her to see the need for younger women to be challenged one-on-one and to be exposed to the wisdom of years and the joy of missions involvement.
- If she has been in a particular leadership role for many years, encourage her to create a new role that is needed in your ministry or church. Help her to see the value in allowing someone else to develop leadership skills with the advantage of an experienced woman's wisdom and advice.
- Ask her to lead a Bible study for younger women. Esther Burroughs once said that younger women are looking for women they know who have their Bibles underlined and know how to find biblical guidance for today's problems.
- Invite her, along with several other women with long-term mission involvement, to participate in a think tank for your women's ministry. Ask them to dream dreams and to set goals for the young women in your church and then to establish a plan for reaching those goals.
- Ask her to coordinate a simple missions project designed especially for younger women, such as giving a baby shower for a crisis pregnancy center, collecting school supplies for underprivileged children, providing personal hygiene gift baskets for a women's shelter, or leading a craft project to be used in a ministry.

Consider these ideas for older women to bridge the gap between the younger generations of women.

Ask her to begin the project with a short devotional thought or testimony about why she's involved in missions.

- Ask her to pray for a younger women's Bible study group.
- Match her up as a prayer partner with a younger woman.
- Help her to identify some younger women who are ready for leadership roles and to include them on their planning team for an upcoming missions event.
- Ask her to share her missions testimony during an event for younger women, such as a Bible study or fellowship luncheon.
- Ask her to share photos and newsletters from missionary friends with groups of women who are not already personally connected to any missionaries.
- Ask older women to be table hostesses and to provide the table centerpieces for your next women's ministry tea or luncheon. Suggest they use items that tie into personal missions experiences. During the event, allow time for older women to share with their table members the meaning and stories behind the centerpieces.

The Prayers of Preparation

Missions involvement in the local church has the potential to help women develop their spiritual muscles. Some may answer God's call to full-time mission service. Others may be called to a one- or two-year assignment. Lead your women's ministry to become a support team through prayer, encouragement, fun and practical gifts, emails, financial giving, phone calls, materials, packages, and learning opportunities.

Short-term mission trips motivate people to consider missions commitment.

It is a fact—short-term mission trips motivate people to consider missions commitment. Traveling out of your comfort zone, whether across town or across the ocean, forces you to depend on God in new ways, to face your own prejudices, and to realize just how valuable your availability is to God's mission. You can discover new characteristics about yourself. You can learn how similar you are to the very people you once thought were different. You can begin to understand God's love for all people and gain a deeper appreciation for Jesus' sacrifice.

How do I know? Because it happened to me when I finally allowed God to send me to a foreign country and more importantly, to teach me while I was there. No, I am not a full-time missionary overseas, but I do have a missions calling on my life.

Begin today to ask God to help you develop a women's ministry that will prepare women to hear God's call, that will equip them to answer

122

that call, and that will nurture a heart willing to follow that call. Challenge the women in your church to participate in a mission trip and/or to develop an ongoing missions project with people in your city. The preparation process, the going and the growing can most certainly transform women's lives—thereby transforming your women's ministry.

The Product to Pursue

What is the product your women's ministry is pursuing? You'll know the answer when you determine which parts of the two greatest commandments are most evident in your women's ministry. Missions involvement is the key to helping women fit the whole world into their hearts. Join in the excitement of being part of God's mission!

Missions involvement is the key to helping women fit the whole world into their hearts.

For Smaller Churches
by Martha Lawley

Sometimes in smaller churches, missions is seen as the responsibility of the WMU, not the women's ministry, if they are separate. This approach is unfortunate; in reality, no "either/or" choice can be made. Churches that replace missions in favor of women's ministry are incomplete, just as churches that reject women's ministry in favor of a missions organization are incomplete. Although organizations vary from church to church, women's ministry and missions are indivisible.

Smaller churches have many missions resources at their disposal. Most associations employ a director of missions who can be an invaluable resource. Each state convention also has missions personnel and resources available to local churches.

Working with other churches in your area can open the door to unique missions opportunities. As you share ideas and develop joint projects, what may have seemed impossible becomes reality with more volunteers and resources from which to draw.

Provide various levels of involvement—from bringing canned goods and food to a church gathering to hands-on missions at a soup kitchen or clothing room—so that all women in your church have the opportunity to experience the blessings that come from fulfilling His mission.

Find creative ways to incorporate missions involvement into each women's ministry program. Most of the suggestions offered in this chapter can be used in any size church. Prayerfully seek God's will for missions emphases and involvement in your women's ministry.

Ministering to Special Needs

The Hurting Woman

by Jacque Truitt

[God] "comforts us in all our affliction so that we may be able to comfort those who are in any affliction with the comfort with which we ourselves are comforted by God."
2 Corinthians 1:4 (NASB)

Frightened by a thunderstorm, a child awoke during the night and jumped in bed with his parents. After comforting the child for a moment, his father said, "Don't worry; God will take care of you." The child responded, "I know Daddy, but sometimes I just need somebody with skin on!"

Women in lay leadership provide hurting women God's comfort "with skin on." What causes a woman to hurt? Illness or death of a loved one, broken relationships, loss of a job, past or present physical or sexual abuse, alcoholism, drug abuse, troubled children, and countless other life experiences bring devastating pain and disrupt a woman's physical, psychological, and spiritual well-being.

God did not promise us freedom from pain or loss. He does promise He will provide what we need to survive the hurt. He promised His presence, His guidance, and His comfort. To comfort others, we must understand our role and its limitations. Then we must cultivate the skills of active listening and good communication to minister to special needs.

Establish Your Role

We are all subject to the "Batman and Robin Syndrome"–sweeping in to solve problems while leaving awestruck spectators to marvel at the wonders of "that masked hero." In reality, the person hurting may not even be asking for solutions–only support and reassurance. A superior and controlling attitude can undermine and destroy a hurting person's sense of worth. The woman suffering does not benefit if the one ministering assumes control and imposes her advice. Judgments ultimately handicap the person in crisis.

Be careful that you do not depend on your role as minister to boost your self esteem. A better idea is to empower the hurting person to seek healthy solutions. What is good and healthy for one person might cause someone else anxiety and fear. An effective minister does not supply the answers for others, but provides support and resources for decision-making.

Consider this analogy. A physical injury left untreated becomes infected. If a doctor lances the wound, releases the infection, applies medication, and covers the area with sterile cloth, the healing can begin. In similar fashion, a lay minister can exert the same healing power in the life of emotionally and spiritually hurting women.

First, acknowledge the hurt and help the person identify the cause. This allows the hurting woman to feel safe in opening the wound and releasing her feelings. Then treat the wound with gentleness and care to nurture healing. At this point it is possible to discuss solutions and offer resources for help. Finally, share the covering of God's grace, love, and acceptance that guarantees hope and recovery to all those hurting.

Sometimes words are not enough. Sometimes there are no words. If a picture is worth a thousand words, then a touch is worth a million. Support and care can be transmitted with a touch on the shoulder or a hug. By holding a hand, we forge a bond; we give strength to those who hunger for it. Always remember, however, that touch must be appropriate and comfortable for the person to whom you are ministering.

Know Your Limitations

Lay ministry is not counseling or therapy. Recognize when to refer to a professional counselor or therapist. Often listening and caring are not sufficient help. Some tasks fall outside the scope of lay ministry. A lay minister would not attempt to set a broken leg if she were not a doctor. Likewise, she should not attempt to provide the intense help required for circumstances of rape or an abusive past or present.

Lay people sometimes hesitate to minister because they think they are expected to counsel. Therefore, hurting individuals often fail to receive the help and encouragement they need. One woman said of her church friends: "They didn't know how to fix me, so they didn't do anything. They couldn't fix me so they left me." An effective lay minister understands how to support and encourage hurting women without feeling compelled to solve their problems.

Listen Actively

Most hurting people are dealing with some form of grief. The normal grief process for a severe loss takes at least two years. A grieving person needs time to sort, search, and regain strength. How then should you proceed if you truly want to help? Many times the best help comes from those who simply listen.

You can minister more effectively if you develop the skill of active or reflective listening. This type listening empowers you to help individuals identify their own feelings, which become the starting point for all future

Lay ministry is not counseling or therapy.

actions. Active listening requires intense concentration; it is a process of feeding back or mirroring back that which is said by the person to whom you are listening. Key phrases in this process are: "It sounds as if ..." or "I hear you saying...."

Active listening encourages the person to clarify her feelings. After hearing her feelings expressed by someone else, the hurting woman can correct inaccurate impressions or feel affirmed. In this way, the troubled woman can move beyond surface emotions and touch the hidden or suppressed hurt.

If the person is shy, she may toss out subtle invitations to you as the listener: "I'm confused" or "I don't know what to think." Say: "How are you confused?" or "What is confusing you?" These statements encourage the person to tell you what she is thinking and feeling.

Expressing an idea requires energy and concentration for the person talking. It requires even more energy and concentration to listen actively. It also requires the ability to focus more on the person sharing than on your own thoughts or advice.

Watch for both verbal and nonverbal messages. For instance, when a woman tells you she is feeling great, does she smile? Is there a light in her eyes? Some examples of nonverbal communication are silence, lethargy, withdrawal, and a lack of zest. Although very outgoing in normal conditions, those who are hurting may withdraw or disappear socially.

Trauma creates a real dilemma for most people. On the one hand, we believe no one can hurt as badly as we or understand the depth of our loss, yet we desperately want reassurance that we aren't unique and alone. The minister needs to build a common bond with the person's pain and to offer hope. However, refrain from competing with the person's feelings. The phrase, "I remember when I ..." turns the conversation away from her and toward you. Like comparing surgical scars, it doesn't lead to a better understanding of the hurting person. Share a related personal experience later when the hurting person feels heard and understood.

What a person says may not tell the whole story. As listener, ask questions to gain insight. For example, a woman waiting to hear biopsy results may say, "I wish the doctor would let me know what my chances are." She may actually mean, "I am afraid." Then as a lay minister you can respond by asking, "How do you feel while waiting for the doctor to talk to you?"

"Carry each other's burdens, and in this way you will fulfill the law of Christ."
Galatians 6:2

Allowing a hurting woman to share is like releasing the steam from a pressure cooker. Release is a natural result of verbalizing emotions held inside. Expression is the most important action—even more important than solutions. Exploring the possibilities for solutions comes later.

Avoid Common Communication Barriers

Certain verbal phrases and nonverbal approaches tend to shut down communication. As lay ministers we want to avoid these common pitfalls. Consider the following tactics and statements that become barriers to communication:

- Advising, giving solutions. "Why don't you just tell your husband to spend more time with you?"
- Directing, commanding. "Stop talking such nonsense; you'll be all right." "You get that notion out of your head right now."
- Moralizing, preaching. "You ought to look at the bright side." "You should pray more about it."
- Disagreeing, blaming. "You're not thinking clearly, if that's how you feel." "You're off base to think everyone has deserted you."
- Ridiculing, shaming, and labeling. "You're acting very immature." "How can you say that when so many are worse off than you?"
- Praising, agreeing. "I agree that people have mistreated you." "Well, you're just more perceptive than she is."
- Warning, promising. "If you will calm down, I'll listen to you." "If you stay in that mood, you will just get worse."
- Giving logical argument, lecturing. "Why don't you…?"
- Probing, questioning, interrogating. "Why did you do that?"
- Withdrawing, humor, sarcasm, diversion. "Well, aren't you the cat's meow!"
- Reassuring, sympathizing, consoling. "You poor thing."
- Interpreting, analyzing, diagnosing. "You did that because … " or "I think that dream means …."

Explore Alternatives

At some point the woman must ask herself: *What do I want to do?* It is a freeing question. It raises awareness that she has some say in the future and it opens the door to discovering personal potential.

The process of exploring consequences is linked to identifying desires. "If you do what you want, what is likely to happen?" "Are you prepared to accept the consequences?" Frequently people don't know what they want, or in some instances they may consider actions that would be harmful to themselves or others. At this point you may suggest possible alternatives. Note that I said suggest! This is a crucial point for lay ministers. It's often easier to give advice than to make suggestions.

Remember: it is not your responsibility to solve problems! Never say, "Why don't you … ?" It will be heard as "you should." Say instead, "Have

This is a crucial point for lay ministers. It's often easier to give advice than it is to make suggestions.

you considered ... ?" or "What would happen if ... ?" Provide information to the person to help in decision-making. Provide only information that offers direction, or suggest a therapeutic referral or a support group.

Deal with Unresolved Grief

Grief is a God-given process—as natural as breathing. However, just as breathing can be interrupted by a foreign object lodged in the throat, the grief process can be interrupted.

Recently I talked with a young woman whose father died from a heart attack. The daughter rushed home just as the father's body was being removed. Church friends had already arrived. The daughter began to cry. Unbelievably a lay leader said: "Stop. You can't cry. You need to be strong for your mother." Six months later when this family arrived in my office for counseling, the daughter still had not shed a tear. Lay ministers need to understand and facilitate the grief process.

People in our society are more and more prone to tuning things out. We watch movies, play video games, and activate numerous other mechanisms to avoid life. Tragically, we practice the same tuning-out process in relationships. Blocking or restraining the grief process only creates more pain. It can, in fact, prevent hurting women from receiving God's comfort. Several writers have contributed to what we know about grief, but many still believe that Elizabeth Kubler-Ross's five steps are the best.

People in our society are more and more prone to tuning things out. Tragically, we practice the same tuning-out process in relationships.

Stages of Grief

The stages of grief identified by Elizabeth Kubler-Ross were published in her well-known book *Death and Dying.*[1] She said the grief process includes clearly definable but not necessarily linear stages. Five basic feelings may be experienced in a loss. Some people experience the entire range of feelings while others may experience only one. These stages are shock/denial, bargaining/guilt, rage/anger, depression/sadness, acceptance, and in some cases, forgiveness.

Because the stages are not linear, it is possible to begin the cycle of feelings with depression, move to acceptance, and then experience shock and denial. No one can predict how a woman will handle grief as a result of loss, but feelings must be dealt with as they surface. An effective lay minister validates the hurting woman during each stage of the grief process.

1. *Shock & Denial*— "Oh no, not me." One response to grief is shock and denial. The woman may be unable to believe that this could happen to her. Some people simply refuse to believe and will act as though the circumstance or situation never occurred. If the events occurred in the

past, the individual may have been blocked at this stage for a very long time, as in cases of childhood abuse. Often in these situations a woman will doubt herself.

In this stage of grief, empathize with everything the woman has to say. Encourage communication of thoughts and feelings without judgment. Feelings are a response to the woman's perception of the event or circumstance that caused her hurt or pain. If her feelings are blocked, denied or condemned, they can be repressed. Eventually they may emerge as destructive attitudes and behaviors.

Comments like "Have faith–God has a reason for this" or "You just need to forgive" are not helpful. These provoke feelings of guilt, spiritual inadequacy, and shame. The woman hearing such comments not only hurts from the circumstance, but also believes she is spiritually inadequate and feels ashamed of her own feelings. The lay minister needs to communicate to the hurting woman that she knows she is hurting and believes she is worthy of comfort.

2. *Bargaining/Guilt–* "It happened, but … " At this stage the hurting woman begins to accept the reality of the circumstance, but still refuses to accept the losses associated with it. Hurting people often look for someone to blame–even themselves. She may ask, "Why did this happen?" or think "If only I had … " This bargaining process is an attempt to control the situation and to resolve the confusion caused by the hurt or pain. The woman may be feeling rejected or deserted by God.

3. *Rage and Anger–* "It happened and it matters!" We are created in the image of God. God gets angry. For us to deny our anger is to deny a part of the person God created us to be. Anger is often the one feeling we don't encourage a grieving woman to acknowledge or express. We need to understand that anger is a normal and healthy element of the grief process. Do not misunderstand; I am not saying that all behaviors that result from anger are healthy. Many behaviors and attitudes resulting from anger are sinful. But the angry feelings themselves are as normal as the ability to feel pain. If hurting women identify and express their feelings of anger, then those feelings are less likely to result in angry behaviors and attitudes such as bitterness, malice, and vengeance.

"In your anger, do not sin."
Ephesians 4:26

Forgiveness is important for the healing process. However, urging someone to forgive prematurely may block the grief process. Forgiveness at this stage is basically spiritualized denial. True biblical forgiveness requires acknowledgement of the offense. Remember that God's forgiveness requires repentance. God never said that our sin is "no big deal." In fact, it is such a big deal that it led Him to the cross.

Many women remain mired in pain because someone pushed them to forgive before they could truly acknowledge the hurt. Encourage the hurting woman to acknowledge all of her feelings, including anger. Then she can move to forgiveness. If she never acknowledges the hurt, she will be consumed with guilt and shame and will repeatedly return to this stage only to evaluate herself as spiritually inadequate because she "cannot forgive." If encouraged to feel and verbalize her hurt, she will move through the grief process reaching acceptance and forgiveness.

If encouraged to feel and verbalize her hurt, she will move through the grief process reaching acceptance and forgiveness.

4. *Depression and loss*– "Oh, me!" Sadness is a natural reaction to loss. Provide support at this stage of the grief process. The hurting woman will move through sadness quicker if you will be there to listen and reflect. Mourning is healthy. Eventually the joy will return.

5. *Acceptance*– "Yes, me. It happened to me. I recognize it. I understand it. I was angry about it. I feel great loss but also hope. I can go on with my life." This stage emerges naturally if the woman is not blocked in an earlier stage. However, it is important to remember that grief is not linear. Sometimes a person may feel acceptance at one level, only to cycle repeatedly through the grief process as she encounters new levels of loss awareness.

Deal with Specific Types of Hurt

Hurt May Be the Product of Abuse

Some hurting women may currently be in abusive relationships. Abuse rarely begins with physical violence. Abuse follows an identifiable cycle which both partners usually deny.

- Phase One: Tension-building phase—Yelling, name-calling, put-downs, throwing things, accusations
- Phase Two: Violent episode—Hitting, punching, degrading, more verbal abuse
- Phase Three: Honeymoon phase– "I'm sorry," promises to change, "It won't ever happen again," flowers, gifts

Learn to recognize the signs of a victimized woman. She …

- is afraid of her partner.
- cannot express her own opinion or feelings without being fearful of her partner's reaction.
- must ask her partner's permission to see family or friends, spend money, or make purchases.

- sometimes feels as if she is living with two different people, Dr. Jekyll/Mr. Hyde.
- tries to please her partner, only to be criticized repeatedly.
- constantly attempts to mold her children, her environment, and herself into what pleases her partner.
- stays confused about the difference in the way her partner perceives the relationship and the way she perceives it.
- eventually believes all the terrible things her partner accuses her of and says about her; is unsure of reality.

If you are ministering to a woman and you observe that these actions are occurring or she shares information related to them, encourage her to seek professional help from a licensed Christian counselor. The cycle of abuse continues and worsens without treatment. Remember: safety takes precedence over confidentiality. If the woman refuses or hesitates to seek help, enlist a qualified professional to assist you. Do not attempt intervention alone.

Help Women Deal with Trauma

Sometimes an event is so traumatic or overwhelming that there may be significant reactions to the stress. In these situations talking about the event is even more important. Confronted early, post-traumatic stress can be prevented or mitigated. Every women's ministry needs a list of professionals who are trained to address trauma.

Depression Is Not a Spiritual Problem!

More than just "the blues," clinical depression is a medical illness that afflicts millions of people every year. Depression can cause major symptoms, including severe headaches, stomach pain or nausea, breathing problems, or chronic neck and back pains. In many cases, women do not seek help for depression, but instead, frequently visit a physician complaining of other symptoms such as loss of energy and change in appetite, weight, or sleep patterns.

Fortunately, depression is a treatable illness. Professional treatment is effective in 80 to 90 percent of all depressed patients. Unfortunately, too many people with clinical depression remain untreated. Consider providing regular health screenings for depression as a part of your ministry. These screenings provide a quick way to spot the first signs of serious illness and to reach women who might not otherwise seek help. The LifeWay workbook, *Strength for the Journey* (see page 221) is a group study giving a biblical perspective on discouragement and depression.

Consider providing regular health screenings for depression as a part of your ministry.

Encourage a woman to seek help if she experiences five or more of the following symptoms for more than two weeks:
- depressed or irritable mood that lasts for most of the day and occurs nearly every day, for more than a week or two.
- disturbance in usual sleeping patterns such as insomnia, sleeping too much or too little.
- disturbance in appetite, weight loss (when not dieting), or gain.
- loss of interest or pleasure in most usual activities, such as socializing with friends, academic work, or sports.
- feelings of lethargy, fatigue, low energy, or agitation.
- difficulty with concentration and decision-making.
- recurrent feelings of worthlessness, guilt, or hopelessness.
- recurrent thoughts of death or suicide.
- difficulty functioning in personal, social, or academic matters.

Remember the Importance of Confidentiality

Consider it a privilege when someone turns to you for help. You have received the gift of trust. Do not betray that trust or trivialize it by gossiping about others' misfortune. Always ask permission before sharing someone's privileged information with family members, prayer partners, church staff, or anyone else. Hold your tongue; respect yourself as well as the person who confided in you. The only exception to confidentiality is the rule of safety. If someone shares that they plan to harm themselves or someone else, you are legally responsible to help keep them safe even if it means betraying their trust.

Recognize Your Own Vulnerability

As you minister to someone who hurts, you hurt. When she mourns, you mourn. Don't deny your personal feelings. Feed yourself emotionally and spiritually so you can continue to care for and nurture others.

Evaluate your motives for becoming involved. Do you see yourself as a "rescuer" trying to "save" your victim? What are your expectations of the person you're helping? Do you expect gratefulness? Do you put a price tag on your caring?

In reality, the hurting person may feel embarrassed or ashamed by an admitted "weakness." If she feels she's failed you (although untrue), she may gradually pull away from you, creating an awkward distance. Often in our ministry and love for someone, we may be called to let go, to allow her to grow, to develop, and to reach beyond our own limiting vision. Keep your vulnerability in check as you seek to minister.

Feed yourself emotionally and spiritually so you can continue to care for and nurture others.

132

How to Refer a Person for Help

Learn about the agencies and resources available in your community. Seek professionals and community volunteers who can help you in your ministry. Identify the services they offer and their limitations. Contact extension offices, social services, mental health services, community action groups, and support groups. Be alert for services you can recommend for legal advice, financial advice, or personal counseling.

The following is a suggested format for linking the woman with appropriate resources.

a. Call the agency; ask to speak with the intake worker (if one).

b. Identify your relationship with the person needing help.

c. Describe what you perceive the woman's needs to be;

d. Ask the agency what follow-up action they would recommend and what (if anything) you can do.

Discuss the referral with the person or family involved. You might say, "How do you feel about seeking help from this agency?" If the person or family feels comfortable making the contact, encourage them to do so. If the woman is unwilling and is in some danger if action is not taken, take the initiative yourself.

As we minister to one another, let us reach out in love and comfort the hurting as God has comforted us.

---

[1] Elizabeth Kubler-Ross, *Death and Dying* (New York: MacMillan, 1969).

For Smaller Churches
by Martha Lawley

A good suggestion from this chapter for smaller churches is creating a list of professionals for referrals. Take time to carefully compile this list and keep it up-to-date.

Good news for smaller churches: comforting hurting women with the comfort God has given us does not require financial resources or a large church staff! God supplies this free gift! If you desire further training in lay counseling skills, check with your association or state convention office or with other neighboring churches for training ideas and trainers.

LifeWay Press has a number of resources that can provide insight and practical help in the areas of depression and discouragement, divorce, issues from the past, grief, addictive behaviors, and sexual abuse. These low-cost materials can be used with groups or in individual study. To order, see page 221.

Ministering to Special Needs
Women in the Workplace

by Linda Lesniewski

Excellent resources for Bible study and discipleship are now available to support ongoing training and equipping opportunities for women. However, churches have observed that the number of women available for these opportunities during the day has declined. Where are the women? They're in the workplace!

George Barna predicted that by the year 2000 more than 60 percent of all working-aged females would be employed.[1] If that information accurately reflects our culture, and if our culture is reflected in the church community, then we must ask how it affects our current women's ministry programming. Many churches are discovering that the majority of the budget and programming is designed to minister to and equip women available during the weekday.

> Women's ministries leaders must develop strategies for reaching out to their Christian sisters in the marketplace.

Women's ministries leaders must develop strategies for reaching out to their Christian sisters in the marketplace. As they do, several areas must be examined.

Bridge the Gap

We must first take steps to bridge the emotional gap between the stay-at-home mom and the career mom—the homemaker and the professional woman. Underlying questions, misunderstandings, envy, and guilt between these groups of women detract from developing an atmosphere of support, encouragement, and cooperation. Honest dialogue that examines individual choices and lifestyles must occur before the polarized worlds can join hands with one heart to better equip the body of Christ.

In this task of equipping, the debate of lifestyle choices is best left to the Holy Spirit as He guides each woman to make the best choices for herself and her family. From this neutral position, a structure designed to express God's unconditional love, joy, and peace can begin to take shape.

Identify Needs

Next, we must identify the needs of the woman in the workplace. Her first need is to know the Lord as her personal Savior. So evangelism is our first priority. But what about the working woman in your church who knows the Lord? What are some of the situations and emotions she faces on a day-to-day basis? The list includes all of the issues women outside of the workplace experience plus many more—coworker relationship conflicts, temptations, guilt, unrealistic expectations, discrimination, limitations for advancement, and deadlines, to name a few.

But the number one issue that affects women's ministry planning is time constraints. Like the homemaker, the woman in the marketplace experiences pressing time demands from the moment her alarm clock sounds to the time she resets it at night. The difference is that for a certain number of hours each day, the woman in the marketplace is simply not available for women's ministry events. No matter how she might try to reshuffle her day, she simply cannot attend. How can women's ministry reach out to her without becoming one more demand on her time?

Formulate a Mission Statement

As our own women's ministry prayed and struggled with these issues, we realized that our Christian women were placed strategically throughout the community as God's salt and light. In a very real sense, they were our women's ministry's "missionaries"! What if we could help them see themselves as "leaving for the mission field" each morning instead of just "going to work!" Instead of seeing themselves as estranged from the weekday opportunities in women's ministry, they would be integral parts—strategic partners in fulfilling our Lord's Commission.

One way to touch the lives of women in the marketplace is to design a mission statement for a workplace ministry that renews her spirit where she is every day—at work! A possible mission statement reflecting these goals might be: *Our purpose is to equip and encourage the career Christian woman to be a light of God's grace and mercy in the workplace around her.* Opportunities and strategies previously overlooked will soon materialize as the result of a clearly stated mission statement.

Scriptural Admonitions

The writer of Hebrews admonished us to consider one another "in order to stir up love and good works" (Heb. 10:24, NKJV). Being a witness on the job is a tough responsibility. Often ears and hearts are cold to even the most effective witness. Without a doubt, Christian women in the workplace benefit from spiritual support and encouragement.

Mike and Debi Rogers, authors of *The Kingdom Agenda: Experiencing God in Your Workplace,* believe God desires to mobilize a powerful missionary force in a vast mission field—the workplace. In the Introduction of the study, they say: "God wants to change the way we think about work! Jesus said, 'If anyone wishes to come after me, he must deny himself, take up his cross daily, and follow me!'" (Luke 9:23). God's agenda calls us to:

- abandon a self-focused life and become God-focused;
- accept the sovereignty of God in our work;
- allow God to mold our character into the likeness of Christ;
- abandon human principles, priorities, and practices in conflict with God's will;
- accept and depend on God's provision for us;
- build redemptive relationships through which God shines light into the darkness; and
- trust that following God's agenda will bring God's blessing on our workplaces.

"As He is glorified, He will draw people to Himself. God is offering each one of us an opportunity to join Him as He actively carries out His agenda to redeem a lost and dying world."[2]

Getting Started

Develop a network of Christian women with careers.

Developing a network of Christian women with careers can provide a starting place. Some women in the marketplace often overlook opportunities promoted through women's ministry because of a mind-set that says, "That's not for me—I don't have time—I'm not a 'member' of women's ministry." They admit to seldom reading the women's events promotions. In response, our women's ministry developed a separate career Christian women heading in our weekly church bulletin that lists information specifically designed for them. We also planned and developed specific events and studies tailored to their schedules.

Evaluate Resources

Evaluate how the current women's ministry structure can act as a resource for the career Christian. How can it serve and support them in their daily mission of being salt and light?

Many successful ideas are already in place. For instance, First Baptist Church in downtown Dallas, Texas, realized they had tremendous ministry potential within the surrounding business complexes. They currently host a Business Women's Bible Study each Thursday noon that averages over 300 in attendance. They also repeat some of their special weekday morning events in the evening under the title "Prime Time Dinner."

One church discovered that offering Saturday morning Bible studies provided a creative alternative. A long-time participant said: "My body clock wakes me up at the same time on Saturdays as week days. I find I can attend the study and be back home before the kids are even up—and still have the whole day ahead of me!"

Many churches offer weekend retreats, conferences, and evening seminars that serve as excellent enrichment opportunities for working women. Experienced speakers/teachers often have topics to suggest.

Survey the Women

The best way to discover people's needs is to ask them! Listen for their hurts, interests, and fears. A survey is one method for gathering this data. Morrison Heights Baptist Church in Clinton, Mississippi, enlisted several women to personally administer 10 surveys in a one-on-one fashion. Another option is to distribute surveys at a high-traffic location. You might even offer chocolate kisses or some other inexpensive incentive to encourage participation.

Women Reaching Women includes sample copies of surveys (see pages 46 and 89). Or, you can design your own. Be sure to include questions that target the working audience. For example, questions might include:

- Are you employed outside the home? Part-time or full time?
- Do you currently participate in women's ministry? In what areas?
- Would you be interested in having a six-week noontime Bible study taught in your workplace? If so, is your office available for the study?
- Would you be interested in receiving a monthly newsletter designed for working women? Would you be interested in assisting with its publication?
- Would you be interested in attending a weeknight or weekend Bible study?

Think Creatively

Since this is a time of great societal change in women's lives, we must be willing to try new approaches and experiment with innovative strategies.

- Pair home-front prayer warriors with marketplace "missionaries."
- Designate a special library section that addresses career issues.
- Offer *Journey* magazines for coffee-break rooms (see page 221).
- Plan luncheons to discuss pertinent topics.
- Establish a daily email "Verse of the Day" for encouragement.

Try new approaches and experiment with innovative strategies.

- Utilize Secretary's Day as a special time to acknowledge your support of secretaries and other working women.
- Schedule quarterly breakfasts.

Challenge the wives of professionals to view their husband's office staff as "ready-made ministry opportunities." Nancy Paul, the wife of a family practitioner, Dr. Alan Paul, regularly leads the office staff in studies during its lunch hour. She also makes women's conference or banquet tickets available to the office staff as gifts. She considers the office as a well-defined opportunity to spread God's grace.

Experiment with an electronic Bible study.

Deb Douglas has enjoyed experimenting with an electronic Bible study. She says: "In the past two years, several of our original group moved to various locations around the country. We emailed frequently to sustain our friendship, but something was missing: the bond we had developed through studying God's Word together. We chose *Whispers of Hope* by Beth Moore for our experimental study (see page 221). We completed four devotionals a week. After each one, we emailed everyone in the group with our thoughts, ideas, and questions. In our group we email separately for personal matters. This practice keeps us focused and does not 'water down' the study.

"The response has been tremendous! Each of us has experienced growth. And prayer lives are increasing and growing. It's not just the accountability that is very important, it is the spiritual honesty that is easily revealed when we write rather than speak. It's almost like journaling with accountability!"

The noon group for career Christian women that meets on Thursdays at my church will break during the summer months. One member wants to offer this type of email "keeping-in-touch-accountability" as a summer option. She's willing to try something new and different to provide support and spiritual accountability for her Christian sisters in the workplace.

Pray for Leadership

As you clarify objectives and purpose, a natural prayer concern will be for the Lord to raise up godly leadership. In our ministry, Donna Shay, a gifted Christian woman who deals daily with the competitive pressures of real estate sales, stepped forward with a personal burden. She cared about other Christian women facing the same work-related stressors. Together we prayed and discussed ways she could fit "ministry" into her own demanding schedule. Donna concluded: "I enjoy teaching the Bible and felt called to return to that love. Assuming leadership for the women's noon Bible study was a logical place to plug in my gift of teaching."

The study Donna presently leads is scheduled from 12:15–12:45 p.m. A light low-cost lunch is available or ladies can "brown-bag." The women eat while Donna teaches. As a "career peer," she conscientiously respects their time constraints and eliminates outside homework. She's discovered that the time and materials must be simple and user-friendly.

During this past year, Donna has observed this core group support one another through prayer and God's Word. Donna says, "I see women lighting other women's torches as we carry the light of God's love and salvation to the desks, cubicles, break rooms, and board rooms around us!"

Identify Leaders

This same core group also has seen the birthing of a monthly newsletter featuring inspiring real-life examples of how various women see God using them to communicate God's love within their workplace. I've selected several excerpts from these newsletters as examples of the influence a spirit-filled Christian woman can have in the lives around her.

"I'm a Patient Representative for a local hospital. Twenty years ago, my only child died at 21 months. Because of what happened to my little angel, Jonathan, who is now in heaven, I approach my work with joy and determination. I will be with him again someday, but until then I will touch as many lives as I possibly can with God's message of hope."–Sheryl Coffey

"In public accounting I had many opportunities to visit with clients. The subject matter could be taxes, death of a spouse, divorce, loss of business, or other difficult matters. The Bible tells us that our paths will be directed. I love the way God directs others into our paths. I refer to it as the mild collision. He brings people into our lives for a purpose. It could be so that we can help them or that they can help us. Either way, it is not by chance!"–Nanci Pritchard

"As a chaplain with Marketplace Ministries, I've seen God's grace at work in some tragic situations. In one incident a client had his leg severed on the job. On my way to the hospital I was suddenly overwhelmed. 'God, I can't do this. I'm not prepared for this!' Quietly, the Holy Spirit assured me that He would give me the words ... I was amazed at how God faithfully provided words of comfort, support, and understanding."–Carye Gillen

"As owner of The Frame-Up Gallery, I know without a doubt God was responsible for my purchasing this business. Sometimes I just listen as a lonely widow talks. At times I must pray for patience and choose to be cheerful when dealing with a difficult customer or employee. Experience has taught me that if I will commit each day to Him, He will never let me down."
—Martha Harvey

These women are keenly aware of ways God can use them in their daily sphere of influence. They provide excellent examples of leadership available to connect, nurture, and empower workplace ministries.

Encourage Work-based Cell Groups

Another way leaders can impact their workplace is by establishing a work-based cell group. Christian coworkers gather during lunch, breaks, and before or after work. They pray for God to reveal His strategy for their workplace. They share insights and observations of ways God is working or discuss the application of Scripture to work practices. They also pray for one another and for specific individuals who need to know Christ.

Specific help on beginning work-based cell groups is contained in *The Kingdom Agenda: Experiencing God in Your Workplace* (see page 221).

Expect the Unexpected—Even Disappointment

Prepare to experience lots of trial and error—just like the early days of establishing your current women's ministry! One church planned an evening of "Coffee & Creme." Women brewed and served cappuccinos between selections of individual topics like managing money, decision-making skills, and facing challenges of the workplace. They prepared for 200 participants and 50 attended. Surprised? Yes. Disappointed? No! Those 50 ladies left with renewed spirits and enriched relationships.

Be Flexible

Be accommodating to a wide variety of time restraints. Some shun night activities, feeling weary from having been gone all day! Others prefer evening events as an outlet after the hectic day. Even Saturdays are considered part of the work week for those involved in professions such as nursing, real estate, restaurant management, and retail sales.

Be Open to Feedback

Consistently provide opportunities for feedback. Distribute evaluation

forms at all activities and events. Create an atmosphere of openness that stimulates dialogue and input. Talk openly about failures as being essential to development. Seeking honest information about the effectiveness and relevancy of the women's ministry enrichment programming will accelerate the process of fine-tuning the programming.

Combine prayers for guidance, servants' hearts, and creativity–then leave the results in God's capable hands. What delight He must experience as a result of those yielded believers who work daily in the middle of His harvest fields.

[1] George Barna, *The Frog in the Kettle* (Ventura, California: Regal Books, 1990), 102.
[2] Mike and Debi Rogers, *The Kingdom Agenda, Experiencing God in Your Workplace* (Nashville: LifeWay Press, 1997), 4.

For Smaller Churches
by Martha Lawley

In smaller churches, where separate programs for women in the workplace may not be possible, look for ways to cooperate with neighboring churches to provide opportunities for involvement. For example, consider organizing a weekly noontime Bible study or a monthly breakfast meeting for women who work outside the home.

Look for opportunities to build relationships and understanding between women who work outside the home and those who do not. Women have many needs in common regardless of their workplaces. You may find that women who do not work outside the home would be happy to adjust their schedules to meet the needs of those who can only attend at noon or in the evening. Evening Bible studies give both women who work outside the home and those who do not a chance to study and fellowship together.

One way to find strength in the diversity of the women in your church and community is to look for ways the different groups can help one another. For example, women who do not work outside the home may be able to provide emergency "sick care" for the young children of moms with outside jobs. Providing an opportunity for the care of a sick child on a day when the mom just cannot miss work is a wonderful way for women who do not work outside the home to minister to those who do.

Conversely, women in the workplace often come across resources they can share with moms at home, such as interesting and informative books, magazines, and newsletters; training opportunities; and leadership tips.

God himself is right alongside to keep you steady and on track until things are all wrapped up by Jesus. God, who got you started in this spiritual adventure, shares with us the life of his Son and our Master Jesus. He will never give up on you.
Never forget that.
–1 Corinthians 1:8-9,
THE MESSAGE

Ministering to Special Needs
Moms of Young Children

by Elisa Morgan and Carol Kuykendall, MOPS International

When a child is born, a mother is born as well—and her heart is changed forever. She is tenderized as she experiences not only a passionate and protective maternal love, but also struggles with a fresh awareness of her own neediness—and fears that she will not know enough or be enough to love and care for her child the way she should. For the first time in her life, she may be keenly aware of a need for help and hope from something or someone outside of herself.

Those who care about young mothers recognize this season as a unique opportunity for sharing God's truth and love because mothers of young children experience a heightened need for God. Identifying and understanding who they are and what they need is the first step to reaching the mothers of young children.

Mothers of young children experience a heightened need for God.

Who Is This "Mother"?

Because the choices for women are greater today than ever before, mothers of young children represent great diversity. They are single; they are married. They are teenagers; they are in their 40s. They work outside the home; they work at home. They live in the inner city; they live in a rural community; they live in the suburbs. They have their GEDs; they have their PhDs. They are spiritually mature Christians; they have never attended church and may even resent organized religion.

In spite of these differences, mothers of young children share some universally common characteristics. In general, they feel greatly depleted—of energy, time, and financial resources. They may also feel neglected and confused. These are supposed to be the best years of their lives, and in many ways, they are wonderful. But there are moments when they feel totally surprised by what motherhood has revealed about themselves.

Surprised by Motherhood

First, there's the never-ending-ness of mothering. Suddenly a woman finds herself responsible for a totally dependent being and is surprised by her responses. As one mother stated: "I learned I couldn't punch out at

5 p.m. or 2 a.m. The responsibility never ends."

She also feels a lack of control over her once-organized life. "How can a seven-pound infant keep me from taking a shower until two in the afternoon?" wondered one mother.

Obviously, she is fatigued. "No one ever told me that I wouldn't get a full night's sleep for months or what sleep deprivation would do to me." She is often discouraged that her clothes don't fit because her body has not snapped back into her pre-pregnancy shape; her moods are affected by all the invisible but powerful hormonal changes taking place inside her; and she's confused by the relentless choices which surface. *"Do I go back to work? How will we make ends meet if I don't? Do I let my baby cry ... or pick him up? Why don't babies come with an instruction manual? How will I ever know how to take care of this child? How will I know the right answers?"*

Consider the following analogy: a mother feels like a cardboard-juice box and everyone around her sticks their straws into her and keeps sucking and sucking until she feels totally sucked-dry. The truth is—a mom is a need-meeter and often she's left running on empty.

Surprised by Needs

Moms haven't outgrown their need for individual nurturing. This is one of motherhood's greatest surprises. Helping moms understand this important concept helps them begin to recognize their need for God.

Moms of young children need to know:

- Needs are normal. Psychologists, social scientists, and religious experts agree that all normal people have needs.
- Needs don't like to be ignored. If needs don't receive attention in a healthy manner, they're apt to rear their heads in undesirable behavior. On the other hand, recognizing needs leads to positive development through this stage of life.
- Needs must be met. When a mom recognizes and meets her needs, she is better able to meet the needs of her family.

A Mother's Nine Needs

In the workbook, *What Every Mom Needs: Balancing Your Life,* (see page 221) we describe nine needs unique to this stage of life. The compilation of these needs is a result of MOPS International's 20-plus years of research, interviews, and experience in working with mothers of preschoolers. Each of the nine needs is met—ultimately—through faith in Christ—and as moms are helped to recognize these needs, they begin to recognize their spiritual needs.

What surprised you about becoming a mother?
My temper and impatience.
How much I love my child.
That while I love my children, some days I don't like them.
That a baby can take up my whole day.
How being a mom brings out the best and worst in me.
That a two-year-old can bring an adult to her knees in prayer.
How wonderful it is to be called "Mommy."[1]

As moms are helped to recognize these needs, they begin to recognize their spiritual needs.

1. *Significance: Sometimes I wonder if mothering matters.* Moms need to know that they matter as mothers and that their role as mother has value and makes a difference in the lives of their children. Moms need to know that their "doing" has value. Ultimately, they need to realize that all the "doing" will never be enough to earn the consistent significance for which they long. God alone provides ultimate meaning for their lives.

2. *Identity: Sometimes I'm not sure who I am.* Mothers sometimes lose sight of the belief that they are individuals of value. Their attention is focused primarily on their children, leaving them feeling they've lost touch with who they are. When they see themselves as God sees them, they can drop the burden of feeling they aren't good enough and focus on being all God created them to be.

3. *Growth: Sometimes I long to develop who I am.* Mothers often convince themselves that now is the time for them to nurture their children and they must put their own lives on hold. But they are better moms when they find time and energy to keep themselves as well as their kids growing. Change and growth are life-giving to mothers and their families as they allow God to shape them.

4. *Intimacy: Sometimes I long to be understood.* Intimacy in relationships cannot be put on hold while kids grow, even though relationships must adapt. Moms need to pursue intimacy in their marriages, friendships and with God.

5. *Instruction: Sometimes I don't know what to do.* Mothers are not born knowing everything about mothering. They need information and practical wisdom regarding parenting, relationships, financial matters, and personal development. They need help in learning to make appropriate choices, and they need trustworthy folks to provide this help. But ultimately, they need to recognize that the Bible provides the truth and guidance they need.

6. *Help: Sometimes I need to share the load.* Moms believe they should do it all, do it all right, and do it all right now. But they can't and shouldn't try to accomplish everything alone. They must identify sources of help and learn to ask for help. God provides help no one else can by walking alongside and controlling the uncontrollable parts of their lives.

7. *Recreation: Sometimes I need a break.* Kids aren't the only ones who need to play and have fun. Moms need fun, too, and they need to lay aside their responsibilities for time to be refreshed through humor, exercise, and play. Recreation actually means re-creation. God created us with the need to rest, and when mothers rest, they are refreshed and better moms. As they seek God, He renews and re-creates them.

8. *Perspective: Sometimes I lose my focus.* Moms need to be reminded of that which is eternally important and that which matters over the course of a lifetime. They need balance between control and flexibility. They need an eternal, God-view of life.

9. *Hope: Sometimes I wonder if there's more to life.* Moms get discouraged or depressed and experience hopelessness—as if a dark moment in which they are living will last forever. They need to know there is something beyond this moment and something beyond themselves. They need to know Jesus, the only source of lasting hope.

Ministering to Young Moms: Program Principles

Several program principles distinguish a ministry to the mothers of young children and make outreach more effective. Keep in mind who this woman is, as detailed in the sections above. She is the mother of young children and doesn't have much time, energy, or money. She may be skeptical of church-organized activities. But she has a great need for nurturing. Several principles will help a ministry meet her needs.

Moms have a great need for nurturing.

Lifestyle Evangelism

Lifestyle evangelism involves walking alongside another and sharing our faith through our actions. It leads us to meet felt needs and build relationships before sharing the doctrine and details of faith. It means modeling a lifestyle that reflects the love of God and love for others. Lifestyle evangelism meets physical or emotional needs as a means to touching spiritual needs. Such an approach is captured in the old saying, "People don't care how much you know until they know how much you care."

Lifestyle evangelism is need based. The greatest need for one mother of young children might be physical. She might need someone to keep her children for a morning when she has the flu. Another mom might need someone to listen to her fears or honest ambivalence about being a mother. She might need encouragement or advice about parenting.

Lifestyle evangelism is lived out on common ground. Because mothers of young children share similar needs, it is easy to establish common ground through a ministry that provides a structure or gathering place for these women. This common ground becomes the setting that supports a relationship and allows it to grow. Later it becomes the natural place to open the conversation and receptivity to spiritual matters.

Lifestyle evangelism is guided by spiritual principles. When it comes to the spiritual aspect of lifestyle evangelism, consider the following:

• Recognize the barriers that may prevent many mothers of young children from hearing the gospel. They may have misperceptions of Christianity that grew out of childhood experiences regarding church or God. Their misperceptions might grow out of poor examples or bad teaching. They might experience intellectual barriers that require patient responses. Some struggle with moral barriers, based on fears about being forced to abandon some area of life if one becomes a Christian. In all these situations, women need models of authentic Christianity. They need patient people to answer questions and accept their concerns.

- Avoid Christian-ese. Many of these women don't relate to our lingo, or if they do, they are turned off by it. So interpret terms like *saved, born again, submission,* or *spiritual warfare.* Make God real in their language.

Help mothers of young children on a journey toward Jesus.

- Be patient. Lifestyle evangelism is a process, not an event. We help the mothers of young children on a journey toward Jesus that is lived out over time.

- God is responsible for the results. He merely asks us to be available to be used.

One mother in a MOPS program identified the MOPS tone of lifestyle evangelism in this way: "During the first couple of years in MOPS, I experienced a very gentle evangelism that gradually wore away at some of my barriers. To be honest, anything more aggressive would have sent me scurrying in the opposite direction! I am grateful to the women who introduced me to this ministry."

For more information, see the chapter on evangelism, pages 105-113.

Mentoring

Mothers of young children hunger to learn ways to tackle the challenges they face in parenting, in relationships, in their personal development, and in choosing priorities. They seek out role models who have weathered the same struggles they face. They long for mentoring. An effective ministry to mothers of young children should include some mentoring from older, more mature mothers. This model is biblical, based on Titus 2:4: "they (older women) can train the younger women to love their husbands and children, to be self-controlled and pure, to be busy at home, to be kind, and to be subject to their husbands, so that no one will malign the word of God."

The mentor acts as teacher, role model, counselor, friend, and advisor to the ministry. She may form one-on-one relationships or assume a teaching role before the whole group. A ministry to young mothers may have a team of mentors or a single mentor-advisor. Mentors are a:

- Teacher—When teaching a group of moms, demonstrate warmth and acceptance of each mom. Describe God's truth as it has been worked out in your own life and apply that truth with relevance to a mother's life today. Be humble and vulnerable, speaking as a "fellow learner" who is still learning from God.
- Role Model—A mentor teaches far more through actions, manner, and example than through words. The degree to which you are able to exemplify a godly woman depends on having your own priorities in order. When a young mother watches what God does through you, she'll be encouraged at what God can do in and through her.
- Friend—Strive for a balance between being a teacher, a role model, and a friend—one who listens to how she feels but doesn't advise or tell her how she should feel—or is available merely to give a hug rather than words. As women are drawn to that kind of love, they will be drawn closer to God, and He will be glorified in the relationship.
- Counselor—Sometimes you may have to refer a young mother to a professional. Become familiar with the issues mothers of young children face and with the available resources in your community. When you recognize that help is needed beyond your ability, recommend someone or a specific group or program.

For more information on mentoring, see pages 95-104 or "Ministry One-on-One" in *Women Reaching Women,* pages 71-81. Refer to pages 130-133 for referral guidelines when women need professional help.

Peer Relationships

Mothers of young children often feel isolated in a world that focuses on their children's needs. They feel most understood by other mothers in the same chapter of life. Provide time for the development of peer relationships through fellowship and sharing, such as in small discussion groups. Schedule these immediately following a presentation or teaching talk to discuss questions that grow out of the presentation.

In those discussions, encourage the idea that there are no right or wrong answers; encourage all moms to voice their opinions. Intimate relationships grow out of these small groups as women encourage and confide in one another and share prayer requests. A powerful mom-to-mom ministry may develop as moms come to one another's aid during times of need such as carpooling, child care, and sharing casseroles.

Mothers of young children often feel isolated in a world that focuses on their children's needs.

Skill Development

Intimate relationships grow out of these small groups as women encourage and confide in one another and share prayer requests.

Moms of young children are attracted to programs that offer skill development. They long to grow personally during the time when they are raising their families. Some suggested areas of skill development are:

- *Leadership Skills*—These include such topics as public speaking and communication skills, money management, vision and goal setting, conflict resolution, stress management, decision making, effective delegating, and listening skills. This structure also gives moms skills for future service in their churches or community.
- *Life Skills*—These topics are nearly endless, but include relational skills in friendships and in marriage, parenting, nutrition, self-discovery, critical thinking, dealing with anger, time management, budgeting, and interior decorating, to name a few.
- *Craft or Creative Activities*—A hands-on time of creative learning allows moms to work on a craft or project. Moms rarely get an opportunity to finish anything. Many of their "projects" are unending and most are focused on meeting the needs of others. Making a wreath or piece of jewelry, working on a scrapbook, or decorating a cake gives a sense of accomplishment and completion, while at the same providing a creative outlet.

Child Care

Moms need a break! Providing convenient, reliable child care provides that break. Moms relax when they know their children are safe and contented. Often the mothers of nursing infants want to keep their babies with them, but mothers of toddlers and older children should be encouraged to take advantage of child care, even if they feel reluctant at first. Help a mother to learn that she can leave her child for at least short periods of time and that such a break will benefit her.

Refreshments

Moms need to be nurtured—and food communicates nurturing. When a mom walks into a room and sees an attractive table set with tasty food, she feels valued. She knows someone has prepared for her coming. She also enjoys eating meals she doesn't have to share with a little person who has sticky fingers. Food helps build bridges between moms.

Window of Opportunity

Because of their great vulnerability during this stage of life, ministry to mothers of young children is a vital and exciting challenge. The principles shared in this chapter will launch any outreach to this target group toward success. The following hints for application are also helpful.

- *Keep on the cutting edge.* More than ever before in the history of humanity, women and mothers are educated, technologically savvy, and committed to making a difference in the lives of their children and their world. Invest in "trend training" so that leaders are up-to-date in the latest advancements.

- *Stay season-of-life specific.* Moms of young children experience such intense needs because they are seasonally specific. As their children mature and these moms gain their footing, they will move on to other spots of ministry and experience a variety of other developmental needs. Resist the urge to draw a wide target for your ministry to moms. Allow your moms to grow through and leave your ministry, moving on to other areas. View their maturation as a natural and necessary launching into the next stage of life.

- *Major on hope.* Today's world is extremely fragile in its offering of hope for this and future generations. Mothers are entrusted with the raising of future generations and need a source of hope to hold out to their children. More than any other ingredient, include the ingredient of hope to your ministry to moms of young children. (For more information on MOPS, International, Inc., see page 222.)

> Resist the urge to draw a wide target for your ministry to moms.

---

[1] Elisa Morgan & Carol Kuykendall, *What Every Mom Needs* (Grand Rapids, Mi.: Zondervan, 1995).

For Smaller Churches
by Martha Lawley

In smaller churches, one of the major obstacles to ministering to moms of young children is the ability to provide consistent, quality child care. For specific suggestions on creative child care, see the Appendix, p. 210.

A Mother's Day Out (MDO) program can provide much needed relief for mothers of young children. If your church does not have the resources for such a ministry, consider teaming with a neighboring church that has an effective MDO program to which you can refer young mothers. Also consider offering study opportunities for these mothers while their children attend MDO at another church. For example, offer Bible study classes, fellowship activities, exercise and health classes, crafts and other training opportunities. With the needs of the children being met through MDO, your church can focus its resources on the needs of the mom.

Assisting moms of young children in organizing small play groups is a way to meet women's needs for interaction with other women. These play groups are often mom-led, with each mom taking a turn hosting the group. Babysitting co-ops can also be organized so that moms have free time to shop, volunteer, study, or rest.

Consider organizing a network of people in your church who are willing to provide short notice or emergency child care. Select at least one person who is willing and able to administer this process. This responsibility would include keeping a current list of volunteers, receiving requests for assistance, contacting volunteers, and following up to insure that the need was met.

Utilize resources beyond your women's ministry organization to meet some of the needs of young moms. For example, a senior adult ministry may be interested in an "adopt a grandchild" program to nurture young children and encourage young parents. Men's ministry can provide programs to support and encourage young fathers, offer babysitting while their wives participate in women's ministry programs or projects, or staff a "young parents night out" child care program.

Although smaller churches may not be able to meet all the needs of mothers of young children, God provides the resources we need to do what He has called us to do.

Ministering to Special Needs

The New Member

by Penny Glaesman

In Acts 12:12-16, Mary, the mother of John Mark, gathered the believers into the big room. Prayer and hospitality in this house were common events. Even the Lord himself had visited this upper room.

Rhoda, the servant girl, found a small, inconspicuous spot for herself near the back of the room. The prayer meeting began. Pleading cries for their beloved Peter, who was in prison, permeated the room.

She barely heard it, but there was definitely someone knocking at the courtyard gate. Anxiously, Rhoda looked around. Everyone expected had already arrived. As this young servant cautiously approached the big court gate, she could hear the plea: "Please, let me in!" Rhoda could not believe her ears. It was Peter's voice!

"Peter knocked at the outer entrance, and a servant girl named Rhoda came to answer the door."

Acts 12:13

In her excitement, she ran across the courtyard, through the door, and burst into the prayer meeting, shouting, "He is here! Peter is here!" Suddenly Rhoda realized she had been so thrilled by his voice that she had left him outside! Fortunately no harm came to Peter as he waited for someone to let him in.

Poor Rhoda! Her heart was so right, so what went wrong? What hindered her from helping Peter reach the people he had come to see? What could she have done differently to minister to Peter's need to be inside with the family of believers?

Often, like Rhoda, our hearts are right, but situations, circumstances, or even emotions hinder us from the right course of action. We pray repeatedly for women and their families to join our churches. Yet, when they do join, like Rhoda, we leave them outside the fellowship of the church. Let's look at some issues that might hinder us from opening the door and allowing an outsider to come inside.

New Members' Needs

What are some needs of a new church member? These needs could include a place that is safe, friendly, exciting, growing, prayerful–and a place where she feels needed. The list could go on and on. What would you look for if you were seeking a new church home? Chances are, she is looking for many of the same characteristics. A basic need which must be met by you and the church family is to be allowed "in." You might respond: "Of course she's allowed in. She's a member, isn't she?" But women want to be more than merely members; they need to feel a part.

When a woman joins your church, she is much like Peter standing outside of the gate knocking, desperately wanting to come in. Why did Peter go to that house? He was looking for security, acceptance, fellowship, spiritual strength, understanding, social essentials, and prayer. How could Rhoda's story have been different if she had been prepared to welcome Peter? What can we learn from Rhoda's innocent yet potentially devastating mistake?

We must take the initiative to help the new member feel included. We must open the gate and escort her through the security of the courtyard, to the door of belonging, and into the house of Christian growth and fellowship.

What problems do we face?

> When a woman joins your church, she is much like Peter standing outside of the gate knocking, desperately wanting to come in.

Problems

Not Expectant of Her Arrival
We may not have a plan in place or an atmosphere established that makes an easy transition possible for new members. In our unpreparedness we may inadequately follow-up to meet new members' needs.

Overzealous
We may be over-anxious and overpower the new member with ideas for how she can meet the needs of the church rather than first seeking to meet her needs.

Feeling Inadequate
You may feel inadequate to welcome a new member. There will always be women who have attended your church longer than you, who have been more active than you, or who may even know more people than you. Yet, anyone who has a heart for another and desires a close fellowship with her new sister is more than qualified.

Lacking a Sense of Personal Responsibility
Assimilating new members is not a task assigned just to preachers, teachers, or women's ministry leaders—we are all called to be servants of Christ. Psalms 100:2 encourages us to "serve the Lord with gladness" (KJV).

Inability to Become Vulnerable

Another problem we face is in the area of vulnerability, a willingness to open our lives with a servant's heart. In Richard Foster's book *Celebration of Discipline,* he puts it so well:

"Right here we must see the difference between choosing to serve and choosing to be a servant. When we choose to serve, we are still in charge. We decide whom we will serve and when we will serve. And if we are in charge, we will worry a great deal about anyone stepping on us, that is, taking charge over us.

"But when we choose to be a servant, we give up the right to be in charge. There is a great freedom in this. If we voluntarily choose to be taken advantage of, then we cannot be manipulated. When we choose to be a servant, we surrender the right to decide who and when we will serve. We become available and vulnerable."[1]

It is difficult to open yourself up to someone you do not know well. But as Christians we give up the right to choose whom we will love.

Procrastination

We must be sensitive to new members' immediate and perceived needs. We must open our eyes and see the person, the real person, as a vital part of the family of Christ and respond to her as soon as possible. If no one helps her feel included, she may decide there's no one home or no one who cared enough to open the gate. Either way, she may leave.

> If no one helps her feel included, she may decide there's no one home or no one who cared enough to open the gate. Either way, she may leave.

Potential

Mary, the mother of John Mark, lived in a large house where people gathered to worship and pray on a regular basis. During that time a large home was built around an open courtyard. If you were to visit Mary's home, you would first approach the gated area. It was usually locked and a porter remained there to safely escort you through the court, up a small flight of stairs, and to the front door of the house. It was several steps from the gate to the door.

Churches are structured in much the same way—not necessarily in architectural form but in organizational structure. A new member must take several steps before coming into the house—into the organization of the body. The more steps taken inside toward the center of the body, the more steps required to back out.

In helping the new woman member of your church to assimilate, take the following steps:

The Gate: Where she is knocking to be let in;

The Courtyard: Where she is seeking security—familiarity and friendship (relationships, not just membership);

The Door: Where she is searching for a sense of belonging—of being needed—useful;

The House: Where she is active and challenged in her growth in Christ.

At the Gate

Anticipate her arrival by implementing plans and programs to assist her in assimilating into her new church family.

- *Prepare for her arrival.* Anticipate her arrival by implementing plans and programs to assist her in assimilating into her new church family.

- *Greet her at the door.* Hostesses and greeters play a very important role in creating an atmosphere of comfort and welcome to new members. Instruct greeters to learn, if at all possible, the name of every new member. If you really want to make her feel special, learn the names of her husband and children. If this is an especially challenging area for you, list their names in a notebook to review. Train your welcoming team to offer appropriate greetings. Statements such as "I haven't seen you in a while" or "I hope the church doesn't fall in" are not appreciated. Warm, welcoming words will eliminate countless roadblocks.

- *Consider using "silent greeters."* Choose and train these greeters in advance to mingle within regular meeting groups. Choose women who enjoy visiting and demonstrate a positive attitude. Silent greeters work especially well in a Bible study or discipleship group. A silent greeter chooses a seat or position in the center of the meeting room or area, leaving an empty chair beside her. When a new member arrives she can greet her, introduce herself, and offer the chair next to her. She then uses this opportunity to become acquainted on a more personal level. After the meeting, the greeter can walk her to meet her children or to the sanctuary. She then can invite the new member to sit with her during the service or introduce her to another silent greeter. Silent greeters are a wonderful way to eliminate apprehensions for new members.

- *Leave space for her to sit.* Even if you do not utilize silent greeters, provide easy, accessible seating. Evaluate the room set-up; locate seats that are easy to reach, yet not at the front or back of the meeting room. Consider designating guest seating; however, if a

154

new member knows someone in the group, be certain she sits near her friend. New members need to feel secure and welcome as they merge into a circle of new friends.

- *Utilize seven touches.* It takes more than one person to draw a woman into the fellowship. It also takes more than one way of touching her life. Form a team of volunteer women to exercise seven touches to new members. Here are a few suggestions from Chris Adams:

    1. Extend a handshake, smile, and hello to greet a new member when she is presented for church membership.
    2. Call her and schedule a convenient time to meet with her.
    3. Visit her in her home and share information about the church and women's ministry. Be sure she knows where her and her family's Sunday School classes meet. Share details concerning additional children's and family activities. Explain your intercessory prayer ministry and inquire as to how you and others can pray specifically for her and her family. Encourage her to ask questions about your church or community.
    4. Follow up at least four or more times:
        a. Send a handwritten note welcoming her to your church.
        b. Invite her to the next luncheon, dinner, or other activity with a complimentary ticket (even offer to pick her up).
        c. Invite her to your house or to meet you for coffee.
        d. Invite her to Wednesday night supper and Bible study.
        e. Bring her to your weekly women's group and introduce her to others.
        f. Introduce her to other new members.
        g. Seek her out at church and invite her to sit with you, especially if she is alone.
        h. Take her homemade cookies or bread, or flowers from your yard.
        i. Send a "Thinking of You" card to let her know you are remembering her.

These are only a few suggestions; be creative with the above suggestions and include several women in this "seven touch" ministry. A personal touch that has been successful for several churches is the "Women's Ministry Welcome Bag." Be resourceful and place a variety of articles in the bag. Some suggestions are an emery board, a bookmark, a church ink pen, and a

It takes more than one person to draw a woman into the fellowship. It also takes more than one way of touching her life.

package of tea bags. Also include information and brochures on women's ministries schedules, important phone numbers, schedule of office hours, and perhaps even a city map. Continue to minister to her until she finds her "niche" and is ready to reach out to another woman new to the church!

Into the Courtyard

- *Training for hospitality.* I love the passage 1 Peter 4:9: "Offer hospitality to one another without grumbling." This verse states two specific instructions:

    1) Be hospitable.

    2) Do it without grumbling.

These verses are not suggestions—they are detailed instructions on how to meet the needs of others, to reach the next level, to take an extra step that lets them know how important they are. Hospitality is not how elaborate you set a table or how smoothly you coordinate a specific event at your home or church. Hospitality is much more than that—it's a way of opening your home or church along with your heart—a way of welcoming others to assume an important place in your life. As Christians, it is no longer our choice whom we will welcome or whom we will serve. It is our responsibility to love others as Christ loves us.

Being hospitable is the least difficult assignment in the Scripture; it is accomplishing the task "without grumbling" that often presents the problem. A task is much more enjoyable when we approach it with a proper "heart-itude."Colossians 3:23 says, "Whatever you do, work at it with all your heart, as working for the Lord, not for men." You will experience such wonderful rewards when you give sacrificially of your time and self for the needs of others.

Since these assignments are presented as instructions and not suggestions, it is important that you prepare to offer hospitality to the new woman in your church. Hospitality requires planning for the expected and the unexpected in order to minister "without grumbling." Preparation eliminates pressure and allows your heart the freedom to touch her heart.

- *Opened eyes and opened hearts.* Sometimes we forget that a new member is not just like us; we are all different, unique, and special. We each have our individual backgrounds, histories, experiences, strengths, and weaknesses. Be sensitive to the fact that

Hospitality is a way of opening your home or church along with your heart—a way of welcoming others to assume an important place in your life.

new members may have different backgrounds and may not fully understand the "church scene." Church language is often confusing to those who may not have attended church all their lives. Be as clear as possible when explaining that God is there for them, helps them, forgives them, and loves them.

Some women will come into your church who have troubled pasts, perhaps having suffered rejection, abuse, divorce, handicaps, addictions, and past failures. Like the woman who washed Jesus' feet with her tears and wiped them with her hair, she may be among us. Yet, like Simon when Jesus asked him, "Simon, do you see this woman?" (Luke 7:44), we do not really see her. Jesus had to get Simon's attention to truly "see the woman." Open your eyes and help her to locate a class or Bible study that might meet her specific needs. Open your heart to being her confidant and friend.

Mentoring programs prove to be a great asset in helping to assimilate women into the heart and ministry of your church. Mentors assure women they have someone to pray with and talk to—someone to help them grow. If you are not already enjoying the benefits of mentoring in your church, refer to the chapter on mentoring for information on establishing such a ministry (see pages 95-104).

A new member may not be ready for mentoring but may be open to prayer partners. Introduce her to someone with whom she can easily relate, has similar interests, and is willing to be her partner in prayer. Be careful to pair her with a mature Christian woman, one who can be trusted to keep prayer confidences.

• *Small Groups.* To assimilate a new member into your church, accompany her though the various levels of Bible studies—from new member classes to in-depth studies. Help her take one step at a time over a period of time.

If your church offers a new members class, encourage her to participate. Explain its purpose as a means to help her understand her new church and its beliefs. It is also a place where questions can be answered. Inform the leader of the new member's interest. As a way of encouraging a new member, offer to meet her ahead of time and walk with her into the first meeting, introducing her to the group.

A women's Bible study or discipleship group is a wonderful way to introduce new members to other women. The class is a small group easily organized for implementing welcoming procedures, greeters, and silent greeters and offers closeness and care. This is expressed in ways as simple as arranging chairs in a circle or around tables, or providing informal snacks. In this setting she will have the opportunity to meet other women, become more intimate, and feel comfortable sharing about herself. Teachers of small-group classes should be sensitive to comfort levels and refrain from asking new members to pray or read aloud until they know women are willing to do so.

Perhaps your church offers support groups for singles, widows, mothers of preschoolers, or others special needs groups. The small group offers opportunities to bond and provides new friends and a feeling of belonging. The chapter "Small-Group Leadership Skills" will further assist you in the area of developing and utilizing small groups effectively (see pages 50-58).

At the Door

Now that you and others have walked with the new member through the gate and across the long courtyard, it's time to walk her through the door of fellowship, drawing her closer and closer to the heart of the ministry.

- *Spiritual Gifts.* By this time she is likely more willing to become involved in the variety of available church activities. To help her better serve in areas of personal interest, assist her in identifying her gifts and talents. A woman with a creative spirit might prefer serving on the decorating team rather than the budgeting team. Discovering her gifts benefits not only herself but also the church as a whole. You can find help in this area in the chapters on spiritual gifts on pages 59-84.

- *Involvement.* Once you've helped her to identify her gifts and strengths, include her in ongoing ministries or in an upcoming event. Suggest smaller tasks at first, not overwhelming her with duties she may not yet feel comfortable with. She might choose to work behind the scenes by volunteering in the women's ministries office, making phone calls, typing, or any number of jobs. Or, she may feel confident to work on a small team or project. It is most important to involve her in some way. Using her talents in partnership and responsibility will encourage her to serve not only in your ministry but also in other areas of your church.

Inside the House

The time a new member spends waiting at the door can be shortened considerably if it is a pleasant experience—not overwhelming or threatening. She will realize that her desire to achieve true belonging to this family is only a step away. With you by her side from the gate to the door, she will step through with confidence, knowing that she is safe inside the house.

Now that the new member is familiar with the structure of the church, is acquainted with more people, has participated in several groups, and has even served in some capacity using the gifts she's discovered, she can pursue other interests and avenues of service within the church. She is ready to serve as an effective team member—teaching, administrating, or any role that best utilizes her gifts. God gave her those gifts in order to serve Him. Allow her the chance to spread her wings and fly.

A Story to Tell

I want to tell you about my experience with a newcomer to our church. After she joined our church, I was blessed by watching her develop into a stronger Christian, particularly as the women of the church ministered to her and her family when her brother died. Later, we rejoiced with her when her parents and another brother were saved and baptized. Her strength continued to grow as both parents and brother struggled with serious health problems. She and her husband shared the joy of watching their children accept the Lord and be baptized. Just recently I learned that her sister has also accepted the Lord. Now this woman, once a new member, opens her warm heart to other women. My friend is just that, a friend—one with whom I've had the blessing of sharing life through the women's ministry of my church.

The woman who was new to your church a short time ago has grown and changed since you first met her. She has a story to tell, the story of how God came into her life and transformed her. She has a story to tell of the changes in the lives of her family since she came to your church.

Her testimony, her life story, her life struggles contributed to who she is now and can be used to minister to the needs of others in the church family—and the cycle continues. God sends women into our lives who change us, challenge us, encourage us, and love us into becoming more godly women.

Preparation ... What a Difference!

Let's consider a different scenario for Rhoda's story. This time, prior to the prayer meeting, Mary and Rhoda met and prepared for Peter's arrival.

> With you by her side from the gate to the door, she will step through with confidence, knowing that she is safe inside the house.

Mary spent time planning and equipping the others to minister to his needs or the essentials of any other unexpected arrival. Rhoda waited by the gate, ready to let Peter in. Another helper was located in the courtyard and helped Rhoda escort her treasured friend to the door. Yet another person waited at the door, opened it, and walked the group of friends inside the house. Once inside, Peter was seated in a place left especially for him. The warmth and welcoming hospitality of Mary and the household reassured Peter that he had indeed chosen the RIGHT HOUSE.

---

[1] Richard J. Foster, *Celebration of Discipline, Revised and Expanded* (San Francisco: HarperSan Francisco, 1988), 132.

For Smaller Churches
by Martha Lawley

Smaller churches do not need a formal structure within their women's ministry to bridge the gap for new women in the church. Utilize church programs that are already in place. For example, your church may have a new members class, or perhaps deacons deliver information packets to new members. Talk with the leaders of these ministries to insure that your women's ministry is included in their presentations or printed materials. Ensure that written information about your women's ministry is available at your welcome center, or in Sunday School record boxes or department meeting rooms.

To help assimilate new members into your church, consider using LifeWay's *Taking the Next Step: A Guide for New Church Members*, by Jerri Herring and Ralph Hodge (see page 221). It is a practical, easy-to-use resource to assist new members in learning more about your church and the opportunities available to them. Another resource is *Basics for Baptists* by Ernest Mosley and Betty Hassler (see page 221).

A welcome basket or bag as discussed in this chapter is a great idea for smaller churches. These bags can be made up in advance as a part of a fellowship time, then teams of women gifted in hospitality can take turns delivering them.

In smaller churches, the need for a formal system of greeters may not be necessary. However, encourage women gifted in hospitality to serve as unofficial greeters or silent greeters as they participate in the life of the church. Do not assume that a new member will automatically feel welcomed. Emphasize the need to include and encourage new members at every opportunity.

Leadership Development

Communication Skills

by Betty Hassler

*A*t Tuesday's Bible study Angela had announced plans for a mentoring ministry. Well, not really plans—more like ideas off the top of her head. The women's ministry council was up-in-arms because she had not discussed the idea with them. But Angela was sure this plan was directly from the throne of grace. After all, it had come to her during her prayer time Tuesday morning.

❧ ❧ ❧

Karen forgot to send out a meeting notice, but she called everyone the night before. Only two of the five team members attended.

❧ ❧ ❧

Beth had agreed to share a devotional at the beginning of the ministry team meeting. Now, as she stood before the group, her mouth tasted like ashes, and she was sure everyone could hear her heart pound. "Why did I ever say yes?" Beth thought.

What do Angela, Karen, and Beth have in common? Communication problems! We may call some of them relationship issues, but usually a breakdown in communication is the source or the symptom of our people problems.

What Is Communication?

Communication denotes more than speaking or hearing. Communication is an exchange of meaning between two or more persons. When I speak, I want more than to be merely heard. I want to be understood. I want my meaning to be clear to those who listen.

Often we assume that if we are heard—that is, understood—our listeners will agree with us. Actually, we can be perfectly clear in what we say and completely at odds with what our hearers think or believe. Yet we still have communicated; we just may not get the response we wanted.

Good communication, then, will not necessarily de-stress your lifestyle. It does not guarantee followship, cooperation, or good will. However, good communication is essential to building followship, cooperation, and good will. Good communication is the foundation of people skills that produce effective leadership.

Good communication is the foundation of people skills that produce effective leadership.

Although we can usually pinpoint the problems with other people's communication styles, often we overlook our own shortcomings. Clear communication begins with taking the fog out of our meaning.

Avoid Foggy Communication

Communication problems generally grow out of five false premises.

1. *Making assumptions without checking them out.* When you communicate instructions, invite the other person to repeat them before you end the conversation. In addition, a clear agreement on the task and the deadline does not guarantee that the other person understands your expectations. Have you asked for the quality you expect as well as the quantity? Ask yourself if you made any assumptions that you did not check out for accuracy.

2. *Confusing silence with agreement.* When possible, check with each person privately. You will be more likely to get true opinions. Maybe the nod of her head simply meant, "I hear you," not "I accept what you said." Without feedback, we cannot know what the hearer is thinking.

    Many people hesitate to speak negatively about an idea in a group setting. Their silence may be taken as consent.

3. *Expecting to be the exception to the rule.* These common rules of thumb apply to you as well as to others:
    – If you tell a secret, it won't be secret for long!
    – Don't give advice unless it is asked for.
    – Don't ask for favors that are not available to everyone.

    When we put ourselves in the position of trusting another person to keep a confidence, then we have to assume equal liability if the confidence is broken. When we offer advice or ask a favor, we must be aware that we risk offending the other person. Never assume you can predict someone else's reaction.

4. *Mistaking feelings with facts.* How one person feels about "the facts" of a situation may be entirely different from how you feel about those same facts. I have a friend who was just laid off from her job. She is delighted that she will have a few weeks of summer to spend with her daughter while she collects unemployment. In the same situation, I might feel scared or depressed.

    The fact that someone, got pregnant, or received a transfer across country is news—we just don't know if it is good news or bad news. Don't presume you know how the other person feels. For example, a death in the family could be a blessed end to painful suffering.

5. *Talking more than listening.* A good talker is not always a good listener.

162

Remember that communication is two-way, not one-way. Listening helps us clarify what the other person heard, how she feels about it, and what further information is needed. Listening gives the other person value. It communicates respect and other-centeredness.

If you find your mind wandering, here are some suggestions:
–Take notes; that's right, carry a pad and pen in your purse.
–Ask questions.
–Look the person in the eye; focus your attention.
–Paraphrase or summarize what you've heard; check it out.

If you can avoid these five common sources of communication fog, you will be well on your way to clear communication.

Practice Clear Communication

Clear communication involves the right information delivered to the right person at the right time.

- *The right information*—Have you announced a meeting and forgotten to tell the meeting place? Have you communicated the day of the week but not the date? Many communication errors result from incomplete information. Answer the five basic questions of good reporting: what, where, when, why, and how.

- *The right person*—The right person may not be the woman's husband or children! Family members may intend to deliver the message, but you know about roads paved with good intentions. Getting the message to the right person may involve several phone calls, but it eliminates the possibility of miscommunication through a middle person.

- *The right time*—The right time may not be in the middle of a church hallway or the parking lot. Giving information when the receiver is distracted or hurried almost insures that it will come back garbled. Be sensitive to the mood and situation of the other person. Ask: "Is this a good time for us to talk?"

Conversations should remind us of railroad crossings: Stop, look, listen. Watch those assumptions! Give your thoughts time to simmer before you rush to share them.

Practice Godly Communication

For the Christian woman, it is not enough to say the right thing to the right person at the right time. We must adhere to a higher standard than that of the world. Our communication must be God-honoring; it must glorify our Creator.

"Do not let any unwholesome talk come out of your mouths, but only what is helpful for building others up according to their needs, that it may benefit those who listen."

Ephesians 4:29

Godly communication builds up the hearer. As you speak, ask yourself if your communication is uplifting, encouraging, inspiring, and empowering. I know a woman who can share criticism or bad news in such a way that it takes the edge off her remarks. She has learned the art of graciousness in her speech.

Godly communication is truthful. Truth-telling does not require us to hurt someone's feelings. But we should not tell ourselves that sparing someone's feelings excuses a lie. Satan is the "father of lies" (John 8:44). On the other hand, Jesus is the Truth (see John 14:6). Peter said of Jesus, "No deceit was found in his mouth" (1 Pet. 2:22). In Ephesians 4:15 Paul gave us the standard of "speaking the truth in love." When we encounter situations where truthfulness may cause hurt, our words will be better received if they are bathed in love.

Godly communication is morally pure. Paul raised the bar on what passes for entertaining stories, jokes, or bantering. Paul encouraged believers to get rid of these characteristics of the old self: anger, rage, malice, slander, filthy language, and lying (see Col. 3:8-9).

"Whatever is true, whatever is noble, whatever is right, whatever is pure, whatever is lovely, whatever is admirable—if anything is excellent or praiseworthy—think about such things."

Philippians 4:8

When we are in the presence of those who are engaging in unwholesome talk, "We take captive every thought to make it obedient to Christ" (2 Cor. 10:5). By not participating, we are resisting temptation. We do not have to preach a sermon or look self-righteous. Seek to change the topic of conversation to one that honors God.

Godly communication reveals a grateful heart. A grateful heart recognizes that "every good and perfect gift is from above" (Jas. 1:17). We are less critical and more accepting. We are more likely to express gratitude to others, as well as to God.

Know Your Communication Style

Each of us communicates out of our unique personality style. You have probably taken a personality profile that helped you determine the strengths and weaknesses of your style. See "Negotiating with Grace," pages 181-190 for an explanation of four styles.

In communicating, women generally tend to be aggressive, assertive, or passive. We may use all three, depending on whom we are addressing, or we may blend them. I've given these styles a name to help you recall the primary characteristics of each style.

1. *High Energy Edna*—Ednas are risk takers, competitive, outgoing, and aggressive. They set high standards for themselves and others. Ednas get things done; however, they can be pushy and a bit overwhelming to a person with a meeker disposition.

Ednas need to avoid a know-it-all attitude, fix-it mentality, or "snoopervision." They may appear hurried and harried or stubborn and unwilling to compromise. Ednas generally dislike detail and may leave small but significant tasks unattended. If you are an Edna, learn to balance your ability to get things done with a kinder, gentler approach that encourages dialogue and team work.

2. *Capable Callie*—Callies have negotiation skills. They are organized, practical, and responsible. Callies excel at creating a climate of acceptance and affirmation. They tend to develop peer relationships rather than over-under hierarchical structures.

Callies can be rigid rather than flexible, plodding rather than timely. Callies are good at detail work, but they can also get mired in it. Callies provide stable leadership, but they may be uninspiring. If you are a Callie, add emotional fervor to your predictability. Seek to develop that charismatic side of your personality that will inspire others.

3. *Hesitant Hannah*—Hannahs are peacemakers. Often thrust into leadership, they prefer the background. Generally well-liked, Hannahs have a servant spirit. They will go out of their way to meet needs and fill holes in the organization.

Hannahs can be indecisive people-pleasers when decisions need to be made. Hannahs can easily become defensive out of a threatened posture or keep people at arm's length to avoid intimacy. They may be "polite listeners" but unable to share ideas for fear of confrontation. If you are a Hannah, seek to develop your self-esteem. Learn to value your opinion and share it freely. Develop confrontation skills that will help you feel more at ease when differing opinions are expressed.

If you have seen yourself in all three of these communication styles, assess the degree to which you have overcome the weaknesses and maximized the strengths of each one. If you are predominantly one of the styles, seek to balance your personality by cultivating one or more of the other styles.

Examine Your Inner Motives

Often, we are more transparent than we want to be! Our "hidden agendas" come out into the open. Our motives show like a slip beneath a skirt. The old adage, "Who you are speaks so loudly I can't hear what you say," rings true in leadership situations. Character does count!

The greatest boon to communication is trust. Others must feel they can trust us with their hearts and emotions. We must communicate: "I regard you. I really do want your best. I am for you." That's why it is

"Whatever you do, whether in word or deed, do it all in the name of the Lord Jesus, giving thanks to God the Father through him."
Colossians 3:17

essential to know the difference between manipulation and motivation. Manipulation is getting people to do what you want them to do. Motivation is helping people to do what they want to do.

Think about situations in which you have felt manipulated. Often the aftermath leaves you with feelings of having been used, perhaps even trampled underfoot. Manipulators successfully use guilt-riddled terminology to lead persons who have a hot button that can be pushed: "You ought ... should ...." They may also use a lot of God-talk to build a following: "God told me to ask you ...."

Think about situations in which you felt motivated. Did you leave feeling empowered, enhanced? Afterwards, did you feel capable and effective? If so, you were probably motivated. Motivators help others achieve their dreams. They do not need to rely on guilt because they are building on a felt need or goal within the individual.

Motivators are trust-builders. Motivators are trust-builders. Here are some key ways to build trust:
- Be dependable. Keep appointments and arrive on time.
- Keep confidences.
- Know all the facts before you leap to conclusions.
- Respond with compassion. Until we have walked a mile in another's moccasins, we cannot know what we would have done in the same situation.
- Demonstrate trust of others. We are more likely to trust those who trust us.

Overcome Communication Fears

Several of the communication problems we have uncovered are based on deep-seated fears that will not go away by wishful thinking or determination. Let's expose the myths behind many of these fears that control or contort our communication.

Fear of conflict is based on the myth that if we are in a conflict situation, it will automatically get out of hand and result in hurt and pain. Many persons who fear conflict grew up in homes in which one or both parents reacted with extreme anger in situations that called for a more moderate response.

Children growing up in such a setting usually try hard to avoid conflict. Conflict avoidance leaves a person vulnerable to anyone and everyone who can use that fear to manipulate or control them. Since conflict is an inevitable component of relationships, it is best to learn how to manage it in such a way that issues are resolved. For more information on conflict resolution skills, see pages 171-180.

Fear of rejection is based on the myth that if people get to know me, they will find me inadequate. In order to be liked, I must be perfect, or at least try for perfection. Any imperfection will be held against me. When our self-esteem is at stake, we find it harder to discuss ideas with others because we confuse criticism of our ideas with criticism of ourselves.

Strangely, people who fear rejection generally do not reject others when they make a mistake. They may be among the most forgiving and accepting of all your friends and coworkers. Yet they are plagued by questions such as: "Will people think this is a dumb idea? Will I look stupid if I do this?"

"God did not give us a spirit of timidity, but a spirit of power."
2 Timothy 1:7

One way to break through this fear is to work on building self-confidence. When I like myself, I have more self-respect. A confident person can hear her ideas critiqued without feeling defensive. As a matter of fact, she may even come to agree with the objections! She is free to learn and grow and improve her plan through every reaction.

One way to improve self-image is to practice positive self-talk. Tell yourself you do not have to be perfect. Let yourself off the hook when you make a mistake. Realize that others will get over it and life will go on.

Fear of public speaking is based on performance anxiety. All performers—whether speakers, singers, or instrumentalists—have some degree of anxiety or butterflies before a performance. Adrenalin kicks in and provides energy for the task. Persons with performance anxiety have exaggerated symptoms—uncontrollable shaking, nervousness, panic attacks, memory lapses, and so forth.

"Perfect love drives out fear."
1 John 4:18

One technique is to picture yourself before the performance successfully completing the experience and looking back on it with satisfaction. This picture is opposite of one that assumes failure and feelings of inadequacy. Here are some other suggestions:

- Outline your talk. "Winging it" is not a sign of spirituality. The statement, "I'm just depending on God," may be an excuse for poor preparation. Preparation gives confidence.
- Use notes. There is nothing magical about memorizing your speech. Notes are appropriate—refer to them as needed. Memorized speeches can sound "canned."
- Use visuals when possible. Visuals help visual learners to retain information shared. With the availability of computer-generated presentations public speaking can be entertaining and inspirational. Match the visual to the size of the room and the size of the audience. A small poster in a large room will not help your cause.

- Use illustrations, examples, testimonials, quoted material, Bible passages. These keep listeners attentive and mentally engaged.
- Avoid distracting behavior. Body language can enhance or detract from clear communication. Pushing up glasses repeatedly, playing with your hair or jewelry, licking your lips, or tapping the podium are mannerisms that distract from what you are saying. Always be aware of what you are doing with your hands.
- Abide by the time allotted. Time your speech beforehand. Short presentations are always more memorable than long. With the 7 1/2-minute attention span of most adults; making one lasting point is better than three points that will not be remembered.

Lead Effective Meetings

For a women's ministry leader, meetings are key vehicles for communication. An effective meeting will go a long way toward eliminating confusion or misunderstanding and building confidence and commitment. Here are some strategies for leading a productive meeting.

- *Publicity*—Some meetings are held at the same time, day, and week of the month or quarter. A simple reminder by phone or mail should be sufficient notification. If the meeting is called or irregular, give attendees at least two weeks notice and follow up with a call or note.
- *Agenda*—Meeting publicity should include the purpose for the meeting, agenda items, and an opportunity for attendees to add to the agenda in advance. Then they can think through many questions and issues that might not come to mind immediately.

  Print beside each item the approximate amount of time you intend to spend on the issue. As the meeting progresses, track the time each item takes. If an item takes more time than allotted, make notes about which items can be tabled for discussion at the next meeting or can be handled in a shorter time frame.
- *Length*—Generally, meetings that last longer than one hour are self-defeating. If you must meet for two hours, schedule a short stand-up break. Always begin on time and end on time. If you wait for latecomers, those who came on time to this meeting will be late for the next. Even if only one person is on time, begin! You will be training latecomers by your example.
- *Follow-up*—Minutes of the meeting should be kept by someone other than the presider. Minutes should be typed and distributed within a week of the meeting. Minutes should include the time,

An effective meeting will go a long way toward eliminating confusion or misunderstanding and building confidence and commitment.

day, date, and place of the next meeting.

- *Polity*—Some meetings are governed by simple majority rule. That system works well in a democracy, but it may not serve the purposes of women's ministry. Consider consensus as a more viable alternative. Consensus means the group will continue praying and discussing an issue until almost everyone is in agreement. Do not wait for total agreement. If you hold out for complete consensus, one person can prevent a ministry or an event from happening. Consensus assures that the group is united in purpose and commitment. Attendees do not leave a meeting feeling run over or unheard.

- *Presiding*—The person presiding must have a clear idea of what is to be accomplished. Are we to discuss an event or come to a decision on it? Can this suggestion be tabled or is there a deadline we must meet?

  Keep the meeting moving. Share leadership when possible by assigning portions of the agenda to persons with an interest, ability, or responsibility in that area. Above all, prevent one or two persons from monopolizing a meeting.

Give Meaningful Devotionals

Many meetings and events begin with a devotional. Not only do you lead these times of inspiration, but also you enlist others to do so. They may be apprehensive if this is a new responsibility. Share with them the tips on public speaking from page 167. Here is a plan for preparing a devotional:

- Pray for direction. Seek God's leadership and trust Him to know the needs of those who will be present.
- Know the purpose or the goal of the group. If possible, tie your remarks to that overall purpose.
- Know the target audience. Is the group co-ed or women only? Is it made up of young mothers or retirees? Will there be new Christians in the group with limited Bible background? The more questions you can ask and answer about the group, the better you will keep their interest and meet their needs.
- Determine a theme (topic). Once you have a topic, research its biblical meaning in a concordance, word study, or topical Bible. Find a verse or passage that supports your primary emphasis.
- Develop the topic. A devotional of 3-5 minutes allows for one well-developed point. A 5-10 minute devotional can sustain two

169

or three points. Don't give a laundry list of multiple ideas.

- Illustrate the ideas with a real-life situation, a personal example, a case study, a newspaper report—or draw from a book, television, or movie plot.
- Apply the topic. Your hearers should leave the room knowing how they can implement the Bible truths you presented. If they cannot, the devotional will be forgotten and ineffective.
- Identify quoted material. Do not try to pass off as your idea something you retrieved from another source. Do not tell a joke as though it happened to you. Persons who have heard the joke will question your credibility.
- Have a memorable closing. A key thought, passage, quote, or question should connect your thoughts. Avoid rambling, repeating yourself, or trailing off as you leave the podium.

Depend on God's Resources

"Now go; I will help you speak and will teach you what to say."
Exodus 4:12

Remember Moses standing before the burning bush? He told God to find someone else for leadership because he was not a good speaker. God's reply in Exodus 4:12 is encouraging. God never calls us into ministry without providing His resources to accomplish the task. As you seek to communicate, remember God's promised help. Call on Him to speak through you and thank Him for the opportunity to be His spokesperson!

For Smaller Churches
by Martha Lawley

Effective communication takes time and energy—both of which seem in short supply in the smaller church. In reality, poor communication results in the loss of even more time and energy. Put another way, your ministry does not have the time not to develop better communication skills. Learning and adopting the suggestions detailed in this chapter will ultimately save you time and energy.

The suggestions for leading effective meetings are helpful for churches of all sizes. Making the most of your meetings will open the door to clearer communication with your leadership which, in turn, will open the door to clearer communication with all the women of your church.

Consider offering communication skills training as an outreach tool for the women of your community, as well as for your own leaders. Involve other neighboring churches and/or community resources as needed.

170

Leadership Development
Conflict Resolution

by Chris Adams

Life without conflict would be nice, but the prospect is very unrealistic. Since all of us are created uniquely by God, we have different opinions about how life's situations should be handled. Thus, we must learn to deal with conflict.

In Philippians 4:2-3 we read about two women working in the church at Philippi who had a broken relationship with each other. Since many had become believers through their efforts, this problem was a major issue. Even Christian women in leadership, committed to furthering God's kingdom, can have broken fellowship with one another. But there is no excuse for remaining unreconciled.

Conflict can cause anger, hurt, confusion, fear, and even physical separation in relationships with those on our women's leadership team as well as other women involved in the church's women's ministry. At the same time, if approached correctly in a God-honoring way, conflict can also bring stimulation, healing, resolution to problems, and building of relationships. It can prevent stagnation and bring about needed change in a ministry and in the lives of those leading or involved in that ministry.

Conflict can't completely be avoided, but it can be managed and resolved, and it can help us grow in our own skills and relationships with others—a win/win solution. If the problem causing conflict is not confronted, the conflict can escalate and lead to more difficult problems in the future.

First we must consider our own attitudes about conflict. We are responsible for our own skill development in the areas of communication, relationship building, and problem solving. We should evaluate ourselves to see if we are flexible and willing to make changes, if necessary. Do we really listen to others and hear what they mean as well as what they say? Do we communicate clearly our own thoughts? How do we really feel about conflict—is it something we seek to avoid, considering it to be a negative aspect of a relationship? Or do we evaluate conflict in a positive light to see what good can come from dealing appropriately with it?

"I plead with Euodia and I plead with Syntyche to agree with each other in the Lord. Yes, and I ask you, loyal yokefellow, help these women who have contended at my side in the cause of the gospel."
Philippians 4:2-3

What Is Conflict?

Conflict is a struggle over opposing ideas or values. Quite often it involves a struggle for power; it also serves as a sign that we must attempt to resolve a problem. Even though we usually associate conflict with an action, it often results from miscommunication (see previous chapter). Here are some reasons conflict occurs:

- We cannot control a situation. When we feel we have no control over a situation's outcome, we tend to get defensive.
- Our rights are threatened. Although Christ says to put others' needs before ours (see Phil. 2:4; Mark 9:35), in our world we are taught to stand up for our rights. When we feel as though someone has tried to take away or infringe on one of our "rights," we may react with hostility and anger.
- Our self-esteem is questioned. Many individuals have a low self-esteem. When someone questions our worth, we may feel challenged to protect our egos.
- We feel taken for granted. One of our greatest needs is to feel valued by others. We want to be needed and useful. When we feel as though others presume upon us, we may become emotional and even irrational.
- Fear of change. For many of us, status quo means security. Change means uncertainty. When someone asks us to change something we do, fear may cause us to react negatively.

For these and other reasons, our needs or expectations of someone are unmet. The result is conflict.

Questions to Consider

When conflict occurs, we may ask ourselves these questions:

- Why has God allowed this to take place and how does He want it resolved? According to Romans 8:28, as believers, if we are obedient, nothing happens to us without His permission. We must view the situation through His eyes.
- How much time and effort should I spend trying to resolve this issue? Is it important enough to use valuable time and energy to resolve, or is it so incidental that it should just be dropped?
- What do I stand to lose in this situation? Count the cost before pursuing resolution.
- Is this a repeat problem or is it a first occurrence? If it happens regularly, research the history for any pattern behind the occurrences before confronting the issue.

172

• Do I have the authority to make a decision regarding the problem? Or does the authority rest in the hands of the opposing party? Knowing who can make the decisions is important to settling the issues.

Barriers to Conflict Resolution

Here are some attitudes or habits that prevent us from bringing about resolution when facing conflict with women on your leadership team or within your women's ministry:

• If we must always win because "we're always right," we have automatically closed the door to considering the other person's perspective in the circumstance.

• Many times we are so busy planning our defense that we do not even listen to what the other person is saying.

• Often we interrupt or respond too quickly. Rather than hearing the other person out, we close the door to that person's communication with us.

• As we listen to the "opposing" side, we may only listen for points of agreement rather than trying to understand.

• Maybe we've lost this same argument before and are determined not to lose it again.

• Perhaps we have wandering minds. Since we can hear faster than we can speak, as listeners we have extra time and may not concentrate on the details being shared.

• We can be judgmental. We may think we already know that person's problem and the solution.

These attitudes will likely shut down communication and possibly prevent problem solving.

Breaking Down the Barriers

Here are steps we can take to break down barriers to conflict resolution:

1. Hear the other person out completely, even allowing time for appropriate "blowing off steam" if necessary. Consider if some of what is being said could honestly be interpreted as constructive criticism. When you listen to the entire message you might be surprised at the validity of some of the opinions.

2. Establish and maintain eye contact with the other person.

3. Observe body language for hidden meaning to verbal sharing.

4. Repeat what you understood her to say.

5. Ask questions to clarify anything you don't understand.

Be open to the idea of
"being wrong" in
some areas of the
conflict, and if so,
accept your part of
the blame for the
problem.

6. Call the person by name when speaking to her.

7. As a leader, model appropriate ways to handle conflict.

8. Be open to the idea of "being wrong" in some areas of the conflict, and if so, accept your part of the blame for the problem.

Difficult People

Sometimes we meet people who are dissatisfied and unhappy about any ideas we suggest or decisions we make in our leadership roles. In *The Empowered Leader,* author Calvin Miller lists several types of difficult people with whom we might come into contact:[1]

The *chronically arrogant* are very strong-willed persons who want to eliminate inferiority and who believe their ideas are the only ones that matter. They believe the church revolves around them, and their agenda is to get their way. "Their ambition may really be their way of masking inferiority."[2] Sometimes the best thing to do is to give it time and turn the other cheek. Eventually this person will meet someone more determined who will tame their arrogance. When dealing with this type person in a team meeting, you may need to re-direct attention by asking how others feel about the issue.

The *congenitally belligerent* have been "upset since the womb!"[3] This type is sometimes aggressive and verbally abusive and always mad. Rather than being afraid or allowing them to control all meetings, effective leaders meet these people head on, demonstrating that nothing will be gained by their belligerence. Before team meetings, identify possible points of controversy and prepare answers.

A *non-negotiator* uses silence and evasion to block progress in a ministry and distract from the major agenda. Move forward with your ministry team's objectives and do not allow this person to control the outcome. Perhaps in a team meeting you can ask her to share ways this topic affects her area of ministry.

A *nitpicker* majors on the minors. She ignores big ideas and erodes the ministry vision. In team meetings, continually summarize important points you have discussed. Help her to focus on the decisions/information/events that really matter.

A *wheedler* whines and groans to have her way, attempting to keep others focused only on her problems. Do not give in to avoid complaining within the team. Instead challenge team members to be more positive in their statements and attitudes.

A *"yes-butter"* approaches new ideas with, "Yes, but it won't work because …"? Their negativity blocks the positive. Allow this person to serve in a less conspicuous role where her negativity will not influence major decisions.

Dr. Miller provides four key questions useful in analyzing our coping efficiency:

- Why has God sent this particular problem person into my life?
- Which of my problem people can be reconciled to the corporate dream?
- How far can I go to satisfy the grudges of antagonists?
- When is my time better spent on finding new support rather than trying to "sweeten up" old belligerence?[4]

We can meet difficult people with respectful assertiveness as well as dignity, never belittling them. We can stand, not sit when addressing difficult persons. Making eye contact and using their names when you speak to them helps to soften and quiet the other persons. Invite them to come to your office to discuss the issue calmly and fully.

Perhaps these difficult people are, as Calvin Miller describes them, just people with difficulties. In facing difficult people, we must be sure we are not also being difficult leaders. In our walk with Christ we must encourage relationship-building and conflict resolution.

> In facing difficult people, we must be sure we are not also being difficult leaders.

Ineffective Responses to Conflict

It has been said that life is 10 percent what happens to us and 90 percent how we react to circumstances. I have also heard that it's not as much how we act as how we react to situations that show others who we truly are inside. Understanding that means we must allow God to guard and guide our responses (as opposed to reactions) to conflict. These are ineffective options when it comes to facing conflict:

- *Withdrawal*—We can walk away from the situation, pout, isolate ourselves, and give the silent treatment. We can just say "forget it" and, therefore, resolution is never achieved. In this case, resentment may mount and cause the problem to grow rather than disappear. If wrong has been done, we have a responsibility to uphold truth.
- *Manipulation*—If our motive is to dominate the other person and control the solution, we will use any means to achieve personal satisfaction.
- *Retaliation*—We can decide to get even or get revenge with our opposition. Neither manipulation nor retaliation results in "win-win" solutions. They only provide a "win-lose:" I win, you lose—definitely not a biblical way to handle the problem.

- *Giving in at any price*—We decide it's not worth it to oppose or confront to resolve the issue. We will sacrifice whatever we must to keep the peace and allow the other person to win. Again, we may forfeit standing up for truth to keep the peace.

The only "win-win" situation is cooperation—working together humbly and with love to achieve peace and solutions.

Conflict Management Styles

In *Just Between Us,* a magazine for women in leadership edited by Jill Briscoe and published by Telling the Truth Media Ministries, the writer describes conflict management styles this way:

- Sharks—I win, you lose (domineering, aggressive, causing others to give in to their strong will)
- Foxes—Everyone wins a little and loses a little (may leave people half satisfied and half committed to solution)
- Turtles—I withdraw (peace at all cost, neutrality in conflict)
- Teddy Bears—I'll lose so you can win (surrenders own interests to accommodate others and believes all disagreement is bad)
- Owls—Let's find a way for everyone to win (sees this as a problem to solve, not a battle to win; collaborates to find mutually satisfying solution).[5]

Which style do you use? Which styles do your women's ministry team members exhibit? Awareness of different styles, regardless of terms used, will help you anticipate responses from team leaders during meetings.

A Biblical Response

How then would God have us resolve conflict in our personal relationships and within our women's ministry leadership team?

First, do nothing. Take a break, think it through and pray about your response. Ask God to help you love and value the other person as His unique creation. If we pray and think before responding, right off the bat we may prevent crucial mistakes in relationship building.

Exhibit self-control. Scripture affirms that *self-control* is a fruit of the Spirit. Angry responses do not honor Christ. We are encouraged to respond slowly to conflict rather than acting on impulse, resulting in regret. Proverbs 29:11 says, "A fool gives full vent to his anger, but a wise man keeps himself under control."

Stop, think—and pray. How does God look at this situation? How does He view the other person? He is a God of wisdom and compassion. Seek to exemplify those traits. What does He want to happen in your

"My dear brothers, take note of this: Everyone should be quick to listen, slow to speak and slow to become angry, for man's anger does not bring about the righteous life that God desires."

James 1:19-20

relationship as you deal with this issue? Could this be a growing experience for all parties involved?

Ask yourself, Is the issue worth pressing? Is it worth your time and effort, or is it of no real consequence? "Count the cost" of spending any more effort. If resolution does not count for much in the long run, perhaps you need to overlook it and proceed with more important issues.

Evaluate your own attitudes, strengths and weaknesses. Matthew 7:5 admonishes, "You hypocrite, first take the plank out of your own eye, and then you will see clearly to remove the speck from your brother's eye" (NIV). Ask yourself, Is the problem more mine than the other person's? Prayerfully seek God's perspective about your role in the disagreement to understand why you feel as you do about the situation.

Follow scriptural principles. Once you've considered all the previous elements, seek specific direction in God's Word for handling the resolution process. Matthew 18:15 provides direction for approaching someone we feel has instigated the problem. Face-to-face, one-on-one confrontation is not easy. Share feelings and viewpoints honestly and in love. Listen carefully and acknowledge each other's feelings and opinions. Remember—attack the problem, not the person. Rather than addressing old issues, focus on the current issue and ways to resolve the problem. Praying together is a positive way to initiate resolution.

Ask questions for clarification. State the problem. Assimilate the facts and clearly define the issue. Is it perhaps a matter of miscommunication or incorrect information? Ask, Who else or what other factors are involved in this situation? Complete research prior to your meeting.

Discover together those things on which you DO agree. Consider compiling a list. Then, evaluate the big picture—how does this situation affect the ministry? How does if affect the church? Brainstorm possible solutions that will result in mutual benefits.

Take some time apart. Think through the possible solutions and pray separately. Come back together to determine actions to take. Be willing to admit individual mistakes and failures that might have contributed to the problem. Ask for and give forgiveness where necessary.

What if this approach doesn't work? If anger erupts, language is inappropriate, the person is unreasonable, or she won't listen, you may need to take a different approach. Matthew 18:16 provides direction. Invite mediators to hear the issue and help to make decisions.

In *To Live Is Christ,* author Beth Moore, gives four steps for handling a dispute:

- Identify the real source of argument.

"A man's wisdom gives him patience; it is to his glory to overlook an offense."
Proverbs 19:11

"If your brother sins against you, go and show him his fault, just between the two of you."
Matthew 18:15

"But if he will not listen, take one or two others along, so that every matter may be established by the testimony of two or three witnesses."
Matthew 18:16

- Submit the issue to God.
- Resist the temptation to sin in your anger.
- Pray for the person involved, and if possible, with that person.[6]

At times you may have to agree to disagree.

Remember—at times you may have to agree to disagree. You cannot change anyone else—only yourself. You are not responsible for anyone else's response to the problem—only your own. Be sure, however, that when you respond, God is honored and the truth is upheld. For those who CHOOSE to be consistently disagreeable, you may be forced to say you are truly sorry they feel that way—then waste no more time trying to fix what they do not want to fix. Humor is also a good divergent in dealing with disagreeable people. It has a way of cutting the tension!

Some Do's and Don'ts:

Do
- have Christ's attitude
- speak truthfully
- seek reconciliation
- forgive
- be loving and compassionate
- listen
- confess any part you may have in it
- put the person above your pride
- put yourself in their shoes
- explain your feelings
- describe what you'd like to see different
- be willing to compromise
- develop creative solutions to problems
- agree to disagree if at an impasse
- accept differences as normal rather than good or bad
- take your time or a "time out" if needed
- use your emotions as signals to help you discern the situation

Accept differences as normal rather than good or bad.

Don't
- sin (give Satan a foothold)
- seek revenge (sin in anger)
- lie, cover up
- swear
- slander
- belittle, call the other person a "fool"
- rage, brawl, hurt, abuse

178

-compromise truth

-blame

-assume you know their motives

-give silent treatment

-act like a victim

-try to "win"

-act impulsively

-let your emotions control you

-crumble and untruthfully take all shame and blame

-presume to change the other person

-pay back insult for insult[7]

Build Conflict Resolution Skills
Within the Women's Ministry Team

- Use your monthly team meetings to provide training. For several consecutive months focus on dealing with conflict.
- Circulate a set of conflict management tapes among team members, then meet to discuss what they've learned. Consult your public library, bookstore, or browse the Internet for possibilities.
- Share books that address the topic of conflict management. Use the resources mentioned above.
- Use role play to demonstrate different scenarios they might encounter in their leadership responsibilities. Consider a role-play situation based on a possible but not actual conflict. Let team members role-play various roles (agitator, peace-at-all-costs, withdrawn, reconciler). Trade roles. Ask team members to offer different perspectives on the best approach.
- Train your leaders to effectively communicate ideas and to listen to others.

Choose Peace

Romans 12:17-21 teaches: "Do not repay anyone evil for evil. Be careful to do what is right in the eyes of everybody. If it is possible, as far as it depends on you, live at peace with everyone. Do not take revenge, my friends, but leave room for God's wrath, for it is written: 'It is mine to avenge; I will repay,' says the Lord. On the contrary: 'If your enemy is hungry, feed him; if he is thirsty, give him something to drink. In doing this, you will heap burning coals on his head.' Do not be overcome by evil, but overcome evil with good" (NIV).

Christians are commanded to pursue peace with others. Peace is a fruit of the Spirit (see Gal. 5:22-23). Peace honors God. As we approach conflict and work for peaceful solutions we must seek His best for all concerned.

Though our differences can sometime cause broken relationships, it can also stimulate energy and encourage growth within our women's ministry team and in the ministry to women in our churches.

[1] Calvin Miller, *The Empowered Leader* (Nashville: Broadman & Holman, 1995), 141-150.
[2] Ibid., 142.
[3] Ibid., 143.
[4] Ibid., 151.
[5] Norman Shawchuck and Robert Moeller, "Animal Instincts: Five ways church members will react in a fight," *Just Between Us,* Fall 1998, 16-17, 30.
[6] Beth Moore, *To Live Is Christ* (Nashville: LifeWay, 1997), 76-77.
[7] Ingrid Lawrenz, MSW, "Conflict: What You Can Do and What You Can't Do," *Just Between Us,* Fall 1998, 15.

For Smaller Churches
by Martha Lawley

"Whether you eat or drink or whatever you do, do it all for the glory of God."
1 Corinthians 10:31

Conflict occurs in every church, regardless of size. Mismanaged conflict is dangerous in any church but can be particularly devastating for a smaller church where information travels fast and long-term and familial relationships are in place.

Do not draw others into the conflict if it can be avoided. All of us have a natural tendency to choose sides, and this division will begin to take on a life of its own. The best way to avoid division is to follow the biblical model that will result in containing the conflict as you seek God's will for restoring the situation.

For most individuals, conflict resolution is a learned skill. Many resources are available to help people learn these skills. This type of skill development can be effective for all women in your church, not just those in leadership. Also, conflict resolution training can be an effective outreach tool for women in your community who desire to learn how to properly respond to the conflict they experience in their daily lives.

"The fruit of the Spirit is love, joy, peace, patience, kindness, goodness, faithfulness, gentleness and self-control."
Galatians 5:22-23

If it is not practical for your church to offer training in conflict resolution, consider association-wide or state-wide training opportunities. Also look for opportunities to join with other churches to provide conflict resolution training for women in your church and community.

As women in your church grow in spiritual maturity and learn to surrender to the leadership of the Holy Spirit, the characteristics of the fruit of the Spirit will become more evident. These qualities are God's best resource for resolving conflict among Christians.

Leadership Development

Negotiating with Grace

by Rhonda Kelley

Leaders who work successfully with other people must develop the art of negotiation. Whether facing conflict or communicating a vision, an effective leader must learn to build a consensus and motivate people to work cooperatively. Women's ministry leaders must negotiate in a godly manner with grace.

According to *Webster's Dictionary, negotiate* means "to confer with another so as to arrive at the settlement of some matter." Negotiation is an ongoing process of exchanging ideas and managing decisions. Successful negotiation involves give and take.

Christian negotiation implies communicating with grace. Women's ministry leaders who speak with grace are better able to meet needs. Because Christian women often enter leadership in women's ministry with little if any previous experience–and women are typically hesitant to confront–negotiation skills must be developed by those who want to be godly leaders. In this chapter, we will discuss negotiation from the Christian perspective and suggest biblical principles to help you learn to negotiate with grace.

"Let your speech always be with grace, seasoned, as it were, with salt, so that you may know how you should respond to each person."
Colossians 4:6, NASB

Information will be provided to help women's ministry leaders better understand those with whom they work–other women, team leaders and members, and church staff members. In addition, you will be encouraged to treat yourself with grace as you seek to work through difficult situations. You can grow personally as you learn negotiating skills that are "seasoned with salt."

The Role of Grace in Building Negotiation Skills

Grace is unmerited favor extended by God to His children. It is undeserved acceptance and love (see Eph. 2:8). Salvation is by grace through faith. Jesus Christ offered His grace to all people. He desired that God's redeeming grace be poured out on all people. In the greetings for each of his New Testament letters, Paul extended "grace" to all believers. The grace that provides salvation is the same grace which provides reconciliation for broken relationships. One entire Pauline epistle is devoted to the theme of grace in action. Read the brief Book of Philemon to receive biblical insights on negotiating with grace.

Using his typical greeting Paul began a personal letter to his friend Philemon: "Grace to you and peace from God our Father and the Lord Jesus Christ" (Philem. 3). He continued with a plea for Philemon to forgive Onesimus, his runaway slave who had received Christ. Grace from God and Philemon were necessary to restore the broken relationship. Paul's steps in negotiating with grace offer us help today in reconciling broken relationships. Examine each step carefully.

1. *Affirmation* (vv. 1-3). Paul affirmed Philemon for who he was: "a beloved friend and fellow laborer." A leader must affirm her followers for who they are in Christ.

2. *Appreciation* (vv. 4-5). Paul thanked God for the love and faith of his friend. A leader must give thanks for the dedication of others.

3. *Acknowledgment* (vv. 6-7). Paul acknowledged the work of Philemon in sharing his faith. Leaders must recognize the contributions of those they lead.

4. *Appeal* (vv. 8-11). Paul appealed to Philemon to forgive Onesimus. Leaders often must plead for action by their people.

5. *Approach* (vv. 12-14). Paul recommended an approach to Philemon–receive Onesimus in love. Leaders should suggest solutions to problems among their people.

6. *Acceptance* (vv. 15-16). Paul accepted Onesimus as a beloved brother and encouraged Philemon to do the same. Leaders must accept others as children of God.

7. *Action* (vv. 17-20). Paul encouraged action by Philemon and Onesimus. Negotiating with grace requires action by all parties.

8. *Advice* (vv. 21-22). Paul's advice to Philemon was threefold: be obedient, prepared, and trusting. Leaders are to respond likewise.

9. *Approval* (vv. 23-25). In his final words, Paul expressed approval as well as greetings from his fellow workers. Leaders must publicly express approval of those who follow.

Ministry through the church and to your leadership team requires negotiation with grace. The biblical model of reconciliation between Philemon and Onesimus is helpful, but there are other practical principles for negotiating with grace.

Principles of Negotiating with Grace

Your interaction with others and relationships with your leaders will improve if you follow these guidelines for grace.

1. Share your vision. As God gives you direction, share the vision with your leadership team. They will claim ownership and follow your lead.

2. Instill passion for the work. Your enthusiasm about the work can be contagious. Passion is the fuel that propels the ministry.

3. Communicate your objectives clearly. State the goals and objectives of your women's ministry in understandable words. Lack of clarity promotes confusion.

4. Listen for feedback. Watch the responses and listen to the comments of your team members. Their feedback can provide valuable information.

5. Offer support and encouragement. As the work begins, a leader must give words of encouragement and affirmation. Don't allow your team to become discouraged.

6. Help solve problems. Problems will be encountered as programs proceed. Be actively involved in helping to resolve problems.

7. Confront conflict as it arises. When differences of opinion are expressed, deal with the differences before the problems escalate. Though confrontation is rarely pleasant, early intervention can prevent major conflict. For more information, read "Conflict Resolution," pages 71-80.

8. Minister to their needs. Notice the personal needs of your leadership team. Minister to them through prayer, words of appreciation, notes of thanks, and acts of kindness.

9. Recognize accomplishments. Successful work needs public and private recognition. Give recognition to those team members who do their work with excellence.

10. Pray for them. Remember to pray daily and specifically for your leaders. In order to pray with purpose, you must know them well and communicate regularly.

Negotiating with grace is not a natural human response. However, Christian leaders are to imitate Christ who always offered grace. Follow the example of Paul who extended grace to all. Negotiating with grace is a true testimony of the power of God's grace to transform lives.

> Negotiating with grace is a true testimony of the power of God's grace to transform lives.

Negotiating One-on-One

As a women's ministry leader consistently casts the vision and leads in love, she will be a godly example and an effective leader. As you seek to negotiate with grace, employ three important resolution skills.

1. Listen effectively.

   The opposite of effective listening is listening to prove a point, to insert your opinion, to explain, to divert, to soothe, or to appease. Each of these represents listening with an agenda. Your role is first of all to hear the other person. Often, when persons feel heard, the conflict is resolved simply because they no longer feel alone or isolated. Another human being has acknowledged their hurt or disappointment.

   Effective listening involves the following actions:
   - Paraphrase or restate the speaker's views (without elaboration or interpretation).
   - Summarize the speaker's viewpoints and concerns.
   - Neutralize the language of the speaker. For example, soften harsh or highly critical language with phrases such as "you understand the situation differently."
   - Maintain eye contact and attentive body language.
   - Avoid assumptions; listen from a non-judgmental stance.

2. Ask open-ended questions.

   Encourage the speaker to fully describe her experience. Ask questions starting with who, what, when, where, and how. Do not ask why questions, which can put the speaker on the defensive, asking her to justify her actions.

3. Take responsibility for what you can.

   No one is totally right or totally wrong in any situation. Find areas of agreement without buying all the responsibility or negating the speaker's role in the disagreement. Be patient, humble, and willing to learn. Arrogance can undo all you are trying to accomplish.

   End the conversation with an action plan. What do you intend to do to follow-up or what do you expect the speaker to do? Don't leave a disgruntled person hanging. Often, that will result in her sharing her pain with others who are not directly involved in the situation.[1]

Negotiating in a Group

Don't allow yourself to be dragged into a negotiation for which you are unprepared.

During a meeting or group session if you find yourself negotiating between two diverging sets of opinions, you may want to postpone the discussion until you have had opportunity to talk with each "side" and formulate an approach to resolving the difficulty. Don't allow yourself to be dragged into a negotiation for which you are unprepared.

At the appropriate time, gather the parties and discuss in a deliberate and prayerful fashion. Seek balanced representation (an equal number for

each opinion). Remind those present that your purpose in being here is to primarily honor God and secondarily to resolve the situation.

Emphasize that "winning" or "being right" is a worldly perspective; call attention to the fruit of the Spirit from Galatians 5:22-23 as the attitude the group wants to convey as they seek God's will. Then, remind the group of the end result (the ministry vision) for what you are about. Say, *Let's not lose our focus on our goal as we discuss ways of accomplishing it.* Ask each group to present their views without interruption.

Ask, *What would it take for [side 2] to agree with [side 1]?* Then ask, *What would it take for [side 1] to agree with [side 2]? What would a compromise (middle) position look like?* Often, a third opinion—a solution not yet considered—will grow out of the discussion.

If the groups are not yet ready to agree to a position, dismiss the meeting with prayer and reschedule for a later time. Negotiation should not be a "forced march" where parties are conscripted to take a certain position whether or not they agree. If time is a factor, look for ways to give yourself more time. Rescheduling the beginning of a new program or an event is much easier than dealing with the fallout from disgruntled participants.

Although negotiating situations will always present themselves as you work with people, an emotionally charged or volatile scene should become less frequent when trust is built with your leadership team. Often, trust-building is a by-product of a shepherding role.

> Negotiation should not be a "forced march" where parties are conscripted to take a certain position whether or not they agree.

Negotiation as Shepherding

The role of the women's ministry leader is often that of a shepherd—one who is responsible for the well-being of a specific group of believers. Many women's ministry leaders discover they have the spiritual gift of shepherding. On some spiritual gift inventories, shepherding is equated with pastoring. This terminology may cause surprise and confusion. How can a woman serving in the local church use this specific gift?

The spiritual gift of shepherding is the special ability to assume long-term personal responsibility for the spiritual welfare of a group of believers. Specific responsibility is to build up, equip, and guide Christians in spiritual growth and maturity. While the pastor is the shepherd of the entire flock (a church congregation), a women's ministry director is the shepherd of a portion of the flock (the women of the church). Under the authority of the pastor and in total submission to the Lord, the women's ministry leader is to build up, equip, and guide the women of the church in spiritual growth and ministry. Thus, the spiritual gift of shepherding is used to glorify the Lord.

Build Up

As a women's ministry leader you are responsible for promoting the personal growth of the women in your church. Growth takes place when a person is built up spiritually, physically, emotionally, and mentally. You must challenge women to grow in the Lord through Bible study, prayer, service, and witnessing. You must encourage them to take care of their bodies through proper nutrition and regular exercise. You must promote mental growth through reading, education, and life experiences. A women's ministry leader nurtures the spiritual growth of women.

Equip

As the women on your leadership team grow spiritually, they will volunteer for service. However, willing volunteers are not always equipped for service. Provide training and motivation for the leadership team. In *Jesus on Leadership,* Gene Wilkes says "Encouragement without training is like enthusiasm without direction."[2] Equipping gives specific direction and focus. Skills are required to work effectively to accomplish a mutual goal.

Lead workers on your team to know their areas of responsibility and accept the challenge to work. They must be taught how to do the work and then to do it well. Your leadership team needs to continue learning, networking, and sharing in order to minister in effective ways. If your team members resist training, then you must negotiate with grace.

Guide

A women's ministry leader must also guide the team members. The most important issue in negotiating with grace is a clearly defined vision of the future. The group must learn to resolve differences in light of the overall goals and objectives set for the ministry, not by personal opinion.

Team members need a leader who commands respect while guiding them in a specific direction. When a leader guides with integrity, team members willingly follow. At times a women's ministry leader may be able to lead in a gentle manner; at other times that same leader may need to drag or push team members. Perhaps they are tired or uncertain or resistant to following you as you attempt to follow God's will. The dragging or pushing may at first be painful, but if they follow in obedience, joy will ultimately prevail. Push in love according to God's will. Strong guidance honors God and promotes unity of purpose. The ongoing process of exchanging ideas will promote trust and loyalty. If you negotiate with grace, your women's ministry leadership team will usually follow.

John Maxwell has identified several leadership limitations because even

The most important issue in negotiating with grace is a clearly defined vision of the future.

the strongest leaders can't do everything. In leading your team members, remember these limitations:

- I cannot lead people longer than they're willing to follow.
- I cannot lead people farther than they're willing to go.
- I cannot lead people faster than they're willing to change.
- I cannot lead people higher than they're able to climb.[3]

The shepherd of a local women's ministry must build up, equip, and guide the flock. As you do, you will grow and they will grow. God will give you direction and grace to navigate even the most difficult waters.

Negotiation with Staff

Growth in women's ministry often results in the need for a full-time or part-time women's ministry director or at least a volunteer coordinator. Complete cooperation and clear communication with others on the church staff are essential for a thriving women's ministry. Although staff members are Christians who are called to ministry, they may not always be easy to work with. Problems in staff relations may arise. Effective women's ministry leaders must negotiate graciously with staff members.

Be sensitive to the different opinions and personalities among the church staff. Remember the general principles of negotiating with team members because the church staff is a leadership team. But also consider gender differences when working with a mostly male church staff. Many women's ministry directors are the only females on an all-male church staff. In most cases, the women's ministry leader is working directly under the supervision of a male staff member.

Some differences between men and women are obvious. Scripture teaches the uniqueness of men and women. While created in the image of God with equal worth and value, men and women are different by design and function. Gender differences are apparent physically and behaviorally. Men and women differ in the way they think, feel, act, and talk. These gender differences are important to remember when working with a mostly male church staff.

Communication methods are strikingly different between the sexes. Men and women use different content, style, and structure. Concerning content, men often talk about sports, money, and business; women most often discuss people, feelings, and relationships. Concerning style, men often talk to resolve problems; women most often express themselves in an effort to understand, support, and connect. Concerning structure, men typically use precise and to-the-point words, without descriptive details; women are more detailed, apologetic, and vague.

> Complete cooperation and clear communication with others on the church staff are essential for a thriving women's ministry.

In her book, *You Just Don't Understand,* Deborah Tannen introduced the term *genderlect.* Genderlect is the language of the sexes—the conversational style unique to men or women. Tannen identifies 12 basic differences between male and female communication.

1. Men communicate to maintain status, women to maintain intimacy.
2. Men offer solutions to problems, women complain about problems.
3. Men give information, women give affirmation.
4. Men report-talk, women rapport-talk.
5. Men lecture, women listen.
6. Men use conflict to negotiate status, women avoid conflict to establish connection.
7. Men interrupt, women overlap.
8. Men talk more in public, women talk more in private.
9. Men talk about their accomplishments, women are hesitant to boast.
10. Men use silence, women avoid silence.
11. Men speak with confidence, women often apologize.
12. Men use body language indirectly, women use it very directly.[4]

In 1993, Judith Tingley proposed a response to genderlect. Men and women should learn to "genderflex" or adapt their conversational style when talking to a person of the opposite sex.[5] A women's ministry leader who can genderflex when speaking with a male staff member will often be more effective in communicating ministry vision and less defensive when responding to questions about various programs.

Understanding gender communication promotes healthy working relationships. If you desire to negotiate with grace with male church staff members, consider the basic differences between men and women.

• Adjust your conversational style to clarify message and intent.
• Adapt to the context to determine if your statements are appropriate. Don't assume that the opposite sex understands you. Try to communicate clearly in his language. And, don't criticize others who communicate in a different way. For more information, read "Communication Skills," pages 161-170.

Negotiation as a Personal Growth Issue

Be sure to extend grace to yourself in the same way you negotiate graciously with the women in your church, with staff members, and with team members. Leaders often encounter great personal struggles as they

A women's ministry leader who can genderflex when speaking with a male staff member will often be more effective in communicating ministry vision and less defensive when responding to questions about various programs.

identify problems and find solutions. But treating yourself with kindness (grace) promotes tremendous growth and gains well-deserved respect.

An effective leader must carefully evaluate her own leadership style. While there is no one perfect leadership style, each specific style has inherent strengths and weaknesses. An effective leader maximizes her strengths and minimizes her weaknesses. Ken Blanchard suggests four basic styles of leadership in his book *The One Minute Manager*:

1. *Directing style*—gives specific instruction and closely supervises.
2. *Coaching style*—continues to instruct and supervise task accomplishments but also explains, supports, and delegates.
3. *Supporting style*—facilitates and supports subordinates toward task accomplishments and shares responsibility for decision-making with them.
4. *Delegating style*—turns over responsibility for decision-making and problem-solving to subordinates.[6]

Once a leader has identified her own leadership style, she can accept her limitations and maximize her strengths.

In addition to growth in leadership skills, women's ministry leaders must negotiate through some personal challenges of leadership. Leadership is hard work without guaranteed success. However, as the Lord blesses the ministry, there is a tendency toward pride and power and personal recognition. Many years ago, J. Oswald Sanders wrote about the perils of leadership in his book *Spiritual Leadership*.[7] His warnings remain relevant for today's Christian leaders.

Women's ministry leaders must beware of these perils of leadership: pride, jealousy, popularity, infallibility, and elation/depression. As a women's ministry grows, there is a tendency for leaders to take credit for success and accept the accolades of others. It is natural for people to elevate leaders to a pedestal, who then in turn may become intoxicated with the recognition. This often leads to pride, followed by a fall. A sense of infallibility is a peril of leadership. Women's ministry leaders may be prone to jealousy or envy of other churches which have successful women's ministry programs. Leadership has extreme highs and lows; discouragement and frustration may follow success and acclaim. Each of these perils of leadership must be negotiated with grace. Turn to the Lord for direction, seek out others for counsel, and hold yourself accountable to be a godly leader. Only Jesus was a perfect leader.

> Women's ministry leaders must beware of these perils of leadership: pride, jealousy, popularity, infallibility, and elation/depression.

John Maxwell has also identified some personal limitations in leadership. Even the greatest leaders cannot lead beyond their weaknesses. Remember these personal limitations as you lead your women's ministry:

- I cannot lead people beyond my leadership skills.
- I cannot lead people above my level of trust.
- I cannot lead people past my level of commitment.
- I cannot lead people around my undisciplined lifestyle.
- I cannot lead people without my willingness to serve.[8]

The power of the Holy Spirit helps us to overcome our limitations in leadership so that all we do glorifies the Father. His grace covers our sin in salvation and forgives our mistakes in leadership. When His grace is evident in our lives, we can joyfully serve, treating others with acceptance and love.

When His grace is evident in our lives, we can joyfully serve, treating others with acceptance and love.

[1] Betty Hassler, *Leading Criminal Justice Ministry: Bringing Shalom* (Nashville: LifeWay Press, 1998), 53.
[2] C. Gene Wilkes, *Jesus on Leadership* (Nashville: LifeWay Press, 1996), 90.
[3] John C. Maxwell, *Developing the Leaders Around You* (Nashville: Thomas Nelson, 1995).
[4] Deborah Tannen, *You Just Don't Understand* (New York: Morrow, 1990).
[5] Judith Tingley, *Genderflex: Men and Women Speaking Each Other's Language at Work* (New York: American Management Association, 1994), 39.
[6] Kenneth Blanchard, Patricia Zigarmi, and Drea Zigarmi, *Leadership and the One Minute Manager* (New York: Morrow, 1985), 30.
[7] J. Oswald Sanders, *Spiritual Leadership* (Chicago: Moody Press, 1980), 23-26.
[8] Ibid., Maxwell.

For Smaller Churches
by Martha Lawley

The guidelines for grace described in this chapter can be effective in any size church. Adopting these guidelines, individually or corporately, does not require spending money or starting a new program—welcome news to smaller churches.

Sometimes the lines of responsibility and authority are less obvious in smaller churches, yet a proper understanding of these lines is important in negotiating with grace. A general agreement concerning areas of responsibility and authority among leadership provides a necessary framework for responding to conflict or communicating a vision.

Look for leadership training opportunities offered through your denomination. For example, associational or state convention workshops offer valuable training for lay leadership at little or no cost. For information on upcoming training opportunities or to offer suggestions on needed training, contact your local association or state convention office.

Training can be important in teaching skills; however, it is the supernatural work of the Holy Spirit that allows us to extend God's grace to others. Each church, regardless of size or location, and each individual has access to the same supernatural power of the Holy Spirit.

Leadership Development

Networking

by Shirley Moses

As a women's ministry leader, do you often feel you have more questions than answers? Have you ever thought, *If I could just talk with other women's ministry leaders, maybe I would get a fresh insight?* Or has God given you a vision to bring women in ministry together within your local geographical area or Baptist association? Then networking is for you!

What Is Networking?

To understand networking, it might be helpful to focus briefly on what the ministry of networking *is not*.

- Networking is not just for churches with organized women's ministry.
- Networking is not just another program for women. We all have busy lives and don't need another meeting to attend.
- Networking is not just a passing fad. Networking is at the core of what we are to be about, a community of believers reaching out to those around us.
- Networking is not just about ministry to women in our churches. It is about reaching women outside our sphere of influence—into the community and the world.
- Networking is not meant to be a clique or social gathering.

Now let's examine what networking *is*. Networking is a term often used in business circles to describe the process of interacting with others who share a common job description, responsibility, or set of skills for the purpose of learning, sharing information, or making contacts that are mutually beneficial.

For example, pastors network when they meet for an associational pastors' conference. Whether formal—through seminars or workshops—or informal—hallway talk and lunch conversations—networking helps pastors to discover what is successful in other churches or how another minister handled a similar situation or opportunity.

In Acts:8:30-31 Philip asked the eunuch, "Do you understand what you are reading?" "How can I," the eunuch responded, "unless someone

> Networking is the process of interacting with others who share a common job description, responsibility, or set of skills for the purpose of learning, sharing information, or making contacts that are mutually beneficial.

191

explains it to me?" Networking is connecting with others to get and give information so that we may all be more effective in sharing the Word with all women in our community.

If you've ever telephoned another woman's ministry leader, talked to one at a conference, emailed someone about a program you have heard about, or been asked to tell what your church is doing at an associational event—you have networked! Networking enables Christian women to form meaningful relationships. Through networking, they can look beyond the borders of their own churches to see what is happening in other churches and denominations. Together, they can look for help and answers to needs within their congregations and the community.

My Journey into a Networking Ministry

Several years ago during my quiet time, I began to feel God speaking to me about starting a network of women's ministry leaders within our association. I knew God had called me to minister to women. In my church, I had taught Sunday school and discipleship groups and had organized women's events, but we did not have a recognized women's ministry.

Some time later I shared with our deacon body my desire to organize a women's ministry in our church. We created an organizing team and prayed for God's direction. Even during the intense period of starting this new ministry, I could not get networking off my mind. I continued to push it to the back burner and promised God I would deal with it later.

One night I was awakened at midnight with a heavy heart for networking—again. God gave me the content for a letter and instructions to send the letter to all churches within my association. The letter was very simple. It was addressed to Women's Leader. I introduced myself and went on to share the burden that God had laid on my heart to reach lost women for Christ and to encourage those in our churches. I assured the women's leader that there were others who had the same desire and asked if we could meet and share our common interest.

The very next day I made an appointment with our Director of Missions and shared my letter and heart with him. He agreed to help and wrote a cover letter to the pastors. The first networking meeting was scheduled and I didn't have a clue where God was leading me!

Day One of Networking

The meeting day finally arrived. Thirty-five women representing 11 of the 63 churches in our association attended our very first networking meeting. At the time I can remember thinking it was not a very good turnout.

I soon discovered that only three churches had an organized and functioning women's ministry—and my church was one of them.

At our first networking meeting each woman received a registration form to complete (example below). This form proved to be a vital networking tool. These names were entered into the computer and we compiled our first mailing list.

Name: _____ Phone: hm _____ wk _____
Address: _____City: _____ Zip: _____
Church: _____ Church Phone: _____
Church size (average Sunday attendance):_____
Check all that apply:
___Our church currently has an organized women's ministry.
___I would like help establishing an organized women's ministry.
___I am willing to be the contact person for our ministry.
___I would like to be notified of future networking meetings.

The women's ministry team at my church provided salads for lunch, and two women from another church led us in worship. This time seemed to bind the women together; everyone agreed that they wanted to continue the meetings. We would meet monthly on the third Saturday, and each church would take a turn hosting the networking meeting. The host church would also mail out the agenda for the next meeting.

Our networking group began to pray about a possible name and a one-line statement to define our purpose. We chose, "Women Connecting with Other Women." Our name became Women's Ministry Connection of Grayson County. This title included not only Women's Enrichment but also Woman's Missionary Union (WMU).

Seven Benefits of Networking

I have identified seven benefits of networking that I would like to illustrate by describing the first networking group in my association.

1. *An approach to bringing women together for encouragement and support.*
   During the first networking meeting, we allowed time for each woman to express her concerns. I was amazed at the honesty. The experience opened my eyes to the struggles of these women, not only in their personal lives but also in their attempts to minister to other women.

   They shared personal concerns for family and church. Others want-

"Therefore encourage one another and build each other up, just as in fact you are doing."
1 Thessalonians 5:11

ed direction for beginning a women's ministry. Still others expressed their excitement at having this ministry offered to them. Yes, women need encouragement.

God will bring women into your lives who need the comfort you receive from Him. Heavenly radar helps you to spot those who are experiencing situations such as those He has already led you through. As you open your heart to those women, you will form meaningful relationships.

2. *A way for women to identify and use their spiritual gifts.*

Many women either do not know their individual gifts or do not know how to use them in the body. Paul exhorts us in Ephesians 4:12 "to prepare God's people for works of service so the so that the body of Christ may be built up." At each networking meeting we encouraged the women to help other women in their churches to discover their gifts and explore ways to use them in the church.

The goal of the networking meetings was to involve as many women as possible in leadership roles. Coming together for fellowship alone will not result in successful networking among women. Each woman must ask herself, What can I do to make a difference? We used two information-gathering forms: one blue and one yellow. The blue form (symbolizing the phrase "talk a blue streak") asked women if they could teach, lead workshops, or be guest speakers. The yellow form (symbolizing the phrase, "sing like a canary") inquired if women had a talent for music. The networking meetings provided a place for these women to serve.

The host women provided food and table decorations. We encouraged simple decorations in order to keep the cost minimal. Some women worked at the registration tables; others greeted guests as they arrived. Everywhere you looked, women were working together, and joy and laughter filled the room. It doesn't matter if you are more like Mary or Martha. There is true joy in discovering your place of service in the ministry to which God has called you.

3. *A way to help women mature in their faith.*

God's Word is at the very heart of networking. Everything we do should originate with God's Word. The study of God's Word and works of service help mature women in their faith. Networking encourages maturity in faith through providing and encouraging mentoring relationships.

Mentoring friendships encourage growth. *Webster's Dictionary* defines a *mentor* as a tutor, coach, or counselor. The key idea is more

It doesn't matter if you are more like Mary or Martha. There is true joy in discovering your place of service in the ministry to which God has called you.

experienced persons help the less experienced. Everyone can use help from those who are further along the road of life. Paul labored to "present every man complete (*teleios,* mature) in Christ" (Col. 1:28-29, NASB). As women network together, they have opportunity to mentor each other. For more information on mentoring, see pages 95-104.

4. *A place to exchange information and ideas.*

During those first days of networking, it was critical that I discover woman leaders in every church in my association. My plan was to have a contact person in each church that could funnel information to the women within her congregation. This information would include details about the next networking meeting and information being shared and learned at these meetings. In turn, the contact person would encourage the other women in her church to participate.

Within our networking group, we established a database which included all women's addresses, telephone numbers, email addresses and fax numbers. This information provided several avenues to send and receive help and ideas. We also provided the women with a resource we titled "Networking Numbers"—a list of telephone numbers for local, regional and state women's ministry leaders. It makes good sense to identify those who can supply answers, to seek their help, and then to follow their advice.

After each networking meeting, I would write an article for our associational newsletter. In the article I summarized the meeting and announced the next meeting place. This information alerted pastors to our accomplishments.

Networking meetings provided the primary opportunity to exchange ideas. When God gathers His women together, borders expand, dreams become reality, and ministry occurs.

> When God gathers His women together, borders expand, dreams become reality, and ministry occurs.

5. *An opportunity to identify the needs in our communities.*

If we are to reach the lost around us and minister to the needs of women and their families, we must first identify those needs. Luke 19:5 says: "When Jesus reached the spot, he looked up and said to him, 'Zacchaeus, come down immediately. I must stay at your house today.'" Jesus identified the needs and met them.

Many organizations are glad to volunteer time and information. Peruse your phone book or other sources of information for organizations that connect best with the women in your area.

One of our monthly meetings focused on community outreach. The director of the Grayson County Crisis Pregnancy Center and the director of the Women's Crisis Center in a neighboring town spoke to our group and revealed ways to support these organizations through our churches and as individuals. There was no fee for their presentations and the information helped us to identify some needs.

6. *A chance to share resources among all churches.*

I quickly discovered that most of the women who attended the first meeting had not participated in the most recent Bible studies and were unaware of the many opportunities available to help them grow spiritually. One network meeting dealt exclusively with the Women's Ministry Resource Catalog published by LifeWay Christian Resources.

I collected extra copies of each Bible study our church had offered in the last few years and created a display for the next meeting. I also distributed brochures, flyers, and booklets. I collected enough resources to fill two large boxes and four milk carton bins. In addition, I provided mailing addresses and instructions for how to order material that would be helpful in their women's ministry.

As a result of sharing resources, the women were excited and began Bible studies in their churches. Within our association, I noticed an increase in discipleship training attendance. I received phone calls from several of the host churches asking me to help them begin a women's enrichment ministry in their churches. God blessed our work.

7. *A place to pray for one another, our pastors, and our churches.*

God has blessed us with men called by Him to shepherd and teach, yet each year an alarming number of pastors leave the ministry. We must be in constant prayer for our pastors; they are under enormous pressure. Encourage the women you lead to pray for pastors and churches. Remember, it is impossible for women to pray too much. Prayer takes you on the high road in your journey with other women.

"For I know the thoughts that I think toward you, says the Lord, thoughts of peace and not of evil, to give you a future and a hope."
Jeremiah 29:11

At the end of each networking meeting we distributed prayer burden cards—one for each woman. After a few moments, we collected the cards and prayed for each request. Oh, how my heart was burdened for those women as I prayed. One card read, "Please pray for my son to come to know Jesus." Another read, "Pray for my husband that he might have a closer relationship with the Lord." "Pray for my sister who is dying of cancer." Still another read, "Pray that I will continue to seek God's direction for my life." Women were pouring out their hearts to the only One who could help them.

At the second networking meeting I met a women who asked me if I would pray with her concerning her church. I was able to talk and pray with her. A bond was formed between us which exists even today.

All of us need to be on the receiving end of ministry at times.

Remember as you reach out to someone with the compassion of Christ that you may one day need someone to reach out to you.

Growing and Developing a Networking Team

Networking was working! The women were praying and fellowshipping with women from other churches. A closeness was created and unity surrounded us.

After seven months of networking, it was obvious the women were enjoying the meetings and attendance was consistent, but we had reached a plateau. Seventeen churches were participating in the networking venture. That meant there were 46 churches still not participating. My goal was to reach every church. Since summer was approaching, I decided we would take a break and begin meeting again in September. I began to seek God's direction and to pray, "What now, Lord?"

Throughout the summer I reflected on my call from God and spent quality time praying and listening to Him. By July I had new direction for continuing the growth and development of networking. I implemented a networking team—a leadership team of women who had a common desire to bring women together within our association. If you recall, there were two women in that first meeting who shared with me a dream of women gathering together for encouragement.

I called those two women, along with three other women, and asked them to pray about forming a team. On July 11, we held our first team meeting, praying and brainstorming for four hours. As I reflect on how our women's network grew as a result of the efforts of this dedicated team, three "P's" were keys to its development.

> I implemented a networking team—a leadership team of women who had a common desire to bring women together within our association.

Participation

Although our networking ministry was growing, the question remained, How could we involve more women in networking?

One of the primary responsibilities of the networking leadership team was to cultivate and nurture friendships with the women in the churches. They communicated with these women, often sharing ideas for developing ministries as well as praying together.

Another idea for participation was to offer retreats or one-day conferences. Because of our geographic location, overnight retreats are not feasible. Instead, the team decided we would sponsor two conferences a year. We would invite all women in the association, not just leadership. Larger churches would host the conferences, with local women speaking and leading worship. As leaders emerged, we would hold a third conference within the year (a forum for leadership).

The time arrived for our first one-day conference and God blessed us in a tremendous way. We added six churches to our networking roll, and 130 women attended.

Purpose

Although our Director of Missions was very supportive, up until this time, our networking group had functioned unofficially within the association. Our DOM suggested that our association acquire a Women's Ministry Consultant and my name was recommended to the nominating committee. I accepted the position and, at last, Women's Ministry Connection was official. Now we needed a purpose statement.

This is the purpose statement we developed for our ministry: The purpose of this ministry is to bring together women from all churches to determine how to reach lost women and their families through the gospel of Jesus Christ. To help women mature in the faith as they serve one another using their spiritual gifts. To encourage and comfort one another in our daily walk with Him and to intercede for our pastors and church families as we seek to bring God glory.

A purpose statement will guide you in the right direction. For more information on developing a purpose statement, see pages 201-202.

Partnership

Networking is partnering with other women in other churches to reach and serve one another and our communities. Dr. John Maxwell said it so well: "Partnership testifies to the Community and the World. Partners demonstrate the unity and love of God."[1]

In a recent article published by the North American Mission Board, Henry Blackaby wrote: "Partnership is the essence of the Christian faith for each believer and each church. Partnership is God's way of touching a broken world!"[2]

One of our networking group's most memorable events was partnering with Women Reaching Texas from the Baptist General Convention of Texas. We offered a one-day associational conference.

Our leadership team had increased to eight members and each of them was a real team player. We agreed on the following plan.

- Each team member was assigned a certain number of churches to contact.
- Each team member was instructed to contact the pastor of those churches and enlist his support for the event.

- These same pastors were asked to provide the name of a woman in his church who would help to promote the event.
- Each team member would stay in touch with their churches' contact women and assist them in publicizing the event.
- All contact women were invited to a coffee to receive promotional materials and registration forms and to meet one another.

Two weeks prior to the conference, only 75 women were registered. I was praying for three hundred—the maximum seating capacity of our sanctuary. It was "a crisis of belief" time. Then heaven's doors opened and numerous registration forms began to arrive. I closed the registration at 350. We added a room with closed circuit TV to accommodate the overflow. All that day I thought, *Father how good You are to Your children.* He gave me a vision, planted a desire in my heart, and partnership grew among His women.

You may be asking, How many are on your mailing list now? At last count our mailing list included 450 women and 35 churches!

Is God speaking to you about networking? Go ahead and take that first step. I've already prayed for you.

He gave me a vision, planted a desire in my heart, and partnership grew among His women.

---

[1] John Maxwell, "The Power of Partnership," *Injoy Life Club,* Vol. 14, No. 7, January 1999.
[2] Henry Blackaby, *On Mission,* North American Mission Board, March-April 1999, 18.

For Smaller Churches
by Martha Lawley

Networking is an effective tool to link your church with women from other churches, to learn new ideas, and to explore ways to share resources. What a blessing for smaller churches.

If no formal networking exists among the Christian women in your community, pray about whether God is calling you to be involved in beginning begin a networking group. In many ways, the smaller the church, the more a ministry can gain from beginning a networking group.

If your church or community is not ready to utilize networking to respond to specific needs, consider starting with a simple partnership between one or two churches in your area. Such a partnership is a good way to learn to work together and experience the benefits of cooperation. It can also be a preliminary step into networking as you allow God to expand the partnership in His time.

Leadership Development
Developing a Ministry Strategy

by Chris Adams

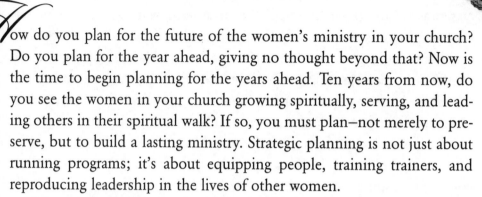

How do you plan for the future of the women's ministry in your church? Do you plan for the year ahead, giving no thought beyond that? Now is the time to begin planning for the years ahead. Ten years from now, do you see the women in your church growing spiritually, serving, and leading others in their spiritual walk? If so, you must plan—not merely to preserve, but to build a lasting ministry. Strategic planning is not just about running programs; it's about equipping people, training trainers, and reproducing leadership in the lives of other women.

If you were to leave your leadership position in a few years, what would you want people to say about you? Would your ministry epitaph affirm what you believe God desires in the way of leadership results? What do you need to do now to ensure those results? The focus of your ministry must not be on you, or any single leader, but on Christ and on the women to whom and with whom He has called you to minister.

The Bible contains many examples of strategic planning, such as Joseph's 14-year survival plan to prevent starvation in Egypt (Gen. 41:28-36), and Nehemiah's rebuilding of the wall in Jerusalem (Neh. 2:11-14). Like these Bible leaders, your leadership team must begin a strategically future-focused planning process. In this chapter, we will deal with a variety of issues that will help you effectively plan for the future.

Purpose

The purpose statement is a sentence or short phrase that explains why your ministry exists.

If you do not yet know the purpose of your women's ministry, you will be unable to plan for the future. In the chapter "Beginning a Women's Ministry" in *Women Reaching Women* (pp. 40-41), you will find direction for developing a purpose (mission) statement for your ministry. The purpose statement is a sentence or short phrase that explains why your ministry exists; it must also support the church's purpose/mission statement.

The purpose must be visible at all times, not only to your leadership team but also to the women of your church. Constant awareness provides focus and direction; it also motivates women to become involved and to serve in a ministry. Purpose also provides a tool by which you can evaluate your women's ministry and establishes a standard as you plan and set goals. It provides structure for the budget, as well as leadership needs and planned activities.

One approach for determining a purpose would be to gather a group of women (all ages and life stages) to pray and brainstorm reasons for ministering to and with the women in your church and community. Study Scripture regarding ministry of women in the church. Discover a scriptural basis for existence and use that as the foundational passage for your purpose statement. Consider including these essential functions in your statement: ministry, missions, evangelism, worship, discipleship and fellowship—all of which must be undergirded with prayer. Share your statement with the church staff and ask for their support and approval.

Objectives

After prayerfully determining your purpose, establish objectives for accomplishing that purpose. Objectives are general areas toward which you direct your efforts. To put it another way, the purpose is the "why" and objectives are the "whats" of ministry.

Using your purpose and objectives, begin to plan how you believe God wants your ministry to accomplish His desires. Develop main objectives, which will last from one to ten years and will be the focus of your time and energy as well as budget money. Then structure your ministry according to these objectives by setting priorities.

Priorities usually focus on the upcoming 12 months and are measurable and dated, driving you in the direction of your purpose and objectives. They guide planning for activities and events that will bring those objectives to fruition and accomplish the purpose.

Involving Women in Service

While developing ministry plans, remember that a priority is to involve every woman in your church in meaningful service. Today's lifestyles involve multiple responsibilities. Women make choices about how and where they will invest their energies. How do we motivate women to discover God's ministry call for them using their spiritual gifts?

According to Royce Rose in *Principles of Church Administration,* there is a 12-point system for motivating volunteers:

1. "Pray ... the Lord ... to send out laborers."
2. Develop qualifications for leaders.
3. Identify needs for leaders.

A priority is to involve every woman in your church in meaningful service.

4. Discover potential leaders.
5. Provide basic pre-service training for potential leaders.
6. Recruit for specific leadership positions.
7. Give specialized training for specific leadership positions.
8. Provide on-the-job training and continuing education.
9. Supervise leaders.
10. Motivate leaders.
11. Evaluate the work of leaders.
12. Recognize leaders appropriately.[1]

In *Church Administration Handbook*, edited by Bruce Powers, Robert Dale states three reasons why people volunteer for a job. *Achievers* find great satisfaction in contributing to a vital cause and feel exhilarated by being "on the team." They love setting and achieving goals. Use this type person to organize new projects, solve challenging problems, and explore ministry options.

Affiliators enjoy the fellowship of like-minded persons. They value warm and friendly relationships and enjoy listening, sharing information, and giving encouragement to others. These volunteers are useful for counseling, greeting, listening, and acting as hostesses.

Power people influence individuals and groups. They enjoy position and hold strong opinions. Place these women in ministries you want to move forward. They can persuade others to join.[2]

Each of these types is motivated by different ministry "rewards." Understanding your leaders and the rewards they enjoy from service will help you supervise the variety of women with whom you will be working.

As you enlist leaders, provide a job description and training prior to and during their service. Place them in groups where they can share their lives with one another, affirm one another's gifts and contributions to the team, set goals for the ministry (based on the vision/purpose you have kept before them), and celebrate together the reaching of those goals. Continue to supervise while delegating responsibilities–giving leaders the freedom to be creative, make decisions, and even fail.

Teamwork is essential. It unites leadership, sets priorities, and helps with evaluation as you build ownership—not only with the planning team, but also with the women in the church.

As your women's ministry expands, you will need additional volunteers and leaders to staff ongoing and short-term programs and projects. Each leader must be able to meet the needs of different types of women.

Some women prefer entry level Bible studies. Others prefer a life-stages group formed around a common need. Some will be seeking longer, more

> Understanding your leaders and the rewards they enjoy from service will help you supervise the variety of women with whom you will be working.

intense discipleship studies. Still others may desire a service group which ministers to others. Offering different levels and types of groups moves women from one stage of spiritual development to another.

Groom potential leaders for each new group. When God reveals the person, provide the necessary training.

Dealing with Change

The rapid pace of change in our world continues to impact ministry in the church. On the following page look at some current changes/trends as compared with the past:

Isn't it interesting that current trends resemble the trends which existed during the time of the early church? Perhaps God is telling us something important: listen to and encourage women to understand the role of laity in the church.

Leadership Network also shares these differences in culture today:

Then:	Now:
Hierarchy and authority	Flat organization and teams
Leadership by position	Leadership by vision and values
Training as linear, one-time,	Learning as experiential, life-life-long, standardized customized
Knowledge by the few over time	Instantaneous knowledge by masses
Verbal/print communications	Visual/digital communications

It's obvious that leadership, training and learning have changed. Focus your women's ministry on relationships rather than programs and include as many women as possible in your leadership development.

Key elements for the future, according to Carol Childress, from Leadership Network, include:

- Relationship, not religion (how women can relate to God personally, daily)
- Authenticity over hype (true stories of women and their faith)
- Connections and community (friendships, mentoring)
- Growth and small groups (not just big events)
- Success to significance (not just achievement, but meaning)
- Times of transition (continual, constant change)
- Soul care and spirituality (caring for the spiritual life of women)
- Burnout and balance (balancing life to avoid burnout)[3]

As changes occur, lead a Bible study on change. Demonstrate that God

It's obvious that leadership, training and learning have changed. Focus your women's ministry on relationships rather than programs.

203

Issue	Apostolic Paradigm (1st-3rd Centuries)	Christendom Paradigm (4th-mid-20th Centuries)	New Apostolic Paradigm (Late 20th-21st Centuries)
Driving Forces	Mission, vision, values	Tradition, loyalty obedience	Mission, core beliefs and values
Mission	Focused on external–reach out to world	Focused on internal–mission was far away	Focused on external–the unchurched, the seeker
Structure	Simple, functional, local church centered	Complex, hierarchical, bureaucracy centered	Flexible, contextual local church centered
Relationship to God	Personal, gets lived out in community	Social, corporate, institutional	Individual, experiential
Role of Clergy	Teacher, Equipper	To be the minister, professional	Teacher, Equipper, Coach Coach to build up the disciples
Role of Laity	Active, engaged in mission	Passive, obedient	Active, deployed in mission and ministry
Communication Vehicle	Narrative stories	Print and proclamator, rational argument	Narrative stories and multi-media
Level of Collaboration	High, informal	High, formalized, denominations	High, short term for specific purposes, networks

204

expects us to constantly change as His calling changes and as we grow spiritually. Attempt to understand how those resisting change may feel. They may at first believe they are losing something important. This loss causes doubt and discomfort. At this point, many will deny that change is occurring or even ignore it. Some may even experience anger or grief. Others will admit that change is occurring and confront it. This latter group will also begin to explore options and regain optimism, becoming a part of the change process.

Enlist the support of influential church leaders by asking them to pray and brainstorm possible and necessary changes to develop a more effective ministry. Explain your vision and the values you hope to promote. These leaders, in turn, will help inform other groups about the necessary changes.

Recognize and affirm the areas that remain stable and are not currently in need of change. Stability will reassure those who are reluctant and fear that everything in the ministry will be different. Focus on reaching individuals for Christ, discipling individuals for Christ, and creating an awareness of where God is working. This focus will motivate even die-hards to consider the positive results of change.

Consider emphasizing situations or actions that have been unsuccessful in an effort to create dissatisfaction with the "status quo." Include as many people as necessary in the discussions dealing with possible change so they will understand, contribute to, and take ownership in "new" ways of reaching more women.

Allow women to release the former and embrace the future. This process may require some time since you will have women in all stages of transition. Exercise patience while listening, empathizing, and responding positively to all concerns. Continue to emphasize that the positive results of the past will influence the future.

Use the worksheet, "Determining the Change Process," on page 208 to help you process changes you feel are necessary in your ministry (reproduce as needed).

Leadership is the key to effective ministry when dealing with transitions. Carol Childress provides "Five Windows into Effective Churches for the 21st Century":

1. Have effective leadership—gift-based teams that foster ownership of the mission, built around empowerment of others in ministry.
2. Equip people for service—preparing and releasing women to serve, assisting them in using their passions and gifts to serve others.
3. Connect them to culture—understanding the global, urban, and

Attempt to understand how those resisting change may feel.

pluralistic culture in which we reside and customize our worship, ministries, and outreach to our demographics.

4. Build authentic community—providing for the needs of women and developing women as a primary purpose for the ministry while programs become secondary, simply the way we achieve our purpose; strengthening group life for caring, learning, support, accountability; intentionally sharing our spiritual growth process with others.

5. Pursue missional impact—seeking to transform culture as we minister; joining others (churches, denominations) to learn and reach the world for Christ; evaluating effectiveness by the transformed lives in the church and community.[4]

We must be willing to make the changes God reveals if we want to continue to go with Him—both individually and in women's ministry.

Someone once told me, there is risk in change, but there's greater risk in standing still. In *Experiencing God,* Henry Blackaby makes the point that we cannot stay where we are and go forward with God. We must be willing to make the changes God reveals if we want to continue to go with Him—both individually and in women's ministry.

Proposals

If you are beginning or changing your existing women's ministry, or if you are adding a new aspect of an established ministry, you may need to present a proposal to your pastor or other responsible staff minister. Use the form on page 209 as you prepare. Reproduce as needed.

Master Plan

Masterplanning by Bobb Biehl is a strategic planning resource. The areas of planning presented in this book are as follows:

Needs–What needs does your leadership team feel burdened by? What needs do they feel uniquely qualified to meet? What needs make you weep (compassion) or pound the table (anger)?

Purpose–Why do we exist? Why are we committed to meeting the needs we have identified? What is the best single measurable indicator of the health of our women's ministry? Begin your discussion by agreeing on a single word that best describes your ministry. Next use 3 words that define your focus. Then write a 5-10-word sentence that describes why your ministry exists.

Objectives–To identify what you will do to meet the needs identified and your purpose, answer these questions: In what 3-7 areas of women's ministry will we continue to be actively involved in the future? What categories of ministry are we going to be involved in over the next few years?

Milestones–List and date any major milestones you have already accomplished in each of the objective areas you have identified.

Ideas–Brainstorm ideas that may result in a priority. List ideas to consider for each identified objective. For each objective, list specific actions you will take to move in the direction of your purpose and objectives.

Roadblocks–What are the top three roadblocks in each of your objective areas that keep you from reaching your full potential as a leadership team? Is there a pattern of roadblocks you can identify?

Resources–Identify three resource people per objective area. Choose people who will help implement ideas and achieve priorities. Add these people to your leadership team. Define the strengths of each team member. Which resources can be used to eliminate your roadblocks?

Priorities–Priorities are measurable and specific plans (goals) to achieve results in a specific amount of time. Begin with the end in mind. Divide your priorities into long-range (5-20 years), mid-range (2-5 years), short-range (0-2 years), and quarterly (90 days). For each time frame, list an objective/dream and three priorities.[5]

As you identify tasks for the next 90 days and move toward your short-range objectives, your plans are ready to be set in motion. *Masterplanning* provides additional information to accomplish this method of strategic planning. It includes forms designed for use in planning.

[1] Royce Rose, *Principles of Church Administration* (Nashville: Seminary Extension of the Southern Baptist Convention Seminaries, 1993), 55.
[2] Bruce P. Powers ed., *Church Administration Handbook* (Nashville: Broadman & Holman, 1997), 60.
[3] Notes taken from seminar by Carol Childress, Leadership Network.
[4] Ibid.
[5] Bobb Biehl, *Masterplanning* (Nashville: Broadman & Holman, 1997), 97.

For Smaller Churches
by Martha Lawley

Strategic planning is not just for larger churches. It is an essential tool for churches and ministries of all sizes. The eight areas of planning from Bobb Biehl's *Masterplanning,* are very useful for smaller churches. They provide a road map for evaluation and strategic planning for a women's ministry of any size.

In a smaller church, the need for volunteers is an ongoing challenge. In the midst of this day-to-day challenge, one can easily it is easy to forget that God's priority is not on getting things done, but rather on our spiritual growth. Ask God to help you to stay focused on His priorities. Allow God to show you that His way will always work.

Determining the Change Process

What area of the ministry needs to be added or changed? _____

_____

What is the purpose of the ministry? _____

_____

Why is this change necessary? _____

_____

Who needs to be notified? _____

_____

What key leaders are needed for support? _____

_____

Who may resist? _____

_____

What difficulties are there to overcome? _____

_____

How many leaders and what specific spiritual gifts are required for this change?

_____

When can we schedule a celebration kick-off? _____

Evaluation Notes _____

_____

_____

Proposal Worksheet

Title of ministry _____

Purpose of ministry _____

_____

_____

Purpose of proposal _____

_____

_____

Pros _____

_____

_____

Cons _____

_____

_____

Other thoughts/details _____

_____

_____

Promotion plans _____

_____

_____

Appendix
Creative Child Care

by Chris Adams

A frequent question when developing women's ministries in the church is how we will handle the issue of child care. Unfortunately, there are no easy answers, but if you want to include mothers of young children, child care is essential for all women's events and programs.

Church Policies

Begin by checking with your church staff to discover if there are any policies concerning this issue. Be sure to abide by them.

Have written guidelines for mothers in your women's ministry so they will know ahead of time what is expected, including opening and closing times, as well as extra charges for late pick-up, if necessary. Inform mothers of your sick child policy, perhaps using the guidelines from the Committee on Control of Infectious Diseases of the American Academy of Pediatrics:

> *For the protection of your child, the other children, and the teachers, we request that you not bring a child who is or appears to be ill. Upon recommendation of the Committee on Control of Infectious Diseases of the American Academy of Pediatrics, that means when any of the following exists: fever (currently or within the previous 24 hours), vomiting or diarrhea, any symptoms of a childhood disease (scarlet fever, German measles, mumps, chicken pox, whooping cough), common cold, sore throat, croup, any unexplained rash, any skin infections (boils, ringworm, impetigo), pink eye or other eye infections.*

Church Budget

The ideal situation is when the church budget covers child care during ongoing women's activities as well as periodic special events. If this is not the case now, meet with the Finance Committee to plan for the future.

Funding Child Care

If your church does not have the funds for child care, there are creative ways to deal with this issue:

- Charge a minimal amount per child ($1-3) to defray the cost. To insure you have enough workers, sell tickets ahead of time.

- Ask for donations from all attendees at the activities to help share the financial burden for mothers of young children.
- Make the financial needs of child care known to your church. There may be members who would gladly help fund this ministry so mothers can attend women's ministry activities.
- Make scholarships available to those who cannot pay for their own child care. Some churches offer coupons that are redeemed as they attend a women's meeting. The coupon may not pay the full amount, but at least it will help those on a tight budget who truly desire to fellowship and grow with other Christian women.
- Add the cost of child care into the ticket price at all special events so all those attending share the expenses* (see p. 213).
- Use your childcare needs as a fund-raising pledge event for a high school, college/career or singles retreat. With the approval and cooperation of one of other areas of ministry, turn your child care into a money-making event. Find out what special events are planned. Then ask the group to act as childcare workers for your event. Once this is agreed upon, let that ministry group ask church members to pledge to individual sitters a set amount for the total number of children the group ends up caring for during the women's ministry events. Many church members are willing to make pledges toward retreat/event funding.*

Existing Child Care
- Find out when your church normally offers paid childcare workers for other ongoing church activities. Perhaps this would be a good time to offer weekly group studies as well as special events. Extra funds would not be needed if the workers are already enlisted and hired for these particular time slots.
- For daytime groups find out who offers a Mother's Day Out program. Offering weekly groups during this time will eliminate having to conduct another childcare program at your church.
- You may be able to "exchange" children with another church. The other church could handle child care for you at your church and you would return the favor on another day of the week.
- Schedule your event at the same time as a children's event. Coordinate this with the children's ministry leader.*

Finding Workers

If finding workers is a problem, there may be others in the church who could help out if they were enlisted.

- If you have youth who are raising money for a mission trip or camp, perhaps they could be "hired" with the money for their time being given toward their trip. Remember: when using youth you must also have at least one adult in the room with them at all times. Check your state laws regarding legal issues related to child care.
- If you live in a college town, check with the local Baptist Student Ministry (or other Christian organization) to discover college students needing to earn extra money, or who are needing to fulfill community service as a part of their ministry programs. Depending on their needs, the cost to the church or mother may be minimal or non-existent.
- Sometimes fathers may be willing to donate their time either at home or at the church so their wives can attend a women's function. A good rule of thumb here is to have a woman present also if the men are watching several children at the church.
- In your publicity for women's events you might include the need for childcare workers. Even though you desire that all women participate in the activity, women who do not plan to attend for whatever reason may be willing to offer their time as a ministry for those moms who would like to attend. Many grandmothers do not live close to their grandchildren and would love the opportunity to interact with small children to help fulfill their "grandmotherly" longings!
- One church formed a missions/ministry baby-sitting co-op. It is made up of women who want to do ministry activities but need child care.
- When your event has several sessions and child care is not an affordable expense for your women's ministry, allow those needing child care to select a session during which they would be willing to stay in the childcare area. This way they can experience the majority of the event instead of missing out entirely because of lack of child care.˚

Reservations Only!

Offering child care by "reservation only" assures that you won't be paying for workers who are not needed because of a low number of children

present. Have a deadline for making reservations as well as a cancellation policy. For instance, if a reservation is made and the children do not show up, the mother could be responsible for helping to pay the expenses. Exceptions could be made for emergencies and illnesses.

Purposeful Child Care

An added benefit to both mom and child is to plan purposeful child care. The spiritual life of their children is important to women who are attending activities to help them grow in their own spiritual life. Offer special Bible activities and stories during this time. Many workers would rather be busy while attending children and only need a little encouragement and some creative ideas to make the time more than just baby sitting. If the lesson can use the same Scripture the mother will study that day, it's even better! On their trip home each time they can discuss what they both learned.

Helpful Ideas

Other ideas that will help you develop effective child care include:

- Clearly defining age ranges;
- Varying the places you have child care;
- Providing a clean, cheerful setting;
- Providing for security measures, such as identification cards/badges for children and mothers
- Properly labeling all of the child's belongings
- Always knowing where the mothers are in case of emergency;
- Finding out if the child has any special needs (allergies, dietary limitations, biting).

Special Note: Many ethnic groups do not place their children in child care. They prefer to keep the children with them at all times. Keep this in mind as your ministry offers activities to diverse groups of women in your church and community.

Ask God to help you plan for child care so women will feel comfortable leaving their young children with responsible workers in a safe environment. Women will then be able to focus their attention on their relationship to Christ, fellowship with other Christians, and service for Him as they attend women's activities.

---

* These ideas were submitted by Judy Bates, who coined the term "Bargainomics" (the wisest possible use of time, money, and resources for the glory of God) and is a regular feature on WAKA-TV in Montgomery, Alabama.

Budgets
by Chris Adams

Whether you are just beginning your women's ministry or are already established, budgeting is an issue you must consider. If your ministry is new, chances are you are not in the church budget yet. But your goal should be for the church to support women's ministry with budget money as it does other vital church ministries.

When There Is No Budget

If you are given no budget money from the church at the present, you will need to be creative in the way you conduct finances for the ministry.

- Each event or activity must be cost recovery by selling tickets and workbooks/materials and charging for child care.
- Decorations can be handmade or purchased and resold at the event. Women are usually willing to bring items from home or donate them.
- When conducting Bible studies that require the purchase of leader books, leader kits, and workbooks, each woman should always purchase her own workbook as an investment in her own spiritual growth. Additionally, group members could be charged a few extra dollars each to cover the cost of leader materials.
- Perhaps your denominational state, regional, or associational office has a copy of the materials (videos, tapes) they will loan to your church.
- Two smaller churches may join together to purchase the materials, then stagger their starting dates by a couple of weeks so both can use the resources at the same time.
- Some larger churches may have already purchased a set of videos and would be willing to loan these to smaller churches.
- For special events, make the needs known to the church. There are many in your church who have the gift of giving and the means to do so. If they know about the needs they would gladly contribute money, time, or other resources to help with your ministry activities and special events.

Scholarships

Occasionally a woman may not be financially able to purchase tickets for special events or workbooks for Bible studies. Partial or full scholarships should be available. Make your scholarship needs known so those who

can afford it will be aware of the need. Publicizing this fund also lets those who need help know how to find assistance.

Documentation

As you look toward the future, document all expenses you have incurred. When annual church budget time arrives, you will have facts and figures to back up any financial requests you may be proposing. Finance committees will want to know you have thought through and documented items on your proposal rather than just pulled figures out of the air.

What are some areas you might consider as you summarize your budget needs?

1. Publicity (promoting and advertising) such as brochures, posters, fliers, newspaper and radio ads

2. Literature (purchase of curriculum, resources, devotionals, magazines)

3. Spiritual growth (enrichment and growth) such as retreats, workshops, support groups

4. Special events (supplementing or funding for food, facility rental, honorarium and travel for speakers, publicity, and decoration above recovered costs) such as banquets, holiday events, conferences, retreats, and luncheons

5. Fellowship (supplementing fellowship/social outreach)

6. Leader training (training, developing, and equipping leadership for women's ministry) such as national, regional, or associational training conferences

7. Discipleship resources (purchase and rental of resources for discipling, training, and equipping individuals for ministry and evangelism including audio, video and film resources)

8. Transportation (supplementing or funding any transportation needs), especially for out of town training and enrichment

9. Food service (purchase of supplies, rental of equipment, and labor above recovered costs)

10. Printing (purchase of paper, layout, printing of newsletters, brochures, handouts, conference materials, and correspondence materials that communicate and promote women's ministry):

11. Postage (mailings) for newsletters, outreach, and correspondence

12. Supplies (general administration office supplies, bulletin boards, photography supplies)

13. Conventions/conferences (transportation, lodging, meals, conference fees, incidentals for continuing education and professional development of women's ministry director)

14. Professional improvement (subscriptions for magazines, newsletters, journals, and purchase of books and other resources for the development of women's ministry leadership team)

15. Hospitality (expenditures related to hospitality) such as food, decorations, and miscellaneous for ongoing activities

16. Child care (expenses for ongoing weekly meetings and special events)

17. Community ministries (expense for outreach to community to meet physical, emotional, and spiritual needs):

Outreach luncheon/banquet	Tutorial program
Mother's program	Nursing home
Food pantry	Hospital
Clothes closet	English as a second language

As you begin to document expenses incurred, do not feel like you must have all of the above included. These are just suggestions to consider as you seek to further develop your women's ministry.

Remember that God is able to provide for any needs you have in the areas of ministry He has directed you to offer.

Easy Promotion
by David Tiller

Promotion techniques are an important set of tools to help you maintain the successes and reverse the failures of your women's ministry. Promotion principles and techniques keep close kinship with what businesses call advertising. Businesses communicate and create awareness via promotional campaigns. We know that promotion attempts to grab your attention and appeals to your emotions and some logical reasoning, and we hope that you are persuaded by the pitch—that is, trying the product or service.

One of the most effective principles of promotion and advertising is also a fundamental principle of learning—repetition. The repetitive principle does not mean to pick one medium and use it forever. It means you should put your message in simple terms and choose several mediums to convey the message to your target audience.

Before discussing the types of promotional mediums, consider the purpose of promotion. An important question to ask yourself is, why am I promoting? Break the word *promotion* into two parts—*pro + motion. Pro* means *yes* and *motion* means *move.* Therefore, if you do not have a valid reason for the women of your church and greater community to move

from their houses to your house (location or place of ministry), don't ask them to come at all. If you proceed without a purpose, you will experience failure and people will be wondering what you are doing.

You want to connect with the target group by conveying in a split second that there are good reasons to consider participating in the women's event. Logistical information (what, when, where) can be sprinkled into the promotion, but only after you have hooked minds with a benefit.

Five Principles of Promotion

Consider these five principles, regardless of the medium (brochures, flyers, bulletin inserts, poster, bulletin boards, displays)

- size grabs attention
- less is more (teasers)
- hook 'em
- extremes work for people under 25
- show me

Size

Answer the initial question of all promotion (and especially when it is in public space): can people see it? Size matters. In many ways size helps you to keep things simple and to achieve the "less is more" principle. A practical rule is to allow between 30-50 percent of your promotion space for the heading, the catch phrase, or the main idea of what is going to happen. If you are mailing a brochure in a regular business envelope, the entire front panel should be dedicated to the main idea. While that is only one of the six panels in your brochure, it is the most important. When you are creating your promotional items with a presentation software package (such as Microsoft's PowerPoint) be sure to use font sizes well above 72 point for your headings. It is better to use a second or third poster than to cram everything into one poster.

Hook'em

Next, read advertising from grocery store circulars, women's magazines, and newspapers (*USA Today* is one of the best) to identify phrases that are used to catch people's attention. Many phrases that play off seasons of the year or special events in your area would also work. Try the following for your next event's leading hook: "Sleep 20% More and Worry Half As Much." We're not suggesting you cheapen the gospel. Rather, you are grabbing attention to create an opportunity for women to hear the gospel.

Show Me

Third, because you have used between 30 and 50 percent of your space to grab attention with special words, you have reduced the amount of copy for people to read. Advertisers tell us that people will read the ad if you can stop them for just one second. People are busy and it takes an arresting idea, phrase, or graphic to grab our attention.

Less Is More

Consider this technique to reduce copy. Ask a friend to function as your reader/editor. Agree to contribute $1 to Lottie Moon Mission Offering for every extra word this person identifies in your promotion. This approach allows you to drop the articles and adjectives and head straight for the action and benefits in your promotion.

Extremes Work

Advertising and promotion ride the fashion waves as do clothing, cars, and entertainment. There has always been room for the extreme or edgy side in promotion. One of the more stable promotional mediums is the outdoor billboard. An extreme in this highly fixed environment is to build an extension that goes outside the 12- by 24-foot space. Simply said, the extreme game has only one rule—and that is "break all rules." You can develop you "edginess" or "shock-value" by perusing magazines targeted at people age 25 and younger. Color, font selection, presentation on the page, and all other sensibilities are up for grabs. Let's take a look at some of the rule-breakers.

1. *Graphics and Clip Art*—A graphic is any item reduced to its simplest form and still recognized as that item. The question is, what will I see that will grab and hold my attention? Professional advertisers tell us an idea must grab the viewer's attention in one second or the idea is ignored, overlooked, or trashed. A second concern is, Will the audience recognize and understand your graphics or symbols? For example, you can use stop signs for letter "O" only if the viewer understands symbolic language and is acquainted with traffic signs. The visual message becomes "stop and look." A variety of clip art is easily available at affordable prices. Be sure the images you select support your message and your audience will understand them.

2. *Typeface, type size, text treatment*—Once we look, words and their placement keep us moving to find out more. Consider these guidelines:
   • RESIST USING ALL CAPS EXCEPT FOR EMPHASIS WORDS AND PHRASES. Caps treat every word the same. On interstate highway signage only the repetitive words like "Exit" and "Speed Limit" are upper cased, while road names are in both upper and

lower case—the easiest to read at high speeds.

- You can use more than one typeface in a brochure or mix hand-writing with computer print in the same promotion idea. Use different sizes for titles or headers, subheaders or bullet points, and copy text or explanations. Another choice affecting readability is typeface or font. Choose a font that not only looks good on the computer screen but also looks good when photocopied. Avoid excessively enhancing typefaces with what I call "cuties." Furthermore, resist the temptation to use the features of bold, italics, script, and centering except for very special words or phrases. This mistake is rampant in church newsletters. You do not want to look as if you went to a font sale and bought out the store. Do not use a script font that has been emboldened, italicized, and centered.

3. *Layout and Design*—Grab your favorite mainstream magazine and consider some layout principles. The two most read corners of any media message are the upper right and bottom left. This usage follows our conventional reading patterns of starting at the top and ending at the bottom, as well as the left-right reading pattern. Also, the eyes tend to scan across the information/article in a "z-pattern." As a result of the "z" tendency, most magazines provide choice statements in large print placed intermittently across the page or pages. Keep the "z" pattern in mind as you place text.

In your brochures and flyers you will want to use flush left and ragged right margins to aid readers. Use "white-space" (areas of the promotion that are void of treatment) to your advantage. Too often, we wonder what can be added rather than what can be left out. Design your promotion on the principle, if only one phrase or one graphic could be used, what would it be? Come Enjoy. Go Find. Seek the Lost. Share Your Faith. Or, could these ideas be better represented by graphics? If you had the luxury of a second sentence, what would it be? The presence of a few words coupled with an arresting visual is more powerful than many words.

A final tip regarding layout is to box the information only when the situation absolutely demands it. The effect of boxes is confining to eye flow. Avoid boxing the message and trapping the eye. Give the reader "white-space" and allow the eyes to flow without encumbrance.

4. *Medium or Media*—Another consideration is where your message will be received. Will the viewer be in public? … at home? … in familiar surroundings? Can the message be delivered in multiple media, such as

posters, newsletters, bulletin inserts, or announcements. Professionals say that combining media makes for the greatest impact on your event.

A sophisticated promotion event might include flyers mailed to the target audience. Flyers contain some but not all of the information. Flyers direct readers to look for posters at the church or event site. Posters provide more information, but not all. Posters direct readers to listen to announcements made at church, to listen to a tape-recorded message, to dial a telephone number that plays a recorded message, or to listen to a live person at a designated area who will greet them and provide complete information. This promotion could have great impact and persuasion!

5. *Placement/Environment*–When debating where to place your promotion message, consider these public areas: hallways, corners (half on one side and half on the other), half on one side of a door and half inside the door, bathrooms, stairways and landings, rent-a-sign, church sign(s), and outside entrances. The traditional means of communicating privately include letters, newsletters, flyers, handbills, phone calls, and emails. Consider the difference in effect if the message medium was changed to balloons and mailed with the following instructions. Readers would inflate the balloons and read the message: "Remember: This event rises or falls with your effort. Now either tie a knot or let the air out and be a not."

6. *Time*–Most of these ideas are two-dimensional. What advantages exist in using the third or even fourth dimension? Time can become a design element when you plan a progressive release of information. Advertisers call this "teasing." For instance, the first week of the promotion states only one word–Coming. The next week another word is added–Coming Soon. The third week of promotion adds–Coming Soon to Local Neighborhood Near You. Then, the final week completes the details.

Planning Time and Implementation Time

For best results, begin drafting your ideas approximately ten to twelve weeks out from the event. Then between six to eight weeks away from the event, begin the implementation of the promotion plan. Always submit your ideas to a "second pair of eyes and ears." If a person cold to the idea can read it or hear it and get the message, you have a good promotion idea. If not, then ask the person to suggest ideas for making it clearer. Make the changes and get a second reaction from another person.

Resources

Visit our Web site at *www.lifeway.com* for information about resources and ministry development for single adults, senior adults, families, men, women, discipleship, health ministries, criminal justice ministry, and prayer ministry.

To order the LifeWay Press resources in this book WRITE LifeWay Church Resources Customer Service, One LifeWay Plaza; Nashville, TN 37234-0113; FAX order to (615) 251-5933; PHONE 1-800-458-2772; EMAIL to *CustomerService@lifeway.com;* ORDER ONLINE at *www.lifeway.com;* or visit the LifeWay Christian Store serving you. Catalog listings include a product number for easy reference when ordering.

For a complete catalog and packet of information on women's ministry resources, contact Chris Adams by email at *Chris.Adams@lifeway.com.*

Events

Information regarding women's enrichment events is available ONLINE at *www.lifeway.com.* To register for any of LifeWay's events, VISIT our Web site; PHONE (800) 254-2022; or EMAIL *registration@lifeway.com.*

Organizations and State Conventions

Missions Organizations

North American Mission Board
Women's Evangelism Office
4200 North Point Parkway
Alpharetta, Georgia 30022-4176
(770) 410-6352
www.namb.net/heartcall

International Mission Board
Box 6767
Richmond, Virginia 23230
(804) 358-0504

Woman's Missionary Union
Women's Consultant
P. O. Box 830010
Birmingham, Alabama 35283-0010
(205) 991-8100
www.womenonmission.com

Other Organizations

MOPS International, Inc.
(Mothers of Preschoolers)
2370 South Trenton Way
Denver, Colorado 80210
(303) 733-5353
FAX (303) 733-5770
www.mops.org

Moms in Touch International
(Organization of mothers who
intercede for their children
and pray that schools may be
guided by biblical values and
high moral standards.)
P.O. Box 1120,
Poway, CA 92074-1120
(800) 949-MOMS
www.momsintouch.org

Leadership Network
2501 Cedar Springs LB-5,
Suite 200
Dallas, Texas 75201
(800) 765-5323
FAX (214) 969-9392
customerservice@leadnet.org

Christian Schools and Home
Schooling
LifeWay Christian Resources
One LifeWay Plaza
MSN 182
Nashville, TN 37234-0182
(615) 251-5749

Women's Enrichment/
Minister's Wives
LifeWay Christian Resources
One LifeWay Plaza
MSN 152
Nashville, TN 27234-0152

Baptist State Conventions

Many Baptist state conventions have a person assigned to women's ministry. Call your state convention office and record this person's name, address, and telephone number for later use. Make sure your name is included on the state mailing list so you can receive information on training and enrichment events.

Alabama
2001 East South Boulevard
Montgomery, AL 36116-2463
Phone: 1-800-264-1225

Alaska
1750 O'Malley Road
Anchorage, AK 99516-1371
Phone: (907) 344-9627

Arizona
2240 N. Hayden Road
Suite 100
Scottsdale, AZ 85257
Phone (480) 945-0880

Arkansas
525 West Capitol Avenue
P.O. Box 552
Little Rock, AR 72203-0552
Phone: (501) 376-4791

California
678 East Shaw Avenue
Fresno, CA 93710
Phone: (559) 229-9533

Canada
100 Convention Way
Cochrane, AB T4C 2G2
Canada
Phone: (403) 932-5688

Colorado
7393 South Alton Way
Englewood, CO 80112-2372
Phone: (303) 771-2480

Dakotas
2020 Lovett Avenue
Bismarck, ND 58504-6737
Phone: (701) 255-3765

District of Columbia
1628 Sixteenth Street, NW
Washington, DC 20009-3099
Phone: (202) 265-1526

Florida
1230 Hendricks Avenue
Jacksonville, FL 32207-8696
Phone: (904) 396-2351

Georgia
2930 Flowers Road, South
Atlanta, GA 30341-5562
Phone: (800) 746-4422

Hawaii
2042 Vancouver Drive
Honolulu, HI 96822-2491
Phone: (808) 946-9581

Illinois
P.O. Box 19247
Springfield, IL 62703
Phone: (217) 786-2616

Indiana
P.O. Box 24189
Indianapolis, IN 46224-0189
Phone: (317) 241-9317

Iowa
2400 86th Street, Suite 27
Des Moines, IA 50322-4331
Phone: (515) 278-1566

Kansas/Nebraska
5401 SW Seventh Street
Topeka, KS 66606-2398
Phone: (785) 228-6800

Kentucky
P.O. Box 43433
Louisville, KY 40253-0433
Phone: (502) 245-4101

Louisiana
P.O. Box 311
Alexandria, LA 71309-0311
Phone: (318) 448-3402

Maryland/Delaware
10255 Old Columbia Road
Columbia, MD 21046-1736
Phone: (410) 290-5290

Michigan
15635 West 12-Mile Road
Southfield, MI 48076-3091
Phone: (248) 557-4200

Minnesota/Wisconsin
519 16th Street, SE
Rochester, MN 55904-5296
Phone: (507) 282-3636

Mississippi
P.O. Box 530
Jackson, MS 39205-0530
Phone: (601) 968-3800

Missouri
400 East High Street
Jefferson City, MO 65101-3215
Information: 1-800-736-6227
Phone: (573) 635-7931

Montana
P.O. Box 99
Billings, MT 59103
Phone: (406) 252-7537

Nevada
406 California Avenue
Reno, NV 89509-1520
Phone: (775) 786-0406

New England
87 Lincoln Street
Northboro, MA
01532-1742
Phone: (508) 393-6013

New Mexico
P.O. Box 94485
Albuquerque, NM 87199-4485
Phone: (505) 924-2312

New York
6538 Baptist Way
East Syracuse, NY 13057-1013
Phone: (315) 433-1001

North Carolina
P.O. Box 1107
Cary, NC 27512-1107
Phone: (919) 467-5100

Northwest
3200 NE, 109th Avenue
Vancouver, WA 98682-7749
Phone: (360) 882-2118

Ohio
1680 East Broad Street
Columbus, OH 43203-2095
Phone: (614) 258-8491

Oklahoma
3800 North May Avenue
Oklahoma City, OK 73112-6506
Phone: (405) 942-3800

Pennsylvania/South Jersey
4620 Fritchey Street
Harrisburg, PA 17109-2895
Phone: (717) 652-5856

South Carolina
190 Stoneridge Drive
Columbia, SC 29210-8239
Phone: (803) 765-0030

Tennessee
P.O. Box 728
Brentwood, TN 37024-0728
Phone: (615) 373-2255

Texas
333 North Washington Ave.
Dallas, TX 75246-1798
Phone: (214) 828-5100

**Southern Baptists
of Texas Convention**
1304 West Walnut Hill Lane
Suite 220
Irving, TX 75038
Phone: (972) 953-0878

Utah/Idaho
P.O. Box 1347
Draper, UT 84020-1347
Phone: (801) 572-5350

Virginia
P.O. Box 8568
Richmond, VA 23226
Phone: (804) 915-5000

**Southern Baptist
Conservatives of Virginia**
4101 Cox Rd., Suite 100
Glen Allen, VA 23060
Phone: (804) 270-1848

West Virginia
Number One Mission Way
Scott Depot, WV 25560-9406
Phone: (304) 757-0944

Wyoming
P.O. Box 4779
Casper, WY 82604
Phone: (307) 472-4087

110925

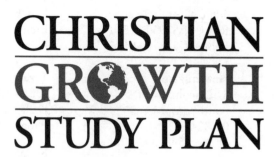

CHRISTIAN GROWTH STUDY PLAN

Preparing Christians to Serve

In the **Christian Growth Study Plan (formerly Church Study Course),** this book*Transformed Lives: Taking Women's Ministry to the Next Level* is a resource for course credit in the subject area Women's Enrichment of the Christian Growth category of plans. To receive credit, read the book, complete the learning activities, show your work to your pastor, a staff member or church leader, then complete the following information. This page may be duplicated. Send the completed page to:

Christian Growth Study Plan; One LifeWay Plaza
Nashville, TN 37234-0117
FAX: (615)251-5067
Email: cgspnet@lifeway.com

For information about the Christian Growth Study Plan, refer to the Christian Growth Study Plan Catalog. It is located online at *www.lifeway.com/cgsp*. If you do not have access to the Internet, contact the Christian Growth Study Plan office (1.800.968.5519) for the specific plan you need for your ministry.

Transformed Lives
COURSE NUMBER: LS-0034

PARTICIPANT INFORMATION

Social Security Number (USA ONLY-optional)	Personal CGSP Number*	Date of Birth (MONTH, DAY, YEAR)

Name (First, Middle, Last)	Home Phone

Address (Street, Route, or P.O. Box)	City, State, or Province	Zip/Postal Code

Please check appropriate box: ☐ Resource purchased by self ☐ Resource purchased by church ☐ Other

CHURCH INFORMATION

Church Name

Address (Street, Route, or P.O. Box)	City, State, or Province	Zip/Postal Code

CHANGE REQUEST ONLY

☐ Former Name		
☐ Former Address	City, State, or Province	Zip/Postal Code
☐ Former Church	City, State, or Province	Zip/Postal Code

Signature of Pastor, Conference Leader, or Other Church Leader	Date

*New participants are requested but not required to give SS# and date of birth. Existing participants, please give CGSP# when using SS# for the first time. Thereafter, only one ID# is required. **Mail to:** Christian Growth Study Plan, One LifeWay Plaza, Nashville, TN 37234-0117. Fax: (615)251-5067.

Rev. 3-03